LIFE IN A WHIRLWIND OF NUMBERS

(26 Years of OCD)

BY

DAVID W. DAHLBERG

Createspace Independent Publishing Platform

North Charleston, South Carolina

To my wife, Judy,
And to all of my family and friends,
Who helped me over the years,
And put up with me.

Preface
The Intent of This Book:

Ever since I was diagnosed with obsessive-compulsive disorder (OCD) in 1999 and was successfully treated, I have been willing to share my story with others. Especially as a schoolteacher and a father, I have been able to relate to other people's similar issues, to inform them that hope exists, and to help steer them toward treatment resources.

No one needs to suffer the effects of OCD.

My OCD started when I was fourteen, and for the next twenty-six years I lived with—and hid quite well—the overt symptoms of this crippling illness. My life was a living hell, and though I could hide my thoughts and compulsions well—as many OCD sufferers do—I could not hide the secondary effects: the withdrawal, the dysfunctionality in school, and later on in work.

Repercussions echo up until the present day, including read-justments to my family and marriage. For eleven years my wife was married to an untreated OCD sufferer. And sometimes the effects still linger—but we are now able to work on them successfully and in context. Just because you are "cured" of OCD doesn't mean old habits don't persist.

Although this book is about OCD, the reader needs to make an important distinction between this account and books written by medical professionals. This is my book, about *my* OCD, so it is autobiographical.

My book gives a very detailed account of my life before, during, and after my OCD. It is my belief that much of my childhood behavior, fears, anxieties, and social skills were predictive toward my later manifestation of OCD. Of course, it is up to the reader to decide. Whether you agree with my thoughts, they may simply be worth studying to gain insight into a mind that spiraled into OCD during adolescence—and may never have returned to normality save for modern medical treatments.

This book is not...

(1) A "case study" such as might be found in a medically-oriented book, which would often include descriptions of many OCD manifestations, as well as treatment options such as medication and various other therapies – such a book steered me through my own treatment of OCD, or (2) a resource to self-diagnose OCD – I was medically diagnosed with OCD, and I am writing only about my OCD, which I feel qualified to do on a personal basis.

Everybody's OCD is different and manifests differently, although certainly by degree. Every OCD sufferer is different both physically and mentally, and environmentally. This is about my mind and body and my environment. I hope it helps you with yours.

Most of the names in this book have been changed for privacy. The exceptions are my family, Dr. Howard Dale, and Sensei Ian P. Harris.

CHAPTER 1

Feelings, Numbers, and Rituals

What's OCD like? Ever had a car swerve into your lane? Or had a dog with fangs bared rush after you? How did you feel when your child came down with a 104-degree temperature? A surge of adrenalin. Anxiety. Physical sensations programmed into your nervous system that require you to respond. And, once the crisis has been successfully addressed, did you have a feeling of relief and relaxation?

Nightmares create these feelings—and nobody likes night-mares. But then you wake up and realize it was just a dream. Again, you have that feeling of relief.

Now imagine a nightmare that won't go away, because you're already awake. It's a nightmare because it's happening only inside your mind. But somehow this nightmare, this fear, even though you know it isn't real, triggers the fight-or-flight circuitry that should be reserved only for reality—like that dog. Let's say it's an image of a loved one dying suddenly—and it won't go away. You can move away from that biting dog. But you can't escape your brain. It goes wherever you go. And somehow your body's incorrect response to this thought becomes a glue that pastes that image to your mind's eye. The image won't go away and it becomes stronger. And your body responds with yet more feelings of anxiety.

The danger is imaginary. But the *feeling* of danger is absolutely real.

You become caught in an endless, inescapable, and debilitating loop. All because your nervous system grossly overreacted to an image that would simply pass through the minds of other, "normal" people. You have the brain chemistry of OCD: obsessive-compulsive disorder.

It started before I can remember. Even as a small child, I had to make things feel right. It was like scratching an itch that wouldn't go away, but it wasn't an itch. I had to put a glass down "just right" in the sink or draw connected figure-eights for minutes at a time until the sensation felt perfect. I would start to take my pencil off the paper then realize I had to do a few more, or many more, to feel the right feeling.

And I'm not saying "good feeling." Being able to *stop* is what felt good.

My first repetitions stemmed from this feeling. Later on, in kindergarten and subsequent grades, I picked some lucky numbers and carried them around in my head. All my friends had them; I just had more. My favorites were seven and eight. But, unlike my friends, they meant a lot more to me, and I began to feel the need to apply them to things I did throughout the day. It might feel good to clap my hands seven times when I applauded or perhaps to take eight swallows in a row when I drank a glass of water. These little number rituals were small feel-goods for me to complete, and they gave my life some order. I mean, it's easier to drink when you know exactly when to stop, right?

I was a math whiz. I mastered addition and subtraction in second grade, multiplication and division tables in third. I could give you the answer to "nine times five" before you could finish speaking it. I became especially fascinated with the idea that any number's digits add up to a smaller number: 1,003 added up to 13, which could further add to four. Just about any number could be transformed into a different, simpler one. This ability, a point of pride, would become a relentless enemy years later.

My childhood took a turn into the dark when I discovered hypochondria. As my awareness of the world around me grew with my years, I began to realize that people everywhere were getting sick and dying—and I knew some of them. It probably didn't help that I considered myself sickly. In first grade, I had strep throat almost weekly, it seemed, until my tonsils were removed that same year. Practically every night, my dad would come home and stick a culture swab down my throat.

My dad was a periodontal surgeon and a commissioned officer in the United States Public Health Service, which treated soldiers and their families. He had access to the medical lab for my strep cultures as well as the pharmacy for my antibiotics. He was practically our family doctor.

My first really big trauma occurred in fourth grade, when my best friend Doug Coleman came down with appendicitis. It frightened me greatly when I heard the news, and when my friend came home and described the experience to me in detail, I nearly went into shock. I was sure I was going to get appendicitis too. Not only would this fear not leave my mind, I actually started to imagine that every little twinge in my lower abdomen was a sign. I began to develop indigestion, which very nicely corresponded to appendicitis symptoms. My dad dismissed my fears and refused to take me to the doctor. He performed some routine tests by feel, and, after a week of this ordeal, pronounced me a healthy hypochondriac.

A child's problems can seem just as big and real to him as any adult's. I think my eventual obsessions with being sick were that I *was* sick a lot. Besides my chronic tonsillitis, I remember contracting rubella—the German measles—and being covered with spots and feverish for days. (After I recovered, I noticed I had slightly blurred vision in my left eye and a slight but measurable high-frequency loss of hearing in my left ear.) I came down with the stomach flu quite a lot—not a pleasant experience at any age.

I think I felt sickness was a natural state of being for me, and I developed a pattern of wondering "what's next?" with a sort of dread. I'd had every childhood disease my friends had, and I would worry whenever the flu or colds were going around.

When my friend had his appendectomy, the "me too" thoughts kicked in with a force previously unknown to me. People could die from appendicitis; people could get complications from appendicitis; and everyone who got it had to go to the hospital and get their belly cut open to remove the inflamed appendix. It was painful to get, and painful to get over. I was convinced it was only a matter of time before I was stricken. The waiting was absolutely terrible. And it was the first time my overzealous fight-or-flight reflex really kicked in.

Initially, I was very open about my fears. My dad had always taken care of my ills: tonsillitis, stitches, a huge wood splinter that lodged one-half inch up my thumbnail. Dad brought home a surgical kit, shot my thumb up with Novocain, and proceeded to use dental surgical tools to extract the splinter.

So I was very willing to share all of my medical fears with my dad. But in the end, he just pooh-poohed them, which made me ashamed.

Having treated myself successfully for OCD, what would I do differently if my own child started exhibiting worrisome obsessions? That was my worst fear as a parent, as OCD tends to run in families. I watched my own girls like a hawk, always looking to see if they worried or exhibited physical compulsions. I knew how treatable it was, especially if caught early, before patterns and fears became ingrained.

If I could go back and whisper in my father's ear, knowing now that I had a treatable *medical* condition, I would have instructed him to tell me my fear of appendicitis was not baseless but had been overwhelmingly exaggerated by my brain and body's reaction. Whereas a normal person might experience a passing fear or apprehension, my fear was based on a near-certainty. This kind of fear should be reserved for *real* near-certainties or *absolute* certainties, where the brain and body rightfully feel and use the fight-or-or flight reaction. In my case, however, this physical reaction occurred with what should be trivial worries—and this rush of fear and adrenaline would embed the thoughts and images further, subjecting me to the ever-deeper spiral of OCD.

I would have had my father start by telling me my anxieties were lies of the worst sort: lies brought on by incorrect brain chemistry, false feelings of fear. The feelings were real to me, but based on others' realities, not my own. I needed to realize that if I did not let myself be affected by these feelings, they would fade. I needed to know I could separate my mind from these physical feelings and practice "stepping out"—that is, pretending I was a neutral observer looking at myself from the outside.

I would have also told my dad to seek medical treatment for me. I needed modern psychiatric evaluation, cognitive therapy, and especially some effective anti-anxiety and anti-obsessive drugs to take the hard edge away and allow me to start beating my fears rationally.

Of course in 1968 these sorts of therapies were unknown; the drugs were yet to be discovered, as were the root causes of OCD. Lucky me. So what did I do? I shut my mouth. I kept my worries to myself, and, as I was a chronic worrier, I ended up keeping to myself a lot. I needed room to worry.

For decades—well into my twenties—I slept with my right hand over where I supposed my appendix was, in order to prevent a cosmic ray from zapping it while I slept.

And here is where you would think someone might ask, if they knew, "Why? Why worry about such ridiculousness? What is wrong with you?" And how would I respond to that? I wouldn't need to. Because if they don't know, they *won't* ask. So I don't have to answer. One of the first OCD sufferer rules is *always hide it.*

I asked myself why—why did I suffer from so much anxiety for so many years and never found an answer. Did you ever have an adrenaline rush, that overwhelming fight-or-flight feeling? If so, it most likely was in response to a real threat. In my case, a ridiculous thought popped into my brain and then my brain grossly overreacted. It sent a false distress signal into my nervous system, which in turn amplified the worry. In some people, this feedback quickly spirals out of control, leading to an all-out panic attack. In my case, I never completely panicked, but my reaction to the distress signal would never stop. I would worry about the same thing nonstop for days, weeks—even years.

After a while, I felt there was no escape from images or words stuck in my head of people I knew who'd gotten sick or died, or from names of the diseases responsible. I couldn't get them out. *They wouldn't go away.* And that's when the real OCD symptoms—what some call *compulsions* or *ritualizations*—started to kick in. Like many other OCD sufferers, I began doing repetitive things to try to get the images to go away. But the ritualizations only made it worse.

It didn't help that I have an exceptional, nearly photographic memory. A variety of images, good and bad, had always been continuously projected in my mind's eye. I saw pictures constantly: pets, loved ones, cars, things I like. Like most people, I paid little attention to these images. It was the ones I didn't like that I spent so much time and trouble trying to eliminate from my mind. And, in attempting to do so, this made them stand out more.

When I was fourteen, I began to develop a complex numerology list, beside which my old lucky numbers paled. Unfortunately, this list included many numbers to avoid. The complete details can wait, but here is my starter list, which ran my life for years, even decades.

The List

1. Okay.
2. Usually bad, but not sure why.
3. Okay.
4. Okay.
5. Bad. A satanic number used in pentagrams.
6. Okay.
7. Okay.
8. Bad. Whenever I counted out an eight, outcomes never seemed lucky.
9. A really good one. Most multiples of three are good.
10. Sometimes good, sometimes not.
11. Okay sometimes.
12. A pretty good one.
13. Unlucky. This was a bandwagon number.

14. Good. The age of a girl I liked at the time I started my severe OCD compulsions.
15. Bad. The age of a friend when he got cancer.
16. Equally bad. Age of the same friend when he died.
17. Bad. Age of a boy, in a book I read, when he got leukemia.
18. Okay. Any multiple of nine was good.
19. Bad. The date in June when my friend with cancer died. When the woman I married turned out to have that date as her birthday, I married her anyway. It became a better number.
20. Once was good, turned bad when I read a magazine article about a young man who had contracted leukemia at that age. Why do newspapers so love cancer stories? I would be shocked and appalled by them weekly, it seemed, throughout the long course of my OCD. But I would still read them, in equally horrified fascination.
21. Okay.
22. Bad. The age of the young man in the previously mentioned book when he died.
23. Was good, then bad. The age of the young man in the magazine article when he died.
24. Good.
25. From *Brian's Song*. The age of Brian Piccolo when he got cancer.
26. Bad? Piccolo's age when he died.
27. Good. Multiple of three and nine.
28. Usually bad. Ended with eight.
29. Good. My birthday in December.
30. Okay.
31. Another magazine article, this time in *Reader's Digest*. The age of a cancer survivor when he contracted testicular cancer.
32. Bad. Multiple of eight. Also adds up to five.
33. Okay.

This is only a partial list. Every number, no matter how large, could be classified either on its own "merit" or on its possible inclusion with one of the listed numbers above or others not listed. For example, 118 was bad, as it added up to nineteen and also ended in an eight.

Most people have no idea how quick and bright I am. Bright enough to be able to classify numbers instantly and to torture myself with them endlessly. The mental ability that had so swiftly allowed me to learn my multiplication tables, understand algebra with ease, and to do mental math faster than I could write it down, also served my OCD well. Worst of all, the process was automatic. I was helpless to stop it.

Now imagine not merely numbers but also pictures and images of all these people—and more—continuously flying into your mind. Then imagine the numbers and the images working in tandem, reinforced by faulty brain chemistry, creating a constant state of near-terror.

For example: Bedtime. I had a digital clock. If any bad numbers were on any part of the display (say 10:19 p.m.—remember, 19 was bad), I could not take my feet off the floor to get into bed. I would wait until a good number appeared: 10:20. Then I had to lift my toes off the floor at least twice, because that totals 20 touches for my toes (a good number at the time). More often than not, however, a bad image would enter my mind as I was completing the act. I would then have to maintain a good image in my head (say, a friend whom I knew was healthy) while I touched the floor again—except that 20 more would total 40, a multiple of 5 and 8. I would have to add seven more touches instead, for a total of 9. At this point, another image might (and usually did) flash through my mind in lightning-like fashion, just as I was completing the modified ritual. And then another counting ordeal would ensue. I'd finally finish, and guess what? The clock would now read 10:34 p.m., which added up to bad number 17. I'd just wasted fifteen minutes of my life. It might be a long night.

There were times that this could take literally hours. And that doesn't even include putting my head down on the pillow the proper number of times. So many little things. So many big rituals.

Getting to bed was just part of it. Studying, practicing music, work—all were hugely affected by wasted time and my inability to concentrate. Often I would seem preoccupied or downright lazy to family, friends, and teachers. Over the years, this list grew to include employers and girlfriends. I seemed preoccupied because witnesses were present. A typical OCD sufferer, I hid my rituals. Exhibiting them was unthinkable. I would do them internally, and any observers would think I had tuned out or simply didn't care. Like a computer with a virus, I was sidetracked and occupied much of the time.

Nobody found out—*nobody*—although the results were there to be seen. Why did somebody who tested ninety-ninth percentile across the board have such trouble studying and applying himself? You can see why.

It's now well known that OCD is genetic. It and other depressive conditions often correlate to high creativity, drive, and intelligence. Being obsessive-compulsive can be advantageous. Many successful people owe their fame and fortune to the relentless, often irrational drive it imparts. It's when the obsessiveness takes a bad turn—visions of awful things rather than desirable ones become stuck in your head—that the fight-or-flight reflex kicks in and locks the image in place.

I was constantly convinced something bad was going to happen. And, in my case, that's when the compulsion would start. Perhaps, I thought, if I repeat an action I am doing at the time, the proper number of times, with the correct image in my head, nothing bad will happen. But if I *don't* complete the ritual, something bad *will* occur. As an OCD sufferer, I just *knew*. And I was literally paralyzed at times until the ritual was externally or internally completed.

Here's another example. Shoelaces. Merely tying my shoelaces could be a Herculean task. What was the proper number for tying shoelaces? If it was okay to tie and re-tie the left one four times, then it would *not* be okay to tie the right lace four more, because that would add up to eight. I could tie it five times to make nine total, but 5 was not an acceptable number on its own.

I could tie the remaining lace twice, but that would result in the end combination of 5-6, one of my "bad" combinations. I would have to tie it at least 6 times for an acceptable total of 10. However, if a bad thought or image popped into my mind as I was finishing the tying, the next acceptable combination would have to be 14. Twelve was good, too, but it would mean tying the right lace 8 times on its own.

Sometimes, in desperation, I would just stop and hold my shoe-laces in the middle of my shoe—completely still—trying to figure out an acceptable number in advance—sitting there, paralyzed, for minutes at a time. I think I spent over two hours tying my shoe-laces once. Shorter but still significant blocks of time I commonly wasted on countless other occasions.

Does this ritual make your head spin? It does mine, and I lived it every day. And this would happen almost every time I tied my shoes.

The important thing to note is that this was the pattern. It could apply to anything—playing or hearing a musical passage, thinking an internalized thought (leading to perceived outward paralysis generally interpreted as tuning out), turning a page in a book, twisting a pair of wire leads together, tightening or loosen-ing a bolt. The possibilities were endless. OCD negatively affected every aspect of my life. And interpersonal relationships suffered worst of all.

When I was fifteen, my family and another family were vaca-tioning at a resort in eastern Washington. My brother, Steve, and I had a lot of fun waterskiing and tubing with another family's kids. The younger sister, fourteen, and I kind of liked each other at the time.

One night, the girl I liked and a friend of hers were camping just above the beach, sleeping under the stars in a grassy patch framed by large, sweet-smelling Ponderosa pine. I was on my way down to the fishing dock, heard them talking, and went down for a visit. She hurled some mock insult at me and dared me to respond. So I went down to the lake and dipped my hands in, cupping the water as I did so. I was very good at trapping water in my hands and then squirting it at any given target.

She knew what I was going to do—she had seen me do target practice in the swim area—so she buried herself deep within her sleeping bag. I sat down next to her and told her I could wait as long as she could.

Eventually, she popped her head out and back in quickly, and I just tagged the top of it. We both laughed, and, in hindsight, maybe I should have kissed her—or at least tried to, for good form. But I didn't, and the game soon took a bad turn. My dead friend's image (15 and 16) popped into my mind when I squirted her, and then I knew I was going to have to squirt her again while keeping the image out. Or I was going to die. So I told her she wasn't going to escape *this time* and went back for more. I squirted her over and over, continuing to do it until I got it right the *ninth* time. I remember hating myself and hating being forced to do it over and over against my will, trudging back to the water again and again until I could finally stop.

At the end of the ordeal, she was no longer fond of me. She told me to go away and wouldn't speak to me for the rest of the trip. Explaining to her why I did it was out of the question. If I did that, soon *everyone* would know. Everyone would think I was crazy—and wouldn't they be right?

CHAPTER 2

Before OCD

P erhaps my greatest predisposition to OCD was my ability to worry continually. I could worry for hours, and it seemed my body could supply itself with a continuous supply of adrenaline to do so. Perhaps my memory is so good because we remember traumatic events much more clearly than mundane ones. Our memories of fear or shocking events can place us back into the sights, sounds, smells, and settings of their exact occurrence.

Where were you when 9-11 occurred? When Mt. Saint Helens blew? When MLK and JFK were assassinated? If you were around then, you remember where you were and what you were doing at such a moment. Imagine someone traumatized in this way every day, either by outside events or their own imagination. How much better should they remember so many details of their lives?

We've all had such personal events. My mother has a vivid memory she has often recounted. When she was in high school, in the late 1940s, geometry was giving her a bit of trouble one day. Sometimes a student, even a very bright one, can find herself stuck on a new or unfamiliar concept—perhaps just needing a different explanation or approach to succeed. Her teacher, trying to help her, became frustrated at my mother's inability to grasp the concept.

Six years before, this same teacher had taught my mother's older sister, my Aunt Marge. Marge was extremely gifted in all subjects; she had been valedictorian of her graduating class. And she had made a lasting impression on her math teacher—now my mother's teacher.

The teacher gave up, and out of frustration, said to my mom, "You're not as quick as your sister, are you?"

Mom went home in tears that day, so visibly shaken that my grandmother extracted the details, took her back to the school immediately, and read the teacher the riot act. Sixty years later, this episode remains one of my mother's clearest memories.

My first vivid memory of an hours-long adrenaline panic comes from September 1965. I lived a short ways from Lake Forest Park Elementary School, with only one street crossing, which was right at the school itself. The crossing was monitored by patrol boys (whom we now call crossing guards), older boys who seemed nearly like adults to a mere first-grader. (Girls were not allowed to be patrol boys back then, any more that they were allowed to wear anything but skirts or dresses.)

First-graders are very energetic, and release from school ups this energy to greater heights. The neighbor kids and I were bursting with energy, waiting for the patrol boys to secure the crosswalk. Right as the flags went out, my next-door neighbor, Rob Stewart, shoved me out into the crosswalk. "Hey," yelled the patrol boy across the street. "Wait until we say go, idiot!" Hadn't he seen me get pushed?

I avenged myself quickly. I had to get back out of the street before I was allowed to cross. This put Rob in front of me. Halfway across the street, I tripped him from behind. He went down, and I ran by him quickly to avoid retaliation. As I made the other side, a strong hand grabbed my coat. It was the patrol boy. He was a large sixth-grader, easily twice my size, and as a preadolescent, he almost seemed like a teacher himself.

He glared down at me. "Jumping into the crosswalk. Tripping another kid in the crosswalk. Running through the crosswalk.

That's *three* major rules broken in a row, junior. Do you realize that any one of these can get you reported to the principal?"

I looked up, far up it seemed. With his police-like patrol boy vest, helmet, and deepening voice, he was *worse* than the principal right then. "What's your name, kid?"

"David."

"David *what?*"

"David Dahlberg."

"David Dahlberg, huh?" He pulled out a notepad and pencil. "Consider yourself on report. I'm turning this in after school, and you can expect a call home to your parents from the principal."

I began to protest. "But I was pushed! Didn't you see—"

"Give it up, kid, and take your medicine, or I'll change it to fighting in the crosswalk. Now go home."

I didn't fear the principal—or even the vice principal, who was renowned for giving out swats. I could handle a swat or two. What I feared far beyond anything was my father's sure punishment for a call home by the principal. The yelling. The announcement I was going to get a good lashing. And then being sent to my room for at least an hour to ruminate on the lashing. The building fear and suspense almost making the lashing itself a relief—except that my dad's lashings with his belt were far too severe to be any kind of a relief at all.

The absolute worst of it was that today was Friday. If the principal called that afternoon, my weekend would be ruined, for I would surely be grounded as well. And if he didn't call until Monday, I would have to sweat the entire weekend out with this twenty-ton weight hanging over my head, waiting to drop. How could I possibly confess on my own, in advance? My sense of self-preservation would simply not let me. And perhaps there was the smallest chance that the patrol boy would forget. No, scratch that. He had written it down.

Arriving home, I found Mom in the kitchen, tending to my three-year-old brother in a high chair. I told her I was heading to my room to read—an activity that would garner no questions. I went to my room, shut the door, and opened a book:

And fretted.

For the first time, the blinding projector of fear in my mind was switched on. As in years to come, instead of the book I was reading, all I could see in my mind's eye was that folded loop of belt. The picture was so clear. And my mind's ear vividly recalled the mechanical bell of our phone ringing, a sound I waited for with horror—but a sound that never came that afternoon. Occasionally my mind would drift to the book, and I would find myself reading part of a page without conscious volition. But then it would quickly return to my visions and worries, a refreshed surge of adrenaline grabbing me.

I didn't last through dinner. Mom was a good cook, and save for occasional experiments or squash, beets, or eggplant, the food was always tasty. Seconds were the norm. Mom would sit at one long end of our dining room table, Dad would sit at the other, and my brother and I would sit facing each other across the middle—Steve still in a high chair.

I can't remember all we had for dinner, but I do remember the peas on my plate. I would usually eat my peas first—although tolerable, peas were not my favorite, so I'd eat them first to get them out of the way. I took my fork and started picking at them. But not only was I not feeling hungry, I was feeling ill. Usually very talkative, I found myself wrapped in a blanket of silence.

"David?" My mom's words broke up my trance a little. "David?"

I looked up.

"What's wrong?" she asked.

In later years I was able to conceal my fears much better. One, people were used to seeing me out in space. Two, I developed more control in order to hide my condition. But in this case I had neither aspect to draw on. I burst into tears.

Soon Mom, in her gentle way, had soothingly obtained my confession. My parents were a very effective good-cop/bad-cop combination. Although confessing to Mom, I kept glancing at Dad, expecting to see a building fury. Instead, he started to look amused. In hindsight, I believe Dad had quickly developed an appreciation for the methods of this patrol boy—fear and humiliation, a chip off the old block.

I was quickly assured that I had punished myself already far more than was necessary. "He's not going to report you," my dad assured me. "He was just trying to talk some sense into you. I expect it won't happen again."

I finished my peas.

This remains one of the most anxious few hours of my life—but, most importantly, the first memorable ones. I had friends who would have given the patrol boy lip and would have not worried a whit about a phone call home. My dad wasn't the only one who spanked his kids. In fact, I didn't know of a friend who hadn't been spanked at one time or another. Some of my friends got it far more than I did.

But none of them, as far as I could tell, had the ability to create and sustain the levels of fear I seemed to possess. Was it a natural lack of self-assurance on my part? Or did my irrational and intense fears already demonstrate the excess anxiety that would later become OCD?

Monday morning. The same patrol boy was stationed at the crosswalk. "Did you turn me in, patrol boy?"

He looked puzzled for a moment, and then remembered me and went right into his act. "Well, since it was a first offense, I was told to let it go with a warning. But I'll tell you this: if you goof off on my watch again, I'll personally kick your butt during recess. Now get to class!"

My strange way of making friends—and how they looked out for me

As part of my predisposition to OCD, my high academic intelligence was coupled with a severe lack of social intelligence. I picked on smaller kids (including my brother), not realizing that their friendship would prove far more valuable than their fear and anger. I had a big mouth; I thought I was funny, but usually I was simply offensive.

I had a small circle of friends who knew I wasn't trying to be annoying (and who would frequently correct me) and at least put up with me, perhaps due to common interests such as band, skiing, or church. But they couldn't always save me from myself. I found myself narrowly avoiding many fights on account of my mouth.

One fight I couldn't avoid occurred in the summer after fifth grade. We were members of Aqua Club, a summer swim club, and I decided to turn out for the team that summer. Many of my friends, including Doug Coleman, were on the swim team, and, although they were all better swimmers than I, they encouraged me to turn out. I soon found out that the workouts were the hardest thing I had ever done. But I got used to it and benefited from the discipline.

One thing I couldn't get used to was the hierarchy. I was used to the pecking order between my friends and fellow students at elementary school, but the fellows at Aqua Club were far more diverse in age. Junior swimmers ranged from the elementary years up through middle school. There were several cliques, with each clique generally composed of kids of all ages, headed by one of the older boys—kind of like patrols in a Scout troop.

Many of the extremely competitive, year-round swimmers were in the group headed by Arthur Davis, already a star swimmer in his school district league. These boys had an attitude, and you had to prove yourself many times over to have them say "you're one of us." It was a league far out of my range. And one more thing: you didn't mess with Arthur Davis's group.

Although I did not wish to be in Arthur's group, I thought I might at least try to get on friendly terms with them. One day after practice, when we were dressing after showering, I noticed Arthur had swimmer's hair—years of exposure to chlorinated water had not been kind to it. In my mind it was a perfect opportunity to endear myself to Arthur and his gang by making a funny comment about his hair. If I could make him laugh, I thought, I might at least not be ignored all the time by him and his group.

The fact that I thought joking about an older boy's hair in front of an entire locker room could be a good thing tells me I was not right in the head. Arthur had just finished toweling his hair, and it stuck up everywhere. "Hey, Arthur, you look like my dog, just after he's finished shaking himself dry."

The locker room went silent in disbelief. Arthur stared at me for long seconds, stood up slowly, and got right in my face. He was dressed only in his sweatpants, and his upper physique was impressive. He glared down at me. I looked back up at him, eyes wide, suddenly realizing what I had actually accomplished.

"Would you mind repeating that?"

"I was only trying to be funny." What I'd meant to say was "I was only trying to make you laugh," but the correct words escaped me. But then, they usually did.

"Yeah, real funny. At my expense. And what have I ever done to you?"

"Nothing... I was just trying to find a way to get to know you."

Arthur leaned down, putting his face close to mine. "You were better off not knowing me—and me not knowing you. What's your name, punk?"

"Dave." This was not good. I had the impression Arthur needed to know the names of people he pummeled.

"Listen up, Dave, you little runt. I am going to pound the crap out of you." There was a ferocious gleam in Arthur's gaze. "But I'm not going to do it now, because I don't want to get kicked off the team. And don't even think about quitting, because I'll find you and pound you that much worse. Now shut your mouth until the end of the season. Don't even think about talking to me."

During the next two weeks, Arthur's followers apparently had marching orders. I would find my clothes in my locker—thoroughly soaked. I was bumped in passing numerous times. Arthur's group would huddle up, take turns staring at me, and then burst out laughing—Arthur himself nowhere to be seen. Once, at a swim meet, I found some M&M's on my towel. One of my friends, probably. Then I noticed a trail of more M&M's, about two feet apart, leading away. Being eleven years old, I had no compunctions about eating them as I followed the trail. It was just a concrete surface, after all.

So intent was I on following the delicious M&M's that I failed to see myself approaching Arthur's group. I found the end of the trail—a small pile of partially-chewed candies, clumped in a puddle of saliva. I heard laughter and looked up—and there they were, again, absent Arthur.

"You might as well eat those too; the other ones you ate were all spit on as well."

"What a scrounge. Eating M&M's off of the ground. You're disgusting."

I ran away in shame, more laughter trailing behind.

The hazing and upcoming beating took its toll. I was much better at hiding my fears than I had been in first grade, having had quite a bit more practice by then, but swim team had long ceased to be fun. I had been sustaining a high level of fear and anxiety for two weeks, and everything was tainted. All I lacked was some rituals to perform. I was just as wound up as I would be later, when the OCD really kicked in.

I asked my friends what to do. They told me the best thing for me to do was to take it, and eventually things would blow over. I was told this was a good lesson for me, and maybe I would watch my mouth more in the future. My best friend, Doug, who had all the social sense I did not, told me not to worry too much about getting pounded by Arthur. "He's not that kind of a bully. You're really beneath his trouble to beat up."

What I didn't know was that my friends had my back, to a certain degree. Doug's older brother, Brian, who was bigger, stronger, and tougher than Arthur, had already informed Arthur of a painful death if he touched me. Thus Arthur's proxies.

The end came quickly and unexpectedly. As the third week of my torment started, my clothes went missing after practice. Everyone had dressed and left as I was still searching the locker room, looking in lockers, closets, and of course in the toilet stalls, dressed only in my Speedo.

As I came back into the locker room, I saw my clothes sitting on a bench. They had been returned—by Arthur's group, who now closed a circle around me in the room. And this time Arthur was present. "I've let you live long enough, punk. But it's beneath me to lay a hand on you. So, my friend Tom here, more your size, has offered to fight you for me. "

I was trapped. It was death by Arthur or a chance with Tom. Tom was my age, but his mental toughness, excellent swimming, and just a hint of sadism fit him right in with the group. Tom would probably pound me more than Arthur would. And everyone was sure he would.

Tom came at me, and I had nowhere to run. A surge of adrenaline hit me, and I grabbed him with a strength I didn't know I had. I flung him violently into the lockers. I still remember the crash it made. Unbelieving yet appreciative sounds murmured around me. This might actually be a good fight. I just figured Tom would give up then.

But Tom didn't give up. After a few stunned seconds, he got up and started throwing punches, swinging his arms around instead of straight punching. They started landing on the side of my head. The punches lacked power, but they gave the impression to the crowd—and to me—that I was losing. And I couldn't bring myself to hit him back. Hitting someone in the head or face was repugnant to me: what if I hurt him? He wasn't fighting fair. After half a minute of this punishment, I spotted an opening between two boys and ran out of the locker room crying, laughter once again trailing behind.

And then it was over. When I went back to the locker room the next day, none of Arthur's clique would talk to me. I guessed they figured I'd been taught a good enough lesson. I hoped they would leave me alone after this. And then I noticed Tom had a black eye. He wouldn't even look my direction. Well, at least I'd done some damage, I thought, when I'd hurled him into the lockers.

My friends had been busy. Willing to let me learn a reasonable lesson, they were upset at the sneaky ambush that had taken place. Doug was especially infuriated at Tom, who had obviously volunteered for the job to gain some further status. Most of the kids on swim team lived in the neighborhood, and walked to practice. Doug knew where Tom lived, and, leaving for practice a little early that day, he had met Tom on the way to the pool, and beaten the crap out of him. Doug had no compunctions about fighting—he'd been trained by his older brother. Thus the real reason for Tom's shiner.

Doug had also brought a note to give to Arthur, written by Doug's older brother. It instructed Arthur to leave well enough alone, or he would meet Arthur before practice the next day. The note also told Arthur he was responsible for anything anyone in his group did to me—and would be beaten up even worse if such an event occurred.

* * * * *

Do people with OCD really lack social skills? I certainly lacked them, early on by default and later on by becoming a withdrawn zombie at times. I had to learn my social skills; they were not innate. And this learning process was not substantially completed until after I had received successful OCD treatment in my forties.

But in my childhood, I had developed a pattern of pissing people off to the point of violence, putting myself into situations that provided numerous opportunities to worry about having to fight or get beat up. Ironically, this fit right in with all my other hypochondriac's worries—those regarding my physical well-being. Every time I opened my mouth, I became a candidate for a Darwin Award.

I now believe I had a love/hate relationship with anxiety. Although I hated feeling anxious, it was a natural state for me. I believe I deliberately created anxiety in my life because, subconsciously, it was a kind of anchor. It replicated the fear and criticism I often received at home from my strict father. And I am hardwired for extra anxiety; that's what makes OCD so hard to kill.

* * * * *

I believe OCD interferes with social skills. Perhaps the same lack of hardwiring that prevents images and thoughts from becoming overpowering throttles social skills also. Or, the self-absorption, the strong inner focus of the OCD person, prevents sufferers from being able to pick up and then process social skills via the outward observation of others.

Today's society is starting to become much more aware of this type of mental illness, which is really a flaw in brain chemistry that can be successfully treated both cognitively and medically. If only I'd had this type of knowledge and support when I was younger! Well, at least I had some support and sympathy, if not understanding.

* * * * *

On more than one occasion, I smarted off to a bigger fellow, got smacked around, and then ended up being the more powerful person's friend. Kind of like big brothers who pick on their little brothers but stick up for them if someone else tries to bully them.

In fifth grade, I was shoved aside in the lunchroom while trying to get the last seat at a table. The boy, Dennis Morris, was an athlete, stocky and strong. He did not have a reputation as a bully, but he took no crap either. "Hey, quit shoving, you fat ass," I remonstrated him.

In my mind *ass* meant "jackass." In Dennis's mind, it meant worse, and of course "fat" didn't win me any points either. He looked back at me. "What was that you said?"

"I said you're a fat ass."

Dennis didn't even look upset. He just stated evenly, "You're going to get it after I'm done with lunch."

Not wanting to take chances, I ate my lunch quickly and ran out to the farthest corner of the playground, trying to make myself disappear behind some large poplar trees lining the edge. But Dennis had lookouts, apparently. Soon, from my hiding place, I saw a group of the jocks heading my way, straight as an arrow. Behind me was a tall chain-link fence, and I had run out of time to jump it.

Why was I so good at generating anxiety for myself, especially when it came to setting myself up for retaliation? I am reminded of a quote from Captain Kirk. When a being offered to take away all of his bad feelings and pain, Kirk grimly replied, "I need my pain."

Apparently I needed mine too, and quite often.

Dennis soon had me in a faceoff. "This isn't a fight," he assured me. "I'm just going to teach you a lesson. If you don't try to fight back, it will go easier on you." He then walked up, put a hard rabbit punch into my solar plexus, and then threw me down onto the ground.

I'd never been hit in the solar plexus with a punch, and Dennis didn't know his own strength. After I'd been lying on the grass for about a minute, too winded to even cry, he started to get miffed. "Come on, get up. I think you've learned your lesson. I'm not going to touch you again."

But I couldn't get up—I still couldn't really breathe. One of the fellow jocks said, "I think you knocked the wind out of him, Dennis. Let's just leave. He'll get up when he's ready." Dennis's friends walked away, the action over. But Dennis didn't leave; chivalrously, he helped me up. He looked really upset with himself. Dennis was one who liked to play by the rules, and he felt he'd overdone it.

"Look, Dahlberg, I'm sorry I hit you so hard—I really am. But you've gotta watch your mouth! Look, I'll walk you back to class if you need it."

"Thanks, Dennis. I'm sorry I mouthed off to you. I think I can make it now."

I made quite a few friends this way over the years, it seemed. But the story with Dennis was not over yet. Unknowing to me, he understood I had an issue and had become my advocate. What a funny way of making friends I had—annoying them to see if they accepted me.

A few weeks later, at lunch again, an empty milk carton hit me on the back of the head, splattering the remainder of its contents down my neck. I looked around and saw Barry Smitt, a *real* bully, laughing at me. I hadn't been his direct target; he'd thrown the carton at my table, where I was sitting with my friends—not caring whom he hit.

I reacted in my classic pattern. "You fat pig! You messed up my clothes!"

Barry rose immediately to come get me. The lunch supervisor, up on the stage, saw Barry get up with murderous intent. Barry was halfway to my table when… "Smitt! You know better than to leave your tray at the table. Clean up after yourself *now!*"

I'd brought a sack lunch, so I bolted out the door, dropped my empty bag in the nearest trash can, and ran out into the playground and back again to the far end, found a the poplar tree near where I'd tried to hide from Dennis. It was bigger, and I hoped it would hide me better. Besides, Barry had few friends, and it was going to be tougher for him to find me. Looking back, it almost seems like I was in my room at home, waiting for my dad to come whack me.

But I had established a pattern regarding my hiding place. Soon enough, I found myself cornered again. "Come out of there, Dahlberg, you little coward!" Smitt had an intimidating, deep boyish voice. "Come out and fight like a man."

I came out to face him. Barry wanted to fight, not just to teach me a lesson. He was one of those big, tall, and wide kids, bordering on obese, who carried great strength nonetheless. His black shock of hair, dark corduroys, black boots, and grubby denim jacket made him look every bit the thug he was. "It's not nice to call people names."

He was talking to me. I had some small hope that maybe I could reason with him, avoid getting beaten up. "I'm sorry, Barry, I was surprised. I didn't really mean it."

But Smitt was just a large cat playing with its prey. "I think you did mean it. I don't like being called fat, Dahlberg. What makes you think I'm fat? Well, fat enough to kick your skinny little butt." He took his jacket off and handed it to a bystander. "Put 'em up!"

In fractions of a second, several thoughts came and went. I really was no good at fighting. I didn't have the stomach to hit someone. In hindsight, my only chance would have been to punch him hard in the nose or kick him in the groin, but I couldn't have made myself do that. Barry was going to break my face. And my dad would yell at me for not fighting back, as I would certainly come out of this with a black eye or two. How quickly disturbing thoughts could enter my head!

Barry put up his big fists. But before he could move, another impressive figure walked up and stood beside me. It was Dennis Morris.

"Get out of the way," Smitt told him. "We're going to fight."

Dennis looked over at me. "Do you want to fight him?"

"No."

Dennis turned back toward Barry. "My friend is a very busy man, Smitt. He doesn't have time to fight. I have time to fight. If you want to fight, you can fight me."

Barry was bigger than Dennis, but he was no athlete. He knew Dennis was stronger, tougher, and disliked bullies. Everybody else knew it too. The level of excitement increased quickly, vastly.

Instead of watching Barry Smitt beat up someone weaker—boring, but better than nothing—they were going to get to see Barry receive a well-deserved thrashing, a much more entertaining event in everybody's book.

The crowd was bigger now too, as Morris vs. Smitt was a major attraction. Barry looked around. Besides being a coward, he would never live down the public humiliation of badly losing a fight. "I don't have any beef with you, Morris."

"You will if you touch my friend. Now make up your mind. The bell's going to ring soon. Would you like to meet after school instead?"

Barry did not want to meet at all. He grabbed his jacket. "I don't want to be late for class. And I ride the bus home; I can't stay after school."

The crowd dispersed quickly, quietly. No one wanted to laugh at Barry—he could still get you later. But I was forever safe from him—if I could watch my mouth.

* * * * *

Years later, I showed I still had it. My senior year in college, I went to a party in the U district (Near area surrounding Seattle's University of Washington) while I was home from Western one weekend. Two of my college buddies – a couple – were home that weekend, and they invited me to come along. The party was in a house just north of the University that was shared by four roommates. It was a very eclectic household of UW students: an Asian fellow, an African-American female, a young white lady, and a young white male who was clearly gay. We'd had a couple of beers on the way to warm up, and my questionable social inhibitions were already lowered.

When we arrived, my friends Neil and Mary introduced me to the hosts, who were busy preparing food and drink in the kitchen. We said our hellos, and then, noticing the unusual collection of roommates (at least in my book), I made what I thought was a friendly, humorous comment. "So, we have a multiracial household here!"

Nobody laughed. And I did not pick up on the strange—no, shocked, really—looks I received. My subconscious, anxiety-creating genius had struck again.

A few minutes later, Neil found me on the stairwell, talking to a young lady. "Dave, I've got to talk to you *now!*" He urgently ushered me into a corner. "We've got to get out of here!"

"What for?"

Neil's eyes were wide with fear. "Everybody in this house wants to kill you."

I didn't understand, and said so.

"Don't you remember the comment you made? About the multiracial household?"

"Yeah…"

"They took it as a slur."

"I didn't mean it as a slur."

Neil rolled his eyes. "You know it, and I know it, but they don't know *you*. The only reason you haven't been beaten up yet is that I told them you were a black belt in karate and were looking to start a fight and kick some UW ass."

I felt bad. "Look, I'll go apologize to them. Would that help?"

Neil shook his head. "It's too late for apologies. One of the girls called up some UW football players." He looked down the stairs. There was a door exiting the basement. "Go out that door now! Mary and I will meet you at the car. There's no time to waste."

And that was my experience with UW parties. I concluded the UW was far too cliquish; I'd stick to Western from then on. It took me years to figure out I'd really gone too far.

* * * * *

The reader by now might think I had no self-preservation instinct. I certainly let my OCD bully me for years. But I never let it win. At times, I was capable of doing what I need to do. My cumulative experience enabled me to survive over the years and ultimately to beat my OCD., as well as to defend myself physically when I truly felt threatened.

Ironically, this occurred with my best friend, Gary Adams. Gary had a real temper. It could be bad, but it was predictable—he had to be provoked. One of our favorite games was sandlot football, played at a nearby neighbor's yard. Back then we called it the Evans field. Today, a house stands there. The Evanses were very generous with their property. An older couple, they believed neighborhood children should have a place to play. No lawsuits back in the seventies.

This day, Gary and I were practicing football in his back yard. We were in seventh grade. In our neighborhood, sandlot football was played much like rugby, and dirty play was often resorted to. For instance, if you were quarterbacking and you knew you were about to get tackled, a common trick was to throw the football into the tackler's face. So tacklers had to be very careful when they rushed.

We were practicing tackler/quarterback, taking turns. Given ten feet of space to start the play, the quarterback had to find a man downfield and get a pass to him. We were practicing avoiding the tackler and throwing the ball at the last second to an imaginary receiver. On Gary's last turn at quarterback, he threw the ball into my face. Gary loved playing rough. It bounced off my forehead, smarting, but doing little damage. "Ha ha ha!" Gary laughed. "You're such a sucker, Dahlberg."

Gary had thrown the ball pretty hard—as if I were an actual opponent. Pissed off, I threw the ball in Gary's face my first turn— and right onto his nose. "You fucker," he said, holding his nose in pain. And suddenly I could see the anger building. "I'm gonna kick your ass!" he said, and came at me swinging.

He was on me before I could turn and run. We were about the same size, and though he was a much more experienced fighter, I could always beat him wrestling. I figured I'd get him down, hold him down, let his anger fade.

I was soon on top of Gary, but being held down infuriated him. I had his arms pinioned with my legs, but he would get an arm free and start flailing. I'd grab the arm and re-pin it, but he'd often get the other free right then and whack me on top of the head. He couldn't hit me terribly hard, with his arm's travel limited, but I was starting to run out of strength to hold him down. I suddenly realized I wasn't going to be able to hold this infuriated person much longer.

It was like trying to forcibly control an OCD attack.

Everyone has a breaking point. As I looked at Gary's face, twisted with anger and the desire for revenge, I realized it was him or me. So, with a quickly muttered apology—"I'm sorry, Gary"—I drew back my left hand and smacked him pretty hard on the right side of his head, close to his ear.

The results were dramatic. I'd really got him. Gary burst into tears of anger and started yowling, holding his head in pain. "You dirty bastard! You hit me on a pressure point!"

I got off him, but Gary stayed on the ground, cussing me out from sort of a curled-up-ball position. I went and got his mom. She looked at Gary, still flattened, and said, "You'd better go home, Dave." I started walking.

I was back in fifteen minutes; I was too worried about him. He was in their TV room, on its big green mohair couch, lying down with an ice pack on the side of his head. "I'm really sorry I hit you, Gary."

"Oh, that's okay. I'm really the one who started it. I didn't think you had it in you to smack me like that."

This one "victory" made me no more eager to seek out fights. If anything, I think it made me more reluctant to hit someone in such a manner. I never felt proud of it. But I'd found out that, when truly pressed, I was not one to give up.

CHAPTER 3

Details

ounting, images, names, rituals—I have discussed these in detail—but in reality, these are only the tip of my phobia iceberg. I developed an intricately *ordered* system of categorizing illnesses and the people who died from them.

A second category consisted of people who were perfectly healthy.

Most of these OCD thoughts and procedures were internalized and often took place when I was trying to get to sleep at night, when preparing to get up in the morning, when I was alone, or, in the worst-case scenario, in front of other people who had no idea why I had suddenly turned into a vacant zombie.

Here's one of the simpler versions—explanation forthcoming. Can you figure out the sense of this puzzle?

Version one:

Cancer, leukemia, heart attack, heart disease,
Cancer, leukemia, heart attack, heart disease,
Cancer, leukemia, heart attack, heart disease.

This was a common phrase I would repeat in my head. Notice in this case it was repeated three times. This made four terms times three repetitions, for a total of twelve. Somehow I still had to have a "good" number of "bad" things; saying it only twice would make a total of eight, which would give it power.

Why would I say this to myself at all? Well, one of the bad thoughts that popped into my mind a lot was the word *cancer*. This word was my chief tormentor. If nothing else, it seemed like I saw it in the newspaper nearly every day. *Leukemia* was just as bad, perhaps worse, as I had often read about this disease, a favorite of books and articles. If my eyes saw either word, it flew into my mind, and—like wallpaper coated with glue—it would smack the surface and stick there, as plain to my perception as the real world surrounding me. It would often blot the real world right out.

Two other diseases I feared far less, since I was young and extremely unlikely to contract them, "balanced" the gravely-feared ones above. When I said them in a progression, with the least-feared last, it was like pushing them off a ramp altogether, out of my perception.

The problem was the repetition. By saying them over and over, I was only burning the words deeper into my psyche. The very act of repeating the phrase made it much more a part of my brain pattern and then forced me into another time-wasting cycle. Repeating this three times was usually just a start. This ritual could stretch into five or ten minutes very, very easily. I would engage in it without thinking, like a mantra. It got so I would be in the middle of my fourth repetition before I was conscious of it.

And of course the variations were infinite. Another version:

My cancer cell count is zero,
My leukemia cell count is zero,
My heart attack count is zero,
My heart disease count is zero.

Repeat as necessary. I would also do this with the names of people who had died, using the same order of disease/death. Sometimes I would simply repeat their names. Other times I would use the prefix again:

"My John Smith cell count is zero…"

I developed this system early in high school, and it persisted all the way into my mid-twenties, when I received my first antianxiety treatments. I must have repeated variations of this internal ritual thousands of times over the years—my concentration constantly interrupted, my fears contributing to increased dysfunction, and all that precious time wasted.

My senior year in college, a neighbor boy in my apartment complex came by repeating a phrase: "I am free of all diseases." Wow. Was that simple.

"Where'd you hear that, Bryce?"

"My mom's a nurse. And she knows I worry about catching something she might bring home. So she told me to say this whenever I worried."

"Does it help?"

"Yeah."

So, for a short time, my life became simplified by this phrase. But then I counted the syllables. Eight! Bad medicine. I tried rephrasing the sentence to give it the proper number of syllables, but it never sounded or felt right. So I stopped using it.

I often repeated the "healthy" category when walking from one place to another. I recall exactly how this ritual began. It was my first day attending Shorecrest High School. I was a sophomore.

The building was a rambler, a huge, single-story fixture with halls parallel around open spaces and connecting corridors between the main halls, dividing up the open spaces. Most were garden-like, with benches to sit on in nice weather. And one space at the eastern end of campus, by the band room, was mostly filled by a greenhouse. The stoners at school were constantly sneaking into the greenhouse and planting marijuana seeds. The plants could grow quite large before they were discovered, to the ire of the horticulture teacher.

This layout meant long walks between classes. I remember starting to count my steps and the OCD tension beginning to build in my mind. I tried to think of a song I could sing silently—something with 4/4 time—to match the rhythm of my steps: 1, 2, 3, 4, 1, 2, 3, 4. But then the image of my dead friend flew into my mind's eye and spoiled it all—and I knew I would have to prioritize some extra ritual for this. Suddenly, the image of a healthy friend came to mind; his name had four syllables, so I started saying it in time to my steps, two syllables to each step. I managed to focus all of this on the chorus of the song, to make it less complicated: "Steven Williams, Steven Williams, Steven Williams, Steven Williams…"

I concentrated on watching my feet, mostly oblivious to the people in the hall, who were probably mystified at this person marching to class in his own little world. But it did get me to class reasonably intact, with a new self-absorbed ritual firmly established. Like all the others, it would last me for years.

There were only a few people whose names I chose to step by. They had to be four-syllable names or capable of being made into a four-syllable name (Bill Rodgers, the famous and extremely healthy marathoner, became William Rogers). They had to be people I admired. Most were very athletic and healthy. And they were all people I knew personally in some way. This was somewhat ironic, since many of the sick people whose names would pop into my mind were those I'd merely read of in the news media. I'm not sure why this was the case. Possibly because real people were more—well, real. And I enjoyed being around my friends, so thinking of them generally made me happier, or at least more secure.

Replacement

My healthy friends "helped" me in another major way: if the image of a sick person suddenly appeared in my mind (and it was always suddenly, always a mental ambush), I would try to think immediately of a healthy person's image to blot it out, replace it. Unfortunately, I have so much space inside my head that the bad image would pop right in again, next to the good one. So I'd throw another good image at it. And the bad one would step right back into sight again.

You'd think the good images might win in the end, as all my effort was going into generating them, and they should eventually overpower the bad ones. But this actually raised two bigger problems:

(1) The bad images popped into my head out of nowhere, with no effort at all. I'd sweat trying to block one out, and the image

would reappear even more strongly. What was pushing these images into my brain? From where did it derive its irresistible power? At times I suspected some evil entity lurked in my brain, a dark, secret personality that delighted in torturing my own trying-to-be-happy one.

(2) Even worse, soon after I developed this replacement habit, I began counting the number of times I replaced. I had to replace a "good" number of times or it wasn't going to be right. I couldn't replace a "bad" number of times. Therefore I might say to myself, *I'll replace nine times.* To speed things up, I started reconjuring the bad image myself so that I could replace it immediately with a good one. The net result? Now that I was helping Mr. Dark Entity out by supplying bad images myself, the unwanted image would reappear much more so strongly after I had finished this type of ritual.

I could run through this mode of thinking for scores or even hundreds of repetitions when it was at its worst. And, as this was an internalized battle, an outsider would see only the result—an inwardly-focused, antisocial human being.

This was perhaps the most disruptive ritual of all. It would happen in the middle of a chapter of a textbook I was reading. It could disrupt my thought process on a math or chemistry problem. And, worst of all, knowing what was going to happen if I did, I would put off tasks or problems as long as possible to avoid these dreaded rituals. I had gone from one of the fastest students in town to one of the slowest.

Bathroom Rituals

What better place to develop many unique rituals than in the bathroom? Brushing hair and teeth, showering, shaving, washing hands—so many little things, so much time and detail, so many opportunities. I remember my first roommate in college calling the time I spent getting ready for bed at night "The Dave Dahlberg Ordeal."

When I was fourteen, the year my OCD really hit, my bathroom was just down the hall, on the upstairs floor. This floor also contained my parents' master bedroom and my brother's room, just across from the bathroom—our shared bathroom. The bathroom was small and contained a stand-up shower, a free-standing sink and cabinet, a toilet, and a closet with lots of room for towels, Band-Aids, and other such bathroom items. A window looked out; it had no curtain, as it looked out into a solid mass of evergreens, And it was twenty feet up from the driveway at that point.

A heating vent opened onto the floor across from the toilet— excellent for sitting next to and warming one's feet on cold winter mornings. It was a quiet, cozy bathroom. Next to the closet by a window was an old, sturdy bathroom scale that still occupies the floor space decades later.

If you weighed yourself on the scale, it was possible to add a pound or two from your weight by shifting forward, over the front of the scale. This was important during the OCD years. When I was fourteen, I weighed about 130 pounds at one point. But 130 was not the best number, as it was nearly analogous to 13. So, I would lean forward to obtain a reading of 131, which added to make 14, a good number. As my weight changed over the years, I would adjust the scale's reading as such to obtain an acceptable reading.

* * * * *

Perhaps the reader may wonder, Why supply so many details? I think I get the point by now. *And I would answer, They are my details. Everyone's OCD is different, just as everyone is unique. This is a personal account, not a case study. My OCD routines accompanied nearly every "normal" routine, which all took time. What if it cost me two hours per day? For twenty-six years, that's over two years of my life wasted. And I feel this is a very conservative estimate.*

As one reads through my routines (and I can't possibly write them all up), one gets a sense of the overwhelmingness of the OCD in countless thoughts and actions. And it not only wasted time; so much worry and anxiety always accompany the rituals. For example, did I perform the ritual correctly? Maybe I should repeat it again. And often I would. Imagine brushing your teeth in two to three minutes and then just standing there for another two to three minutes, just doing nothing. Imagine doubling the time it took for you to complete any task. Then you might get a sense of the everyday waste of life I was forced to endure.

* * * * *

Tooth brushing: I divided my teeth into eighteen sections: outside, top surface, inside, left/right/front top, left/right/front middle. Each section had to be brushed at least three times and in this order: outside, top surface, inside. I was also a simple perfectionist, as I had to get each tooth perfectly clean. My only saving grace was that my dad was a periodontist. He noticed a little gum erosion around a couple of teeth and made sure I brushed softly with a proper brush, of which he had endless supply. So at least I didn't brush my gums away.

Showering: My showers usually ran to a count of twenty-seven. Get in the shower. Wet my hair. Put in the shampoo. Wash my hair and the rest of myself, generally using multiples of nine; scrub myself nine times under the arms, for instance. Rinse my hair by swishing my head back and forth under the water for total of six immersions. Rinse the left ear, then the other. Repeat. Rinse under the left arm, then the right. Repeat. Use my fingers to wash between my toes three times. Add it up:

7 head immersions

4 ear immersions

4 rinses under arms

12 washes for the toes

27 actions total. And 27 is a multiple of 9. What a nice number!

How long did this take you to read? Imagine having to do it for real. And this does not even count my drying routine, nor does it count having a bad thought ambush me while I was rinsing my hair. There were the occasions when I would have to rinse my hair for minutes more, always counting up to another good number. Rarely (fortunately) I would be forced out of the shower by the hot water running out. And if the attack was especially urgent, I could even stand cold water for quite a while—uncomfortable, even painful, but better than the fear and anxiety driving me.

Shaving, brushing my hair, other bathroom routines: The reader certainly gets the sense by now. Much like tooth brushing and showering, everything had its special numbers and ordering—and extra time.

Hand washing: Although I had not heard of OCD at this time of my life, I *had* heard about compulsive hand washing. It was the one OCD routine I refused to engage in. Certainly I might count a few scrubs, but hand washing was the one place I drew the line. Compulsive hand washing was done by insane, out-of-control, mentally ill people. It was the one thing I absolutely refused to do. My lack of compulsive hand washing seemed to show me I was only weird, not psychotic. It was a small victory in the larger battle—my way of not giving in completely.

Injuring myself

My OCD apparently had its limits. Once when I was at Scout camp, I was cleaning out my tent. The tents at Camp Parsons, an exceptionally beautiful facility on the Hood Canal in Washington's Olympic Peninsula, stood on wooden platforms.

After sweeping out the tent, I noticed a small piece of dirt on the edge of the platform and wiped it off with my finger. As I did so, a bad image flew into my mind. I would have to wipe the spot again. Now my OCD is also tactile—in other words, the replacement action must be performed more strongly than the original, while holding a replacement image in my mind's eye. So I had to wipe harder, and of course, having to count a good number of wipes was paramount.

For some reason, I could not get the bad image to go. I kept wiping, harder and harder. It got to the point where I was literally jabbing at the wood. Then *pop!* I had just sprained my finger. The middle joint of the index finger I'd been using started to swell immediately. I can still vividly remember the sound when it went. And finally the trance was broken. I ran to the bathroom to run my finger under cold water.

In this case, a lasting impression was made. Although I still engaged in tactile OCD, I never allowed it to progress to the point of injury. At least not deliberately.

A fairly severe OCD-related injury occurred when I was in college. I was home for the summer, and early in the break I had sprained my left ankle running down some stairs to my parents' basement. I had caught my heel on the last step, which turned my foot down—and again, the dreaded *pop* of a sprain. I collapsed at the bottom of the stairs, groaning, curled up into a ball, holding my ankle. It was one of those really painful sprains that combines the sensation of being dipped in lava with that of hundreds of needles being jabbed in simultaneously. The X-rays proved nothing broken, but the ankle was still sore six weeks later.

After these six weeks, around the middle of August, I started running again—I ran quite often to stay in shape. During the middle of a run during this time, I was around two miles from home, running along a sidewalk along a busy street approaching Lake Washington. Coming up to an intersection I was going to cross, I turned sideways to look behind me, checking traffic. Not wanting to lose my momentum, I started skipping sideways on my left foot. I had all the visual information I needed by the fourth skip, but decided to go to six skips, as it was a much better number than four or five. During this time, I failed to notice a dip in the sidewalk coming up, a dip commonly used for wheelchair access to the crossing.

My left ankle dropped into the dip with the full force of my body weight hopping onto it, and turned. A horrid sound far beyond a *pop* registered in my ears. I dropped again, the pain in my reinjured ankle far beyond that of the previous sprain. I vividly remember huge anger at my compulsions—as I lay holding my ankle again, I cursed them over and over. I could not move for several minutes, and with no one to support me, I had to crawl to a nearby tavern (fortunately only about a hundred feet away) to find a phone. Luckily my mom was home and was able to pick me up quickly.

I've heard it said sometimes that it's better to break an ankle than to sprain it because the recovery is shorter. But somehow my ankle was not broken, but now was severely sprained. I spent a month on crutches before I could walk again, and it took a couple more before I started jogging. To this day I have to stretch my left ankle regularly to keep it loose. And I never skip while looking backward during a run.

And there's that time thing again. While my ankle was sprained, I lost time on getting back into shape. I lost time on working and recreation almost until school started again. What did I do with the time? Unfortunately it gave me that much more opportunity to do nothing but sit around and obsess, an exact counter to the healthy effects of running and other activities. All because my OCD made me put in two extra skips.

Driving

Driving with OCD can be tough. First, once learned, driving becomes automatic—one of the miracles of the human brain that allows us to make machinery an extension of our bodies. But driving takes time. The automatic part frees us to think—or, in my case, to obsess—while getting to our destination. I specialized in internal ritualizing while I drove.

I remember an occasion when I lost track of what I was doing—ironically, it was right across the street from where I had skipped onto my ankle. The street I was coming down crossed a four-lane arterial. My street had the stop sign at the bottom of the hill. That particular day I made a legal stop. But, as I stopped, in flew a bad image and pasted itself to projector screen inside my head. So I let the car roll a few inches and stopped again, trying to finish on a good image. Many little stops later, I still hadn't licked it. I heard a honk. Suddenly the road reappeared out of my mental fog, and a car whizzed by the front of my own. Where was I?

Quickly I glanced around. The car that honked was in the lane I was blocking (I had inched out that far), with several other cars waiting behind it. In my rearview mirror I saw a few more cars waiting behind me. Fear and embarrassment hit me with brutal force. What the hell had I just been doing? Checking left, I cranked my wheel to the right and moved out properly into the arterial, freeing up the little traffic jam I had created.

Details

In this case I had been fortunate. There was good visibility coming up to the intersection. The driver who I had blocked had seen me inching out slowly from quite a ways, and, certainly puzzled, had lots of time to slow down and inch up to me. Nevertheless it was a severe shock to me, and I never allowed compulsions to control my driving actions again. Another small victory at a cost.

CHAPTER 4

High School

The high-school age effects of my OCD are often described as you read through the other chapters of this autobiography. My experiences with OCD during this time were predictable, and certainly tragic in many ways.

Certainly I could spend an entire book addressing my high school years and my OCD, and yet these three years were but a fraction of the twenty-six I spent suffering from my condition. But high school is a critical time. Many people still look back on high school as the fulcrum on which their present and future rests. "If only I had done this. If only I had done that…"

My OCD effects would have been worse in high school if I had not been active in so many programs. My musical talent allowed me to participate in many bands; I played saxophone, clarinet, drums, and piano. One semester my senior year I took four band classes.

I was also active in athletics. I wrestled for a year and then joined the swim team in subsequent years. I ski raced. My Scouting kept me very busy. And I took challenging subjects: trigonometry, chemistry, physics.

Although not a social butterfly, I had a great circle of friends and acquaintances via my classes and activities, especially through band. I went on only one date in high school, however—a Tolo, a girl-asks-the-boy dance. A young lady asked me. My OCD made me appear (and act) functionally withdrawn in many settings – and, unfortunately, I did so at this Tolo as well. I worried much more than I danced. We did not go out together again.

My OCD limited my ability to concentrate, costing me a high GPA. I finished high school with a 3.3, nowhere close to admission standards to many four-year colleges nowadays, but certainly not too low for Western Washington University, which I did attend.

My parents, teachers, and counselors had one big frustration: how could I score in the ninety-eighth to ninety-ninth percentile in all the aptitude tests and yet do so relatively poorly with my grades? Although I did carry a 3.3 GPA, over a third of that came from A's in my band classes. My average in my "academic" classes was in the high C range.

I could blow away aptitude tests, but they only showed what I *could* do. There was no OCD box to check on the exams.

* * * * *

Looking back, I believe I did the best I could. I never gave up. I gained and obtained many invaluable experiences during high school, all the while fighting through my OCD. I attribute much of this to the fact that my family never gave up on me. If OCD had been known of and treatable, they would have been the first to rush me to see a doctor.

And this is today's bottom line. Although high school can seem a lonely time, a time to find yourself, a time for letting go, high school is also a place where a young person can find a great deal of help. Students can obtain counseling and evaluation in the high school; they can be referred to the proper process of treatment; and the school itself can set up accommodations for such students. *No one needs to suffer the unmitigated effects of OCD*—or, for that matter, the many interrelated problems associated with anxiety, depression, lack of motivation, and the myriad of other "mental" conditions that have a physical basis.

Mom, Dad, Student: This stuff is *treatable!* You can make your child's or your experience a great one, if you are informed. Mom and Dad, it is especially important that you are a driving force behind such treatment—for often, the student is depressed to the point that he or she will not be motivated to find the help on his or her own.

Again, I have written this book as a resource by a former OCD sufferer, and as a teacher. If you feel your child has a problem— if *you* have a problem—see a medical professional. Things have come a *long* way since I went through my OCD.

CHAPTER 5

College Friends

Many of my friends were confident and charismatic. People such as this have social skills bordering on ESP. They somehow were able to see through my surface social idiocy to the person underneath. Is this what makes a charismatic person? The ability so see into everybody, their fears and their hopes, and to play to them? I, on the other hand, couldn't see below the surface. Heck, half the time I couldn't even see the surface itself.

After my OCD kicked in, I believe my social skills regressed still more—my extra maturity more than counterbalanced by the more intense internal world I was so often trapped in. Especially striking to me in hindsight is my behavior in college—especially when I first arrived.

During my first quarter at Western Washington University, I found myself in a faraway dormitory—the Fairhaven section of WU, which was over a mile from the main campus. Not only this, but I had a roommate who might have been more bizarre than me. I moved into my dorm the Sunday before school started (I always did things at the last minute). My roommate had arrived two days earlier, however, and was a music major—a vocalist—and a Barbra Streisand hoarder.

In those two days, he had dedicated our room to Barbra Streisand. Shelves were filled with Barbra Streisand records, tapes, and books. Barbra Streisand artifacts were strewn about his desk, spilling onto the floor. Worst of all, the walls were covered with Barbra Streisand posters and concert flyers. Not just the wall by his bed. All the walls. When I lay down on my bed, posters of Barbara stared down at me from the ceiling. And I'm sure if a Barbra Streisand Barbie doll had been available, he would have had several of those too. There was not a place I could turn in the entire room without seeing Barbra Streisand. I wondered if there was a blow-up Barbra Streisand in the closet.

Although I appreciated Barbra, this was overload. I had to get out. Plus, the walk was simply too long. I was in concert band, and carrying a tenor saxophone to campus, plus my books, was wearing. I had taken to stashing my tenor sax in a friend's room at the Higginson Hall dorm, a very close walk to the main campus. My friend, Tony Weiss, was a year older than I and had convinced me to attend Western because of its musical reputation. Tony and I had played in bands together in high school—both symphonic and jazz groups. It had been an easy sell.

For the first few days, he felt sorry for me, but he finally let me know I was becoming an imposition. He didn't like leaving his room unlocked for me. He suggested I apply for a dorm transfer. Although Higginson, Tony's dorm, had been my first choice, I had applied too late and the dorm was filled. But not everybody showed up at the beginning of the year. There were always openings after the first week of school.

"Hey, there's going to be a party upstairs tomorrow night," Tony told me the first Thursday of school. "Why don't you come along with me, and if you like the people in this dorm, you should apply for that transfer." Tony was a good guy, and one of my friends who looked after me in high school. His advice was always good.

Higginson's architecture was considered ideal for parties. A large, concrete five-story structure, shaped like an L, it had no hallways on the dorm floors. A walkway surrounded the rooms, on the inside and the outside of the L. The rooms themselves were long and narrow. One room would be on the outside of the L, the other would be on the inside. The two rooms were connected by a common bathroom and closet area, and a large shelf extended across on side of the room, with dresser drawers underneath. This bathroom arrangement also made it possible for the dorm to be co-ed by room, not just by floor. Generally, men's suites alternated with women's.

When roommates threw a party (generally a "kegger"), the keg would be placed on the shelf between rooms, with the spigot overhanging the floor, beneath which a bucket would be placed to catch the drips. People lined up for the keg in shared room and took their beers to either of the two outer rooms to socialize. It was unwise to take beer outside a room; although the Western Campus Police could not enter a room, they could and did ticket students who brought beer out in public.

The center bathroom was reserved for girls—the boys' bathroom was generally down at the far end of the L, where it extended into the trees and was dimly lit. It was not wise to stand below this section of the dorm at night during weekends.

The party was on the fifth, top floor of Higginson that night. Tony and I took the elevator up, paid our one-dollar entry fee (well, it was 1977!) and entered. It seemed like Tony knew everybody; his social skills were masterful. (After teaching band for years in the future, he was to do well in upper-level school administration.) He introduced me to several of his friends, and we all proceeded to fill our cups and drink together, to the loud sounds of what is now classic rock. Styx was the hot band at the time, and Boston was still smokin'.

The door opened, and a well-built guy with a striking female companion entered. "Dudley!" Several voices shouted enthusiastically. He and his companion smiled. "You call this a party?" he stated loudly. "Somebody get us a beer."

The request was enthusiastically granted. "That's Jim," Tony told me. "He's sort of the dorm leader."

"How's that?"

"Well, he helps keep people in line. He's a senior, and he looks out for the rest of us."

49

"How do we need looking out for?"

Tony nodded over at Jim. "Well, occasionally at parties, there are people who come in looking for trouble—maybe looking to start a fight. Their idea of entertainment.

"Last spring, when things could get a little wild, some pretty big guys came in from another dorm and started shoving people around. Football players, or crew maybe. Jim arrived right after they had left. Well, Jim and some of his friends chased them down and caught them by the gym. Let's just say that those fellows don't come to any parties around here anymore."

"Who's the girl?"

"That's Allison, his girlfriend. But Jim just calls her Punkin' Eater."

Hmmm, I thought. *There's more to this guy than I thought.*

I had no idea.

A few days later the transfer came through. There was one empty bed in the entire dorm: 512 Higginson. Apparently one guy's roommate had changed his mind about Western at the last minute. The room was Jim's. I asked Tony about rooming with Jim. "Oh, you'll be fine, as long as you don't piss him off," he replied.

I had no idea about the fifth floor of Higginson. Either by some vast coincidence—or, more likely, a check of student records—Higginson's fifth floor was a collection of rowdies, misfits, jocks, ex-cheerleaders, and anyone else who might belong on a topmost floor as far as possible from everybody else. Although I might have been the only OCD sufferer, my lack of social skills was more than matched by the delinquency of at least a dozen others.

The rooms in Higginson had big picture windows that extended from one edge of the room to the door. A few more feet separated the door from the opposite wall. A study desk followed the picture window's length. Across from the shelf-like desk, a single desk was located. The other bed fit into the space between the door and the far wall. Most people left their window shades open, as it was possible to observe the comings and goings of others from your desk. My new room had an ideal view—located on the inside bottom of the L, it was possible to observe all floors from it.

As I walked by the window of 512 Higginson, I could see Jim reading, lounging on his bed. I knocked on the door. Jim opened up. "What's going on?" he asked.

"I'm going to be your roommate. I was just reassigned from another dorm."

I had wondered if Jim was going to be annoyed about a freshman sharing his room space. But he held a complete poker face. "Come on in then," he said nonchalantly.

Jim had to move a few things around to make space for me, but he did so quickly and efficiently. I noticed his weight collection—several barbells and a bar for doing shoulder presses. I could barely do five presses with that bar. Jim could rattle off dozens.

"Johnson!" Jim yelled. "Come in and meet the new roommate."

In strode another freshman about my size, but with much darker hair and the energetic look of a Doberman pinscher about him. Brian Johnson was a baseball player on a partial scholarship. Full of energy, he was generally too lazy to dress himself. His favorite clothing to wear around in his room was a T-shirt and underwear. "Cool," said Brian. We all talked a little about our interests and soon found out we had both been competitive ski racers. Jim was impressed. He liked to ski, although he was an aggressive freestyle skier.

To top off the collection of characters on the fifth floor of Higginson, the two most immature freshmen in the dorm—possibly the entire campus—were now rooming together in the same suite.

Our other roommate, Mark McCleod, was a soccer player and a superb athlete, with inhuman reflexes and a sardonic sense of humor. He had worked for two years out of high school, and was a twenty-year-old freshman. The working world had supplied Mark with excellent focus for college. He was ready for school; he now had the motivation he had lacked when he had graduated from high school. He was actually the perfect roommate to keep Johnson under control, and he was big enough and mean enough when necessary to make Brian get dressed—such as on the occasions when Mark's girlfriend, Becky, came to visit.

Later that day, Brian told me a few things about Jim. Jim was the oldest guy in the dorm—he would be turning twenty-four during this school year. I didn't believe Brian at first—although big and strong, Jim barely looked twenty and got carded every time he bought alcohol (which was frequently, being in a dorm full of mostly underclassmen; the standard arrangement was that older students received a "commission" for doing so, either more alcohol or cash). In fact, Jim had been refused alcohol before—a clerk once looked at his driver's license, handed it back to him, and said "That's the best damn fake ID I've ever seen."

Jim had served in Vietnam, on a carrier, and had been frequently shot at by the North Vietnamese while he fired a machine gun of his own from a helicopter gunship. Thus Jim's navy vocabulary, which consisted of using the F word at least once in every sentence, often several times. Jim used the F word for adjectives, adverbs, verbs, nouns, appositives—every part of speech possible. And, like a properly-trained navy man, he could switch his speech patterns unconsciously—he rarely uttered the epithet around Allison.

Jim was charismatic and a social genius at both winning people over and pissing them off. If Jim didn't like you, he would insult you both to your face and behind your back. And you took it. Nobody argued with Jim. In fact, many of the males in our dorm were terrified of Jim and took great pains to stay clear of him. He had a reputation as a fellow who liked to fight.

Jim saw through much of me right from the start. I believe this is how I lived through my first week with him. Just like he'd been putting up with Brian Johnson, he realized I couldn't help myself. In fact, my second night in my new room, Jim told me he wondered if I was going to kill him as he slept.

That night, a Friday, always saw several parties and social events in Higginson. Mark, Brian, and I returned to the suite around 1:30 in the morning, having watched the last keg run dry in Joel's room down the hall. Joel and his roomies were all rugby players, and the traditional rugby drinking songs had been merrily and obscenely sung that evening.

Jim had been out with Allison and was in his bed trying to get some sleep. And he did like his sleep. He liked to get to bed by nine on weeknights, and he had told me if I wished to stay up later I could hang out with Brian and Mark, who rarely turned in before midnight. As Jim weight trained nearly every day, he did need sleep.

Things were quieting down a little too early this night, according to Brian. We sat on the edge of my bed, discussing options while Jim complained we should just go to sleep. Brian started giving Jim lip, being the one person on campus who could smart off to him. I think Jim saw a little of his younger self in Brian.

"Damn," said Jim. "Now you fuckers have thoroughly fuckin' woken me up." He sat up, bare-chested with his covers still around his lower body.

Brian was encouraged. "What can we do?"

Jim looked straight ahead, not seeing us, his poker face in excellent form. Ten seconds of silence passed. Without changing his look or gaze, he said, "I have some fireworks."

Fireworks! You could get expelled from the dorm for possession of fireworks.

"Whoa!" said Brian.

"You'll have to shoot them off outside. Go down to the lawn in front of the dorm and have some fun. But be careful—security will arrest you if they catch you."

Jim's fireworks—mostly strings of firecrackers and smoke bombs—appeared from a locked suitcase that we had thought only held Pat's liquor supply. He kept a well-maintained Colt .45 semiautomatic handgun in there as well, hidden at the bottom.

"Got any M80s in there?" Brian excitedly inquired.

"Not for you. Now get out and let me get some sleep!"

"I'm going to bed," Mark said.

Brian and I were on our own.

"Which lawn do you want to go to?" I asked Brian.

"The hell with that," Brian answered in an excited, fairly inebriated voice. "I'm throwing them off from right here."

"Are you kidding? Jim will come out and throw *you* off."

"Oh, we'll move over a little, over to the courtyard."

Higginson's L had a hole in it. Instead of rooms completely filling it, the corner of the building had a rectangular space, where the bottom side and the upright side of the L came together.

Although small, this courtyard extended from the ground to the top of the dorm and was unroofed. Surrounding this courtyard were rec rooms and the RA's residence. Steve Harbush, our RA, had a large sliding glass door that opened out into this space. It was a good central location to watch the main entrance to the dorm.

We stood overlooking the courtyard. "You're really going to throw firecrackers down there?' I said. "You're crazy, man!" Even my social skills knew better than this.

Actually, Brian's did too. He was just an expert at causing trouble. He pulled off five firecrackers from the bundle, twisted the fuses together, and lit them. He waited for a fraction of a second to let the fuses burn down, and he dropped them down into space.

BangbangbangBANGbang! The courtyard amplified and reverberated the sound—a sharp, hard. Brian stood there and laughed. I ran back to the room.

Jim had locked the door. The shades were closed. No answer to my frantic knocks. My key was still in my jacket in the room. It was times like this my OCD was completely forgotten. Real threats always took priority over imaginary ones.

"Shit," I muttered to myself. I ran around the other side of the dorm and crouched under the solid concrete rail. Brian was nowhere to be seen. I was hoping Mark would let me in. Fortunately his door wasn't locked. I entered, crossed the suite, and found Jim and Mark smirking in my room.

"You idiot," said Jim to Mark. "I thought you said your door was locked."

"You knew he would do something like this, didn't you?" I accused them both.

"We just wanted you to get to know Brian a little better, that's all," said Mark. "You've only had a couple of days."

Far down the end of the dorm, the rest of the string of the firecrackers let off at once. We could see the flashes right through the shades. We peeked through. It looked like a war zone. Before lighting the firecrackers, Brian had dropped smoke bombs everywhere for cover before he'd lit off the string. Sickly greenish-yellow-brown smoke billowed everywhere. Doors opened as residents checked the commotion, and shut again quickly to keep out the smoke. Mark's door slammed, and Brian ran in gasping, beaming as if he'd just won the medal of honor.

In the end, the disturbance of the dorm was minimal. It usually was, in Higginson. Everybody assumed Jim was behind things like this, but nobody would ever finger him, out of fear for their lives. And even though Brian was the culprit this time, Jim had still provided the ammo and the impetus. He was very good at directing people.

As Brian and Mark finally headed to bed, the adrenaline shock of being trapped outside, easy pickings for the campus police, still held me. It turned to anger. I sat on the edge of my bed, in the dark, stewing. Then I had an inspiration that only my mind could create. I went over to my desk and found some sheets of notebook paper and a lighter. I grabbed our metal garbage can and went back to my bed. I took a sheet of paper and lit the corner. And I started laughing diabolically.

In the days before smoke alarms, you could do things like this. Now, even lighting a cigarette in Higginson would set off the entire dorm's fire alarm.

Jim sat up again. "What the fuck are you doing?"

I only laughed harder. I lit a second paper with the first one and started dancing around the room. Little pieces of live ash cascaded about, even settling on Jim's bed.

I believe that this moment was when Jim came to see my mind was not entirely put together right. "Jesus!" he screamed, and hid under his covers, never to come out again that night. I threw the rest of the burning paper in the can to finish burning.

The next day Jim told me he was actually afraid that I would come after him with a burning sheet next. I don't know if it was exactly respect, but Jim certainly had a new appreciation for me after that. I had joined the Crazy Club.

Besides this incident, Jim soon picked up that I was extremely quirky. l did my rituals before bed, just like I had done them at home—tooth brushing, opening and closing drawers the proper amount of times—unseen but heard things taking place in the middle of the suite, things that took way too long or were not necessary at all. This was when Jim named my getting-ready-for-bed routine "The Dave Dahlberg Ordeal." He observed my tuning out when I studied and my staring into space at times from my bed.

His powers of observation were excellent, and, if nothing else, he concluded I could be very strange and unpredictable at times. The one thing Jim couldn't figure out was why. He watched me, catalogued me, accepted me, and moved on. Jim turned out to be extremely good at working with people. Now a battalion chief fire-fighter, he specializes in "putting out fires"—the person-to-person kind.

Being Jim's roommate had a major perk. Freshmen were subject to pranks and hazing. No one in my dorm dared to bother me; hazing me would be essentially picking a fight with Jim. I was unaware of this aura of invincibility until a rather large junior pulled a simple prank on me one afternoon.

Tony had introduced me to Kurt Fair, a junior who lived on the fourth floor of Higginson. Although not quite twenty-one, he had a short beard and looked older. He was tall and brown-haired, and he had a quick laugh and a bright smile. He was a good two inches taller than me and about twenty pounds heavier.

Higginson had an elevator, used often by upper-floor students. One day as I stepped onto the elevator, Kurt stepped in, grinned a big "hi," punched all the buttons on the elevator, and jumped back out. Whoever had programmed the elevator had possibly just finished a job at a retirement home. At every floor the door would stay open for at least half a minute, and the "close door" button had been disabled or broken.

That night I planned my revenge. It was a school night, and I had Kurt's phone number. Not being the greatest sleeper, I knew I would wake up once or twice during the night. I always did.

I woke up around two. Our phone was a wall phone next to the center room door. I picked it up and dialed the four-digit campus extension. It rang several times.

"Hello?" said a groggy voice. I recognized the voice. It was Jeff Darling, Kurt's roommate.

I lowered my voice a notch. "I need to speak to Kurt. This is his dad."

Kurt was a much better sleeper than I. It took Jeff quite a bit of trouble to wake him up. "Hello, Dad?" His concerned voice rang loudly from the earpiece.

"No, this isn't your dad. It's Dave."

Not quite awake still. "Who's Dave?"

"Dave Dahlberg. Hey, Kurt, I was just calling to thank you for pushing all the elevator buttons today. It was a real fun ride."

Spluttering and swearing on the other side. Then the slam of a harshly hung-up phone. Jim slept through it all.

The next day, Kurt got into the elevator with me as I came back from class. He was livid. He got into my face—as close as he dared. "Dave, that was the most idiotic thing you could ever have done. What if I'd had a test today? As it was, I never got back to sleep very well. Between thinking it was an emergency, then being pissed off at you, I could hardly close my eyes. I swear, if Jim wasn't your roommate…"

Kurt's face had gone red. I'd thought he was a nice guy who would appreciate a prank like this—but once again, I'd gone too far. Nice guy or not, he desperately wanted to pound me. The STOP switch on the elevator had no alarm; how easily he could have flipped that switch, bounced me off the walls a few times, and then throw my limp body out onto the fifth-floor landing. What was it about Jim? Did he put his victims in the hospital? How strange that so soon into college I'd already made another virtually invincible friend by simply acting weird.

Kurt got out on the fourth floor without a backward glance. Even though I was under Jim's protection, I still felt bad about what I had done. It took a while to repair the damage I had done with Kurt.

The Rugby Players

Overlooking the courtyard at the bottom of the L was a suite with three freshmen and one sophomore. All of them had been high school football athletes, and all of them had been starters. But they would have sat on the bench at Western. Wanting better action, they had met some of Western's Ruby Club players at a party and had been convinced to try out. By the second week, they had the rugby attitude mastered. When they threw a party, every time their door opened you could hear howling or bawdy singing from within.

The suite on my side was shared by Don Armstrong and Jack Barnes, both from Longview, Washington. They had attended RA Long High School and were both good athletes—football players and wrestlers—in high school. Don had a partial wrestling scholarship that covered his books.

My first weekend in Higginson, I decided to capture a few memories and got out my Canon SLR loaded with some Kodachrome 64 slide film. I started walking around the building, capturing shots of its interesting architecture. Back near my room, I decided to shoot some angles of the courtyard.

Suddenly I noticed a medium-built fellow in a rugby shirt watching me. He was a bit shorter than me but broader and very athletic looking. He gave me kind of a puzzled grin.

"Why are you taking all of those pictures?"

"I thought the building looked cool."

"How many pictures of the building have you taken?"

"Oh about twenty." In the days before digital cameras, this was a lot.

"I'd think you'd want people in some of those shots."

"Hold still by the railing there. Smile!"

And so I met Don Armstrong. Everyone called him Donny.. He invited me for a visit later on, and, later that evening I went to his room and met Jack Barnes as well. Jack was a formidable specimen—he stood six feet three inches and weighed a solid 190 pounds. His father, a former amateur boxer, had taught Jack to box as well. And he was extremely strong for his size. He had long, curly hair that he wore in an afro. He wore black-rimmed glasses and was good at looking and acting goofy, which was most of the time. But he was an excellent student.

Jack handed me an "animal beer" (the cheap, generic beer sold at stores that had pictures of game animals printed on the cans). Having not really developed a taste for beer yet, I forced myself to sip it while Donny talked rugby and I studied their messy room, so unlike mine.

I think it was Jim's navy training that caused him to insist our room be neatly picked up. Once, when I failed to pick up my side of the room, I came back to find all of my loose items—including my clothes—stuffed into the trash can.

Donny and Jack had no such motivation for maintaining their dwelling. Clothes, papers, underwear, socks, towels, and books lay about on beds, chairs, desks, and the floor (they cleaned up well before parties, however).

Donny and Jack introduced me to Roger Davis and Luke Seivers. Roger was a freshman my height, although built like a linebacker, which he had been. He now played scrum on the rugby team, as did Jack and Luke. Luke was only about five feet seven inches, with close-cropped, dark, curly hair. He was compact and strong. Like me, Roger and Donny were dark blondes.

Roger and Luke were appropriate roommates. They both had steady girlfriends that they were always fighting with. This aspect of Roger and Luke disgusted Donny and Jack. Donny especially was always admonishing Luke and Jake to "just be men" and dump their girls. Donny was a real charmer—aggressive, funny, and cocky, he was the kind of young man that certain girls—especially college girls—seemed to throw themselves at. I'd even heard him referred to as "Don Juan." Donny never committed, however (although he did boast of a steady girlfriend back in Longview). Decades before the first *Pirates of the Caribbean* movie appeared, Donny had mastered the saying "Take what you can. Give nothing back." Grin and all.

* * * * *

I'm not sure Higginson has seen such a collection of characters, including me, since. Nowadays, getting into Western is a highly competitive process—very good grades and test scores are required. Many, many are turned away. Back in 1977, Western's enrollment was less than nine thousand students, down from previous years' enrollments of over ten thousand. The Vietnam War had just ended, and a big reason for many to attend—a college deferment—was over. Tony Weiss always joked about the enrollment requirements: "They laid us down in a long line. They walked down the row and kicked us. If you moved, you were in."

In other words, the population of Western was in some ways much more eclectic in the seventies. Students of many academic levels and capacities were enrolled during this time. Many of the people in my dorm would not have been admitted nowadays. On the other hand, there were many brilliant, disciplined, and capable students as well. Perhaps Western was a better place back then for this.

But it was a busy, active, vibrant place—a place with far less limits and restrictions and a place where my OCD seemed to be right at home. If I'd been hoping that college would chase it away, I soon found out that my OCD thrived in college—under the constant academic pressure.

Donny and Jack became fast friends of mine. They knew I was "goofy," as Jack put it, but at the end of school they invited me to live off campus with them for the next year. After a series of rowdy pranks and loud parties, Western had banned them from living in the dorms. I often wondered what inspired them to ask me to live with them. I believe I was, in part, a mysterious source of entertainment. They could see brilliance at times, but they also saw parts of me that were unfathomable. Or perhaps it was plain paternal instinct.

CHAPTER 6

Classes at Western

My first two weeks at Western were a flurry of tryouts for bands. Western had a nationally-renowned jazz program, directed by a talented musician and professor named Bill Cole. There were three jazz bands—even the third one was better than most of the other college jazz bands in the state.

I tried out both on piano and saxophone; I thought I had a shot at piano, but I really had no chance with the sax. The experience was fun; there were so many good players trying out, it was something to hear them play. My other main instrument was clarinet, with which I easily made the Freshman/Sophomore Concert Band.

I had been looking forward to playing in band as well as taking lessons and musical theory classes. I had been mulling music as a possible major, and this first quarter of school was going to be my test of this desire. I was waiting to declare a music major, because I hadn't quite made up my mind.

This soon changed when I found out lessons were so full by then that only music majors were still being granted access. Much sooner than I thought, I was applying for a major in music. The counselor told me that changing to another major at that point would not be much trouble, if music didn't work out.

Three major problems quickly occurred:

(1) My piano teacher, a professor, didn't like my hand position.

(2) My clarinet instructor, a graduate student, didn't approve of my ambature.

(3) A sophomore clarinet player in my concert band class had been treated for cancer over the summer. He had lost his hair and had surgery scars all over his neck and throat. Though he was apparently in remission and cheerful, the sight of him nearly knocked the wind out of me. I refused to go near him or learn his name (which wasn't a huge issue, as the concert band was pretty big).

I couldn't get his image out my head—and it didn't replace the existing, never-leaving image of my dead friend. No, it pasted itself up beside the image.

I saw this fellow in band around campus and in the cafeteria. There was no escaping the sight of him. Had he been sent to torment me? I asked Tony if he knew anything about him. "I don't really know him. I think his name's Rob. He was here last year, but I think he had cancer."

Just the mention of that word made me wish I hadn't asked. Now I had a name that wouldn't stop ringing in my ears either.

My lesson practices suffered immediately. I would enter one of Western's many music practice rooms, located in a huge underground maze next to the Performing Arts auditorium. The rooms all had pianos, and I would take my clarinet along and practice my music for both instruments. No sooner would I play a line or phrase on the keyboard or my clarinet than Rob's image would pop into my head. I would have to stop and do an internal counting ritual. Or I'd have to play the line over a certain number of times.

It didn't take images to trigger my OCD either. In the middle of playing, I might just hear the name Rob in my head. That was enough to do it. I should clarify this: I never thought there was actually a real voice in my head. But like my mind's eye, my mind's ear could be very vivid. I would hear it, just like I often heard music in my head. Obsessive-compulsive disorder continued to warp my talents.

In forty-five minutes of practice, I might accomplish what I could have done in fifteen minutes when I was younger—sometimes, maybe even in five. My progression was slow.

I don't know who aggravated me more, my piano teacher or my clarinet teacher. The piano professor, Jennifer Reese (whose husband, Kyle Reese, was in charge of much of Western's jazz theory and classes), insisted that I start lifting my fingers higher off the keyboard. She said it wasn't possible to play forte (loud) without a little room for momentum. Why do so many college instructors think they know better than the professional musicians who instructed their students previously?

I demonstrated to her that I could play louder than she could with my existing hand position. I hadn't yet learned the rule that you don't contradict your professors. She assigned me some Bach Inventions to start. *Great*, I thought. I'd memorized Invention IV in less than a week when I was in junior high. It would be easy enough. Well, it had been easy enough back in junior high, but I hadn't figured in my latest round of obsessions.

My clarinet teacher was a sort of blobby fellow who probably spent most of his time sitting in a chair. He had a scraggly beard, glasses, and just as scraggly brown hair running down the back of his neck. Ambature is the angle and pressure one applies to the mouthpiece of a wind instrument. In the case of a clarinet, this involved a tight, precise seal around the upper part of the mouthpiece, varying in pressure and angle with the pitch and/or volume of the note.

He didn't care how I sounded. I was just holding it flat wrong. He wanted me to bring the clarinet into my body, tipping the end of the mouthpiece up into my palate. And my mouth position was appalling to him as well. Instead of applying even pressure around the mouthpiece, he wanted me to draw the corners of my mouth out and clamp more with the top and bottom of my lips. I could hardly get a sound out of it this way. After two sessions, I dropped my clarinet lessons but continued to play in the band.

Besides my band classes that first quarter, I was enrolled in College Algebra (pre-calculus), American History, and Freshman English 101. I was able to concentrate reasonably well in these subjects, as the math wasn't over the top, and history and English were classes where my aptitudes carried me through. By far, my most difficult studies were my musical instruments; I was having a difficult time improving, given my instructional and mental situation. To play well, a musician really has to be able to clear his mind—and those times were few for me.

Leading up to my second quarter at Western, I started feeling some pressure to do something with my life. My father had encouraged me to consider dentistry or medicine. He reminded me that if I was serious about such a career, I should start taking more rigorous classes. I was game to try, as I did want to make a decent living.

During my second quarter at Western, winter 1978, I put the music classes aside for a while and enrolled in first quarter calculus, first quarter chemistry, and a political science class required for graduation. The poli sci class turned out to be an easy A for me—the professor tested mainly out of the book. The night before the tests in this class, I would read the necessary chapters on a roll, with OCD mostly deflected, and then get up and ace the tests. It was Recall 101 for me.

The calculus and the chemistry were considerably more challenging. Although I could follow the calculus lectures, I had extreme difficulty thinking through and setting up the problems on my own, back in my dorm room. Fortunately, I had some help. Jim's original roommate, an old buddy, had finally enrolled, and he and Jim now shared a room down the hall. But Pat and I would remain lifelong friends. My new roommate, Earl Addams, was from Alaska. He was twenty-four. Like Mark, he had gone to work out of high school instead of enrolling immediately in college. And he and I were in the same calculus class.

Earl and I studied quite a bit together. His presence helped prevent me from entering the Twilight Zone when studying, and I helped him when I could pry the occasional flash of insight away from my OCD musings. He told me I should be acing the class, as

I seemed to think so much during our study sessions. If only he'd known what I was thinking about!

Calculus, at least for me, required a lot of visualization to set up the problems. Having so many other visualizations I could not get rid of left a lot less space for the math. I managed a C at the end of the quarter—not the best grade for a possible pre-med student.

Chemistry was just as tough in its own way. It is much like a history class—in fact, you could say the study of science is the study of history—but I could not simply read and regurgitate, as I could do with a history class. Equations and physical concepts and properties are embedded in a chemistry book's reading, as were problems requiring the application of such concepts.

What gave me fits off the bat was dimensional analysis—using the units of a problem to set up the answer before you actually knew it—a way of checking the answer in advance. Here's an example:

> There are 24 carrots in a bag. There are 8 bags in a box. There are 12 boxes in a crate. How many carrots are in a crate?

Now the mathematically inclined would likely see 24 X 8 X 12 = 2,304 carrots as the answer, while the mathematically disinclined might require an explanation, or have no opinion at all.

Although the correct number of carrots is given, this answer would be considered at least partially incorrect if there happened to be a chemistry test on carrots.

Why would it be wrong, at least partly? A further clarification of *dimension* in regard to science is necessary. *Dimension* does not necessarily mean something as measured in feet or meters—it's not just distance or volume. "Dimension" in this case means *what* you are actually measuring. You can measure mass, and a gram is a dimension. Temperature is a dimension. Dimensions are all units of measurement.

Which means in this last problem, "carrots" is a dimension, because that's what we are measuring—how many carrots. But so are "bags" and "boxes."

So if you were to show your work more fully, you would have to write this:

(24 carrots) X (8 bags) X (12 boxes) = 2,304 (carrots) (bags) (boxes).

A "crate" is also a dimension, and it is nowhere to be seen. And what is a carrotbagbox, anyway?

What we actually want, on this carrot test, is an answer that matches the original question: *how many carrots are in a crate?* To rephrase into familiar terms, we could say: *how many carrots per crate?*

Such statements are often represented as a fraction: for example, 60 miles per hour can also be written as 60 miles/hour, or, more formally, $\dfrac{60(miles)}{(hour)}$

In the case of our answer for carrots, we need $\dfrac{2304(carrots)}{(crate)}$

But where did the boxes and bags go? Here's the "fun" part, and here's where my concentration started to fizzle out. We know the answer needs to have carrots over crates. And for this problem, as we are converting upward, the smaller things stay on top. Let's go back to the original numbers.

There are 24 carrots per bag. So, this becomes $\dfrac{24(carrots)}{(bag)}$

There are 8 bags per box. Therefore, $\dfrac{8(bags)}{(box)}$

Finally, 12 boxes per crate. $\dfrac{12(boxes)}{(crate)}$

Ever multiplied fractions? Remember, top multiplies top, bottom multiplies bottom, so the numbers multiply as before. But, when multiplying, top and bottom-like dimensions cancel each other. So bags cancel bags and boxes cancel boxes. Only the number and the final dimensions remain:

$$\frac{24(carrots)}{1(bag)} \times \frac{8(bags)}{1(box)} \times \frac{12(boxes)}{1(crate)} = \frac{24(carrots)}{1} \times \frac{8}{1} \times \frac{12}{1(crate)} = \boxed{\frac{2304(carrots)}{(crate)}}$$

There's that passing score. When I taught chemistry and physics to ninth-graders, I created many examples using common units—"cookbook" examples, to give the students practice lining up their terms. Only then would we start to look at chemical equations.

What in this process gave me fits in college? First, before I even try to line things up, there's that number 8. Just the sight of a bad number in a problem would often trigger a bad image, and I would have to spend up to several minutes ritualizing away. Sometimes I'd simply have to get up from my dorm desk and lie down.

I had a hard time lining up my dimensions. I lacked the concentration while reading and during lectures to establish the dimensions first and then plug the numbers in. I'd always try to run the numbers first and then match up the dimensions afterward.

To quote my chemistry book:

> In this last example, we have strung together a series of conversion factors. When we set up the problem, we link these together by considering what units must be eliminated by cancellation.

Honestly, it just takes practice. But it takes concentrated practice—and even more so if combined initially with simple examples like the one above. But I lacked the concentration to see it all fit together, and college-level classes like this do not set aside the time to start with simpler forms.

Perhaps the best analogy I can give is this. If you really didn't get or skimmed over this last "chemistry lesson" section, go back and study it for a full minute. Then put a chair in a corner, and count the texture spots on the wall or tap a pencil on the edge of your chair for five minutes. Then go back for another minute. Did you lose track? Imagine doing this for an hour. Then you might begin to understand my powers of concentration back then—study, obsess, study, obsess—and never quite getting it.

CHAPTER 7

Projects

Everybody is good at something they hate. I've had A math students tell me they don't like math. If people were not good at doing things they hate to do, or at least would rather not be doing, civilization would probably collapse.

Balancing this is the feeling of accomplishment one gets from looking back on a job well done. Fitness master Jack LaLanne remarked that he hated getting up early out of a warm bed just to exercise, but the results were well worth it and were what drove him.

My periodontist father was also a mechanic and handyman. I was continually helping Dad fix the cars, fix the plumbing, run new wires. We also pulled and rebuilt the cylinder head on our boat, and I learned a lot. And it was fun, for the most part, although Dad's habit of having me clean carburetor parts, wheel bearings, and other gunked-up objects with straight leaded gasoline (no gloves necessary) is a bit nasty in retrospect. At the time, though, I enjoyed the smell of gasoline.

My main job was mowing our half-acre backyard, which, although mostly open, was still home to many fruit trees, garden beds, and rhododendrons. I developed a routine that allowed me to mow it, using a gasoline push mower, in around two hours. But, at fourteen, when my OCD kicked in badly, suddenly this two-hour job became at least thirty minutes longer. I would have to redo portions of mowing, even though there was nothing to mow. I wasn't just cutting grass; I was trying to mow down the bad thoughts as well.

Because much of the yard was visible from the house, my worst showings were at the bottom of our yard, behind a small barn, out of sight of an audience, where many a time I would have to mow a strip or edge of a garden a proper number of times to be able to move on. Mow a garden bed—bad thought or image—and then have to re-mow the same location, say, six times, before I could move on. The yard behind the barn never looked better—or better scalped.

Mowing is actually a perfect example for the effects of OCD—not just in wasted time, and wasted thoughts, but in the character of how I interacted with my environment. Although I had always considered mowing the yard tedious, it had been nice to get outdoors, to smell the grass, to admire the beautiful trees, flowers, and gardens my mother had planted. My awareness was always filled with beauty and the thoughts of its admiration, and about my wanderings among the sights in the distance, as our yard had an excellent view of snow-capped Mt. Rainier and down Lake Washington.

When the OCD came, my thoughts turned inward and downward. All I saw was the grass in front of me and the thoughts and images inside my head. Gone were the external inputs I so enjoyed; they were pushed out of my awareness by worry and fear. I was no longer moving through gardens and light and the views of the outdoors to captivate me; I was now pushing my mower down a dark tunnel dimly illuminated by my fears. Tunnel vision is aptly named regarding OCD. One truly does turn inward, with fears and unwanted thoughts taking over the input channels to your brain.

Mowing the lawn—or any other project requiring manual labor—became something to be dreaded, not so much the task itself, but because of what the task would become—another point-less battle.

Still, I found myself being a handyman for much of my life. It can be a great substitute for paying someone else for something I could not otherwise afford. When my wife and I built our house, I did much of the mechanical work. Although we saved money, I could have completed the work—wiring, plumbing, heating, sep-tic—in half the time if not for my OCD. Crystallized in our house is literally days of OCD—drifting off, stopping, repeating the same task. We finished the house with almost no time to spare on our construction deadline. Now, had I to do it over, I would have fin-ished my part early—and I would have enjoyed it.

Obsessive-compulsive disorder really can take much of the joy out of life. It's like walking through the woods on a beautiful spring day, but wondering all the while if there's a sniper behind one of the trees.

So many things had come easily to me when I was younger, before OCD. I didn't really need to study. In the cases where study-ing was necessary, I could perform the tasks quickly and efficiently. How ironic that when my studies became more challenging—high school and beyond—I could no longer concentrate as well. And every job, paying or not, became an ordeal, sometimes equal parts working and equal parts fighting OCD.

One striking example is my advancement in Scouting. I obtained my Life Scout badge—the second highest rank—in three years, by the time I was fourteen, just before my OCD became seri-ous. It would take me almost another four years to finish off my Eagle rank. I had been on a pace to finish it in another two.

When I graduated from high school, my father told me my sum-mers must shift from Scout hikes, camps, summer swim team, and the like to finding a job and helping pay for my college. My uncle, my dad's brother-in-law, generously offered to hire me on building a house in Eugene, Oregon. My Uncle Dave was a Lutheran family counselor, but he was also one of those people who sleep little and always needed to be doing something. Therefore he also worked nearly full time buying, fixing up, and selling houses—or, in this case, building a new one of his own.

I drove down to Eugene in the summer of 1977, in hot, sunny weather, with the windows down all the way. It was even hotter in Eugene. Week after week it seemed the temperatures hovered around one hundred degrees. My uncle would drag me out of bed in the cool of the early summer morning, and it seemed like we got twice as much work done by noon than we would accomplish the rest of the day.

My OCD symptoms started to diminish a bit as I got into the construction business—because my uncle caught me being weird. My first job had been to pull all the nails from a pile of two-by-sixes he was going to recycle into the new house. He presented me with a crowbar and hammer, and told me to start pulling. Being a generous man, Uncle Dave had stacked the lumber in the already roofed-in garage, so I was out of the direct sunlight. The instructions being simple enough, he departed to supervise the main construction of the house.

I was by myself with nothing but nails to pull—a job I would have enjoyed a few years earlier, as I would have challenged myself to do it quickly. But with OCD, even the simplest tasks can become herculean. I would pull a nail out partway—a bad image would hit—and I'd have to stop my action for a few moments, trying to force something better into my mind before I could finish the job. The net result was that the nails came out very slowly. In the middle of one nail ritual, I realized my uncle had been watching me. He lectured me up and down on how that was not how one works for a living, and that I could drive back to Seattle right that minute if I wanted to. He said he didn't care either way.

I wasn't sure which terrified me more—driving back to Seattle to face my dad or the fact that my Uncle Dave had been *observing* my OCD. What had he really seen? How ironic I couldn't confide in him—his main job was as a family counselor, after all. But I was able to pull nails a whole lot faster after that; there are degrees of terror that surpass others. Ironically, my biggest memory of that summer is Elvis Presley's death. But Elvis's death did not trigger my OCD – Elvis' own choices had triggered his death, not random chance.

And so a pattern developed and held through this job and future jobs. I was a good worker when I was being directly supervised or thought someone could be watching me, but a very slow worker otherwise. Very quickly I learned to internalize my rituals in the workplace, just in case I was being observed. The result was, of course, that my bosses soon figured out I often got little done when unsupervised, and they figured I was lazy. Well, that was the net result. More than once I was caught spacing out on the job, and in one case lost my job working for an irrigation company. My supervisor diplomatically told me that business was a bit slow.

A family friend, a Dutch immigrant who ran a boiler company and installed many steam systems in Alaska, had friends in the seafood business. He practically guaranteed me a job with Peter Pan Seafoods; all I would have to do was apply and use him for a reference. Unfortunately, I also used my former sprinkler company as a reference, and to Jan's (pronounced "Yon") shock and dismay, I was not hired. It was at this point I figured out what my main reference was doing for me. I'm pretty sure Jan knew as well, and he was determined to make a worker out of me. He hired me on personally as an assistant on a boiler job he would be working for six weeks, in Port Moller, a salmon-processing facility in the Aleutian Islands. Although an isolated dot in the Pacific, the place bustled with the activities of fishing and constant construction. Frankly, I was relieved, as the original job would have involved gutting salmon for the entire summer. Mechanical work was much more interesting, and, I would find out later, it would provide me with many useful skills.

I found out sooner, however, that Jan Hendriks was, apparently, geographically bipolar. At home, he was the most courteous, godly man you would ever meet; he had always been so to me and my family. But when I stepped off the small plane in the little Port Moller airstrip, I met Jan the fanatical Boiler Man of Alaska. I immediately grasped why Jan loved Alaska. Up there he was a man's man—uninhibited, working hard and swearing even harder, a relentless taskmaster. He loved the nonstop action and the atmosphere, which reminded him of his WWII Dutch navy days.

In fact, I would hear many an interesting navy tale from Jan, who never talked about the war at home. I had never heard him swear once in all of my life. I thought this pious man was incapable of it. But, as I walked with my bags to our dorms by the dock, he started trotting with a loud "David, quit fucking around" and followed this first epithet with a stream of cussing that ran my laziness up one block and down the other.

Jan liked to hire workmen who kicked ass. If you could work, you were a "piss cutter" in his book. But he had hired me as a project, perhaps even as a favor to my frustrated dad. Yes, Jan was going to make a decent worker out of me.

Therefore he watched me nearly every second. When he sent me to run an errand to fetch a part or tool, he would time me with his wristwatch. And if he saw my mind wandering into OCD space, his first statement to me continued to be his favorite: "David, quit fucking around." It came to be quite endearing, actually, as instead of pronouncing his Rs with his mouth, he rolled them off his palate with his tongue. This tended to make the *around* softer and really put the emphasis on the F word that preceded it.

I began to suspect that not only was Jan watching to make sure I was keeping busy, but I was actually *under observation* of some sort. Was Jan my dad's spy? Was he trying to help my dad figure out what was wrong with me? On the surface I was lazy, no doubt about that. But I think Jan eventually got an inkling there were other issues, issues he couldn't understand or help with. But I'll say this much: even more so than my Uncle Dave, Jan Hendricks taught me how to work.

My uncle, Jan Hendricks, and my father all shared one thing: they were obsessive compulsive. In other words, highly motivated men who enjoyed what they did, rode their tremendous drives to success, and greatly enjoyed both the process and the results. There's nothing wrong with plain obsessive compulsion—except that it can make people into workaholics—but again, they enjoy it.

I did not enjoy my *disorder*, for it made me less successful, less motivated, and *took* the joy I would have otherwise gained from a job well done.

CHAPTER 8

Twenty-Seven Years of Scouting

S couting has provided me with some of my greatest joys and, ironically, my deepest fears and sorrows.

I was a Boy Scout for seven years and a Scoutmaster for nearly twenty. I grew up in Scouting, and I watched many a boy become a young man during my adult leadership. It was a joy and adventure to join Scouting, hard to leave, and an equal thrill to rejoin—and, once again, when the time came, an equal sadness to leave.

My OCD dovetails with my career as a Boy Scout and a Scouter (the term for an adult leader). I developed and lived through the worst of my OCD while in Scouts and ultimately faced it down and beat it while a Scoutmaster.

It is safe for me to say that a singular occurrence in Scouting triggered my latent potential for OCD. Would some other event down the line have triggered it anyway? Quite possibly. My brother experienced crippling obsessions as an adult—his "critical event" just took place later on. But if it had, at least I would have suffered my OCD for a lesser amount of time. My trigger was atrocious to me in part because of the strong bonds I had formed with other troop members, one poor young soul in particular. This is one reason the story of my Scouting is so important to this book.

Troop 348, in Lake Forest Park was already an old troop when I joined in May 1970, having been originally chartered in 1926. I had graduated from Cub Scout Pack 348 that spring, and it was customary for graduated Webelos (the eldest Cub Scouts) to join the troop for a few meetings before summer, to get to know the troop boys and to be eligible for summer hikes. (By the way, "Webelos" stands for "We Be Loyal Scouts.")

Troop 348 held its meetings in the large basement of the Lake Forest Park Presbyterian Church on Monday nights during the school year. Every troop must have a sponsor, and the LFP church was our charter holder. Troop 348 had a reputation as a rugged, outdoorsy troop, a fierce competitor at inter-troop competitions—known as Camporees—and a skilled group of high-adventure hikers that often used established trails as the jumping-off point for hiking into territory where few other hikers ventured.

My first meeting was spent with an older Scout, Craig McCloud, who was nearly an Eagle Scout (Scouting's highest rank), running through the requirements for Tenderfoot with me—Tenderfoot being the first rank and badge earned. I had to learn seven different knots (easy for a boy with no OCD—yet), the Scout oath, law, motto, and slogan, basic information about Scouting such as ranks, and some simple first aid and direction-finding.

I was assigned into a patrol—a mix of boys of different ages, the basic troop unit—and spent the next couple of meetings preparing for the summer Shakedown Hike. This hike made a new Scout eligible for the August nine-day hike, which my father had tentatively signed me up for.

"Three quarters of Scouting is 'outing,'" and Troop 348 added the word *challenging* to this saying. The Shakedown Hike was to be a five-mile hike to Pratt Lake, near Snoqualmie Pass. It would turn out to be quite challenging for me. However, outings meant "be prepared"; the Scout motto had to be followed. So, prior to every hike, a pack inspection occurred the Wednesday before an overnight, with the patrol leaders completely unpacking their patrols' packs and making sure their charges had the list of required items stowed properly. The experienced hikers always looked forward to these first pack inspections, as the new Scouts would quite often pack unnecessary, bulky items that, if nothing else, meant more weight to carry.

I received the first taunt. Karl Roberts, my patrol leader for this hike, held up my toilet paper for all to see. It was a brand-new roll, probably enough to last me a couple of weeks. I'd had to stuff it into an extra-large Baggie. "Oh, a big wiper here, I see!" Karl called out to everyone around, generating some pretty good laughs.

Then he said to me, "When you get home, switch this roll for one that's already being used, that has the least paper left."

Everything else satisfactory, I was weighed. At seventy-five pounds, I was big enough to carry twenty-five pounds, one-third of my weight. My pack weighed fifteen pounds, so I was given food and supplies totaling another ten. I strapped the pack on, and it felt pretty light. Five miles was going to be nothing, I told myself.

We arrived at the trailhead at 7:30 Saturday morning and wasted no time hitting the trail. I felt very Scout-like—I was even wearing a pair of brand-new leather hiking boots. The trail started at an elevation of two thousand feet—over a distance of five miles, it would climb another two thousand vertical feet to reach the four-thousand-foot-high Pratt Lake. In other words, this trail was going to have some steep parts.

We started off at a decent clip. An adult leader up front set the pace, and the other adults usually brought up the rear—to account for stragglers and for the peace and quiet. We hiked and hiked. I was in the middle of the twenty-five or so Scouts, and I was starting to breathe hard. We must have hiked a half hour by then—all uphill, it seemed. I asked a more experienced boy behind me, Scott Johnson, about how far we had come.

"Oh, I'd guess about a quarter mile."

He had to be joking. I would have thought at least a mile. "Really? When do we rest?"

"Oh, about every half mile or so. We've only been hiking about fifteen minutes."

Scott was not one of those older Scouts who practiced much hazing. He had to be right. I had thought every half hour might be reasonable for a stop. The only problem was that half an hour was only halfway gone. And the way I was starting to feel, I wasn't sure if I'd have a lot left beyond then. Suddenly, I didn't much like hiking.

I could feel myself slowing down. You stayed with the leaders or fell back with the adults. If you were holding someone up who was behind you, they would say "Pass," and you would step to the right to let them by. The all-troop stop signal was "Trail!"

By the time Mr. Ames, the front leader, called, "Trail," I was too far back to hear it. Not only was I tired, but the heels of my feet were really starting to hurt—burn, really. I had just reached the troop when they finished their rest and resumed hiking. Scott stayed back for just a minute. "Wait for the adults. This is your first hike. They're used to helping new Scouts along."

It was a small comfort to me, as I was the only one of the "new Scouts" having so much trouble. It was humiliating. Although at seventy-five pounds I was the smallest member of the troop, I wasn't carrying a disproportionate amount of weight.

How much of this was mental? Looking back, taking into account my performance on later hikes and my future martial arts training, I'd have to say a lot. I wasn't into as many sports as some of the other kids; my only main athletic activities were Little League baseball and snow skiing. And it wasn't so much not being in decent physical shape; it was that I had never been physically pushed in my entire life; I had no idea that my body's complaints were well below its actual physical limits. I had never felt this way before. I didn't know where my 100 percent was—or even close to it.

Did this lack of mental toughness also predispose me to OCD? Was it a cause, or was it in fact an early indicator of a latent condition?

I also suffered a bit from exercise-induced asthma, but its effects were minimal at this level. But there was one more thing, as my Scoutmaster, Bill Roberts (Karl's father), would soon find out.

Five minutes after the troop left, Mr. Roberts and Mr. Munson showed up. Mr. Munson was a fit and experienced hiker in his early sixties, whose sons were long grown. He still enjoyed volunteering his time, however. In Scouting, there are never enough volunteers, especially when it comes to outings.

"Oh, setting up camp early, I see?" said Mr. Roberts. It was easy to see where Karl obtained his sense of humor. Mr. Roberts was a powerfully built, experienced hiker who looked at least ten years younger than his actual age of forty-two. He radiated vitality, and Karl had obviously inherited this from his father.

Speaking of mental toughness, Karl was by far the most mentally tough boy in the troop. Only a year older than me and not a whole lot bigger, he was tremendously strong for his size. We would have contests where a group of us would stand in a stream flowing from an icefield—brutally cold, painful water that would drive most people out in less than a minute. Karl could stand in the water all day; he never lost such a competition. Later he would join the US Ski team, and he would help others survive near the top of Mount Everest, where many around him perished.

Karl was a born leader and had every gift of social intelligence I lacked. And, of course, as many people similar to him, he became a mentor and a person who watched my back, knowing I needed it.

I wasn't Karl, and Mr. Roberts knew it, but he didn't hold it against me. "Ready to start walking again?"

"I guess so. Yes."

When I got up, I immediately forgot the weight of my pack. "Owwww! My feet!" Within five steps I had to stop. What was it now?

There's mental toughness and then there's practicality. You have to take care of your feet, or all the grit in the world won't last you through a hike. My new leather boots were not the least bit broken in. I'd worn them only in the store. Neither I nor my father nor the salesman, for that matter, had thought about my need to wear them around for a few days. The boots weren't flexing, causing my heels to rub up and down constantly. Mr. Roberts had me remove my boots. I was going to get more rest than I had counted on.

A half hour of hiking uphill in new boots had done its job. Both heels had pretty good blisters on them. "We'll have to break these boots in," said my Scoutmaster, "but there's no time now and too much uphill. Better get out your tennis shoes."

Tennis shoes were a required item for hiking, and I was now grateful for this requirement. The boots replaced my shoes in the pack. "We need to get moving. I'll carry your pack for a little while, Dave." Mr. Roberts slung my pack under his arm as if it were no more than a lady's purse.

We walked up the hill at a pace so fast, I could barely keep up without a pack. Our long stop had put us way behind the troop, and Mr. Roberts wanted to check in with Mr. Ames to let him know all were accounted for. After thirty minutes of this, it became apparent the troop was still way ahead. We stopped and took a water break. "Well, I don't think we're going to catch them before the lake," Mr. Roberts observed. "We might as well take it easy. Time for you to carry that pack, Dave."

The pack that had felt so light at the inspection and not too bad at the beginning of the trail felt as heavy as a load of bricks. But my feet no longer hurt, and I was becoming a little more accustomed to the fact that it was going to take time and that others ahead of me were surviving just fine.

The trail was muddy and had many small streams crossing it, due to the June snowmelt. I started picking my way around the mud, streams, and puddles. But my feet were still getting wet—there was no avoiding it. "Just walk right on through," advised Mr. Munson. The adults laughed when I started attacking the muddy trail. Soon I had mud splattered up to my hiking shorts.

"That's the spirit," Mr. Roberts said.

As we climbed, I started to notice larger and larger granite boulders about the surroundings, until I saw a bright spot ahead. It was the cirque for the lake. As we emerged into the basin, the trees gave way to a tremendous rockslide. Cliffs surrounded Pratt Lake, as did the boulders that had fallen from them. Very few trees—mostly evergreens, with some vine maple and alder mixed in—bordered the water, so a considerable amount of rock had piled up over the centuries. At the far end of the lake was a treed area surrounding Pratt Lake's main inlet, a decent stream that time of year. The surface of the lake glittered under the sun, its waters the deepest blue I had ever seen.

Karl and the other patrol members had set up quite a bit of the camp at this point. Karl greeted me. "You made it! How are you feeling?"

"Pretty good, I guess. Pretty tired." I'd been looking to kick back and take a real breather at the lake.

"Well, you're still standing. Take off your pack and go collect some firewood."

A Scout's work is never done, and Troop 348 always kept its youngest members busy. Slackers might find themselves accidentally swimming in the lake with their clothes and boots still on. And keeping a young Scout busy, especially on a longer hike, helps prevent homesickness from setting in. Obsessive-compulsive disorder isn't the only thing that takes advantage of time for thought.

After wood collection and lunch, there was extra time. I ended up "helping" Mr. Roberts go fishing. I had not thought to bring my own pole, and spotting him casting from a large rock, I decided to join him to see what mountain lake fishing was about. In the high, clear mountain lakes, the fish hunt by sight—it's not a matter of casting a baited hook into murky water and waiting. This was active fishing, cast after cast. Mr. Roberts used a fly trailed behind a piece of leaded line to keep the lure just underwater. In retrospect, he was a very patient man. He must have answered my numerous questions for over an hour. But then, that's what Scoutmasters do. Don't be a Scoutmaster if you want continuous peace and quiet.

After dinner, there was still plenty of June daylight. I set my wet tennis shoes by the fire, took off my socks to dry, and walked down to the lake to soak my feet.

"Dahlberg!" yelled Karl.

"What?" I answered.

"You're forgetting something."

Oops. I had been assigned cleanup detail. I made my way back up to the campsite—Karl was already gone—and collected the dirty pots and dishes, and a Brillo pad. I went back to the lake and started scrubbing. Cleaning cups and utensils is not so bad, but we'd had macaroni and cheese as well, and part of it was burned to the pot.

Ten minutes later, Karl came back. "Dave!"

"Over here!"

Karl came running down. He looked at my cleanup site. "You idiot!"

"You're *really* new, aren't you?

"What's wrong?"

"Dahlberg, you never do dishes in the lake. You take some other pots with water in them—including one with hot water—and clean up next to the fire. You throw any trash in the fire, including all that macaroni you just dumped in the lake."

"Won't the fish eat it?"

"No, they won't. And the water's so cold, it'll take forever to dissolve. This macaroni will be here for all to see for the rest of the summer. You'll have to pick it out. I'll be back in ten minutes—I'm going to collect more firewood."

When Karl returned, there were still lots of little bright orange pieces of Kraft Macaroni and Cheese decorating the sand under the water. "I'll help you," he said. "I should have got you started on the dishes myself."

Between the two of us, we were done removing the macaroni within ten minutes. I had now spent thirty minutes doing the dishes, and I hadn't even finished. But during this time, my tennis shoes had dried. And heated up. And caught on fire.

Karl saw the black smoke first. "Oh crap!" he yelled. He came running back with what seemed like a mass of flame in each hand and threw them into the lake. I had put my tennis shoes toe-first next to the fire, and the rubber had heated up and burned splendidly. I now had two half shoes, heels only.

The next day I had to wear my boots home. Fortunately it was downhill; I had Band-Aids on my feet; and Mr. Roberts had made me put my boots on and submerge them in the lake. I would be hiking with wet boots, but it would help break them in and relieve any rubbing on the way down—as long as I didn't hike too fast. But Mr. Ames set off at a tremendous pace down the hill—maybe he had a date that evening—and I found myself again being escorted by the two adults.

"How was the hike?" my dad asked me when I returned.

"It was fun." I never did tell him I had burned my tennis shoes.

In fact, the hike *was* fun—looking back. Eventually a couple of years later I reached the point that I enjoyed all (or most of) a hike. But even as a younger Scout, when I thought back on hiking in the rain for hours, being miserable and cold, or just as likely exhausted and overheated, or just plain homesick—I can say I enjoyed having had the experience and was even proud of myself for surviving it.

When I was Scoutmaster, one of the funniest and most inspiring Eagle Award acceptance speeches was by a young man named J. D. Giles, who had never missed one of my feared-by-some hikes. He said that the pain and the suffering were just as important as the fun, and just as inspiring. And he was right.

In some ways, experiences like this resemble OCD: if you make it through, it makes you stronger. But I can't look back and say I ever *enjoyed* having OCD. Although I can vividly remember many OCD attacks, I can't say I have any appreciation for them at all. OCD is edifying, certainly—just like spending years in a prison camp. But there are better ways to seek such self-realization. Scouting kept me busy and kept my mind focused on other things than my OCD. So, it is hugely ironic that a Scouting experience three years later would trigger the worst of it.

Seven weeks later, I was in the middle of a line of Scouts. It was raining hard—practically a gale—and our ponchos flapped around us like sails whipping in a typhoon. It was so foggy I could barely see ten feet ahead. We were at about seven thousand feet of altitude, in the heights of the Cascade Mountains, traversing a trail that had been blasted out of the side of a cliff. The wind chill was well below freezing. It was the next-to-last-day of my first nine-day hike. We were fighting our way through the Goat Rocks, where more than one hiker had succumbed to hypothermia in years past. Up there, seasons had no meaning—you came prepared for winter, even if it was August.

It was nearly the last day for Jim Lansing, another new Scout my age. He was wearing a hat over his poncho, and a hard gust plucked it from his head and sent it flying. Jim chased after the cap like a young child chasing a ball into a busy street—but, instead of an oncoming car, there was a drop of over a thousand feet. "Jesus!"

said Bill Newton, a senior Scout twice Jim's size. He horse-collared Jim and hurled him back forcefully into the side of the mountain on the near side of the trail.

"A Scout is clean," says one of the twelve points of the Scout law, but it didn't stop Bill from cussing Jim out with a few choice words. Mr. Roberts had deliberately alternated older Scouts with younger ones as we headed into the maelstrom, and this fact had perhaps saved Jim's life. I couldn't have caught him, that's for sure.

Just the night before, we had been camped in McCall Basin, a valley near the Wonderland Trail by Mount Rainier. The day preceding it had been the last of a series of hot, sunny days with spectacular views of the Southern Cascade Mountain range, dominated by Mt. Rainier, so close-seeming at times it looked like a well-tossed rock would land on one of its massive glaciers.

McCall Basin was well forested, and, as usual, I and the other younger Scouts had been assigned firewood detail. Back in 1970, most hikers still cooked by campfire, and each patrol of ours carried a saw and an axe for procuring wood. I had made a friend over the course of the hike—a year older, he was almost a mentor. Greg Brooks was an excellent camper and hiker; his father, Dan Brooks, was one of the adults. An avid hiker himself, Mr. Brooks had trained Greg well.

I always enjoyed fire duty with Greg, because he was so good with an axe. He was big for his age and probably outweighed me by fifty pounds. He was tall and powerfully built, with a shock of brown, curly hair. His favorite hiking attire was Levis and a red-and-black checkered, wool logger's shirt. Nearly thirteen years old, his voice had already deepened into a pleasing tenor. His favorite phrase for me, the daydreamer, was "Wake up, Dave!"

Greg's favorite strategy was to find a fallen log, seasoned but not rotten, quickly chop it into manageable pieces for carrying. We were not allowed to cut live wood—even branches.

Everybody had a different stance for handling an axe. I don't mean a hand axe, by the way. To chop a log, you need a real ax. Greg was big and powerful enough to chop like a logger—feet spread a little past shoulder width and a tall stance to really obtain elevation on the axe. He had a good feel and eye for the wood. In a chop or two, he'd have the optimal angle for the grain of the log, and huge chunks of wood would go flying, the log dropping apart in seemingly no time at all.

It takes technique and power to use an axe well, and Greg worked with me on my technique to maximize the power I had. Unlike some other older Scouts, he had the patience to let me take my turn at chopping, coaching me until I could occasionally let a chip fly. I was grateful for this, as most of the time the new Scout would be the one to use the saw on smaller pieces of wood—an often boring task.

We brought in extra firewood that day, which was a good thing, because that night, all of the patrols decided to "sleep under the stars." The days had been cloudless, and the stars seemed to have an extra brightness and glitter. The Milky Way stretched brightly across the mountain sky, untouched by city air or lights, with a mile of atmosphere missing compared to sea level. It was the most brilliant sky we'd ever seen, and, sick of setting up tarps all week, we left the tarps in the packs, eager to watch August meteor showers.

Later on, we were told the extra-bright, almost glassy clear sky that night was due to excess humidity in the air. Unseen clouds gathered quickly at the bases of the mountains, and, at 1:30 a.m., I was shaken awake by an older Scout to help set up some tarps in the squall now parked over us. When we woke up to climb the Goat Rocks trail, we were already wet. The extra firewood had been piled into an early-morning blaze to at least warm up the damp Scouts.

We finished the hike the next day under gray skies. We had covered seventy-five miles in nine days, which, according to the older Scouts, had been "a walk in the park" compared to the troop's usual practice of hiking largely off maintained trails. Apparently, there were so many new Scouts on this hike, they had "eased up."

The nine-day hikes were a big part of my Scouting life. I enjoyed four of them immensely—the hikes of 1970, '71, '72, and '73. Starting in '71, I also spent a week at Camp Parsons, a very large, very old, very spectacular Scout Camp on the shores of Hood Canal, Washington.

Greg also attended Scout Camp and was a mentor to me there as well, serving as an adviser and helper to me and many others. He was well liked by everyone. He never bullied and had a complete lack of ego. There were some older Scouts it was down-right dangerous to cross, but you couldn't even insult Greg—even me, who addressed my usual not-too-well-thought-out comments at him sometimes. He quickly recognized my need for coaching in social skills and always made positive suggestions and corrections.

During the school year, when there were more meetings and fewer campouts, Greg was always there to provide balance. He could get kids with every kind of ego and attitude to work together. I always regretted that Greg never made Eagle—of all the Scouts I met, he perhaps deserved it the most.

In August 1973, our troop took on its most challenging hike yet—a trek through the Glacier Peak Wilderness, starting on the Pacific Crest Trail and ending up on a little-traveled spur of Glacier Peak known as Lime Ridge. The hike was challenging in its ter-rain—we spent one whole day looking for a route—and impressive in its weather, from bright, hot sunshine to the snowstorm that hit us on Lime Ridge. Greg had been my patrol leader on this hike, and I would often take my place in the tarp next to his, where we shared a bond of conversation as we drifted off. In the morning, he'd always be gone when I woke up, busy starting the fire, doing chores, and generally taking good care of his patrol.

I went on three more nine-day hikes as a Scout: 1974, 1975, and 1977; I missed 1976 because of a school-sponsored band trip to Europe. And I wish Greg could have been there on all of them. After the Glacier Peak hike, later that summer, he and some other Scout friends (including an older and wiser Jim Lenker) retraced the 1970 Goat Rocks hike. It was the last hike Greg would ever take.

Life with OCD begins

In the fall of 1973, I entered the ninth grade at Kellogg Junior High School. The Monday-night troop meetings started. But Greg was not in attendance. His younger brother, Kyle, assured us that Greg was just busy with his first year of high school, as a sopho-more at Shorecrest High. It seemed he must have been awfully busy to miss the Scout meetings.

I've talked about how we can recall traumatic memories in the context of exactly what we were doing at the time. It was after school, early in October. My mom called me into the kitchen. I recall the image: she stood with her back to the south-facing windows. I entered the kitchen and stood a few feet across the floor from her. "I have some bad news, David."

"What is it?"

"Greg Brooks has cancer."

Those four words, spoken in my mother's voice, are my most vivid aural memory of all time. All I have to do is imagine that setting, and I can still hear them clearly, so very clearly. And so chillingly—because I also still feel the surge of adrenaline that hit me at that moment, speechless, not knowing what to say.

Finally: "What kind of cancer?"

"It's somewhere in his chest."

Matt Sirota, an extremely brilliant, close friend of Greg's, later told me that Greg had "about a million kinds" of cancer. Basically, his immune system had broken down in a way that left him vulnerable to this extremely aggressive case. Nearly forty years ago, he didn't have a chance.

As a contrast, Karl, over thirty years later, was diagnosed with late-stage cancer as well. But this was in the era of Lance Armstrong, when such cases were treatable. Karl survived and refers to his bout with the disease as a "speed bump."

Greg's case was a mystery, and his younger brother, Kyle, also a troop member, wouldn't talk about it—and nobody asked him to. Greg came to one more meeting, in November of 1973, briefly, just to say hello. He really didn't look sick, although he wasn't very talkative, and my mom said she didn't think his color looked very good. It probably wasn't, although Greg had always been very fair-skinned—he'd never had much color. I had a few words with him, the phrase we always shared.

"Wake up, Greg."

"I'm tryin'!"

I would see Greg only one more time, months later, at the end of the school year.

It was after the November visit that Greg's image began to haunt me. I began to have fight-or-flight feelings of anxiety. Various words would appear, spelled out in my mind's eye, or would sound in my mind's ear: "cancer...Greg Brooks...tumor..."

They would just *appear,* and I couldn't get rid of them. My first thought was to drown the thoughts. I began trying to force good images of healthy people into my mind to drive out the bad—Karl, Bill Newton, friends of mine. I would try to think of as many good images as I could, in rapid succession, to replace what had involuntarily popped in. And as soon as I would finish this early ritual, no matter how many people I had thought of, Greg would still be there. It was like splashing paint at a frictionless wall. It would fall off as fast as I could throw it.

My First Ritual

There's a saying about the car you drive—whether it's a Beetle, a Jeep, a Camaro—once you own one, you suddenly see them everywhere. Only I didn't have a car; I had a friend with cancer. Suddenly cancer was everywhere. It was in the newspapers. Other people we knew had it. It was in movies. I watched *Brian's Song* one night and was haunted for weeks afterward—before the images chiefly turned back to Greg.

And I remember my first manifestation of ritualization. Ironically, it involved a cross.

One of my best friends at the time was Ken Duncan Jr. We were inseparable buddies on the ski slopes. And, for a couple of years, we had been lobbying our dads to take a ski trip together. Imagine our surprise when, in February 1974, Ken Duncan Sr. and Bill Dahlberg announced to us they were pulling us out of school for a week-long trip to Vail, Colorado. Talk about blowing your kids' minds!

Even in '74, Vail was huge, including the town surrounding the base of the hill. Our lodgings were in some tall, A-frame condominiums with steeply-sloping outer walls, which matched the slope of the roof outside. Pine was everywhere—covering the walls and ceiling—and warm carpet covered the floors. Ken and I had the two small upstairs rooms, each with a single bed and nightstand.

During the day, we skied the huge peaks, rode gondolas—not puny chairlifts—and generally forgot there was an outside world. On the hill, I was so elated I generally forgot about my sick friend.

At night, however, things changed. I'd always had difficulty getting to sleep quickly, and after the bright excitement of the day, my mind found itself devoid of all but its own stimulation. It began to pick out images previously unnoticed.

Although my parents would have disagreed, I'd always been a bit of a keep-it-neat person when it came to arranging the objects on my shelves. All of my model cars, books, and various treasures had a certain place and orientation.

My parents had given me a cross necklace when I was confirmed at our Lutheran church. It was a one-by-two- inch metal cross attached to a thin, pewter-colored chain, which I often wore around my neck. Since Greg had become sick, I had taken to wearing it constantly.

At bedtime, I would often slip the chain over my head, and then, holding the cross, slowly lower the end of the chain and move it clockwise, making small concentric circles with it until the chain lay like a perfect circle on my nightstand. I would then lay the cross at a right angle to where the chain ended. It made quite a little work of art, and it provided a small, flowing ritual that provided a neat, comforting end to my day.

When I was extra tired, I would resort instead to an alternative: I would lower the tip of the necklace straight down and let it fall as it may. It usually ended up making some sort of circle, or circular pile, anyway.

Somehow, the remoteness of Vail and the stillness of the condo at night felt surreal. Everything took on extra meaning. The first night in Vail, alone in my room, I was tired. The room narrowed from floor to ceiling—the top story of an A-frame. A single lamp on a nightstand provided a dim yellow light, which reflected off the warm, brown tongue-and-groove wood paneling. Shadows abounded. I simply let the chain drop. And to my mind, still worried about Greg, it seemed to drop into a letter C. Capital C for *cancer*. The word spelled itself out instantly in my mind. And thus began the first of many do-overs—the ritualizing had begun.

I picked it up and put it down again. To my horror, it made another C, although this time it looked more like a Pac Man (which had not yet been invented), a devouring little monster. The phrase "the deadly jaws of cancer" popped into my head. I picked up the chain and had to drop it several more times until it fell into nothing resembling a C. Sweating, I turned off the light and eventually dropped off.

The next night, it took me five tries to get it right. I hadn't meant to count the number of tries—I'm just a natural counter. It then occurred to me that five was the devil's number. So I had to do it six times. And this is when I first felt the feverish, intense feeling of being trapped, out of control, unable to stop what I was doing. Every night, the ritual seemed to get bigger, more unstoppable, and worse.

When it rains, it pours. Vail had a movie theater, and Ken, I, and Steve Williams—the son of a college buddy of my dad, who lived close by and had driven up to join us—went to see a movie. It was *Bang the Drum Slowly*, which happened to be about a cancer-stricken baseball player. Although a very good movie, for me it was absolutely the wrong place at the wrong time. It just reinforced that cancer was all around me, waiting to pounce if I let down my guard even for a second. And for decades afterward, that obsessive-compulsive "protection" seldom gave me a moment's rest.

When I returned home, I left the cross on my shelf, never to arrange it again, never to *have* to arrange it again. But the die had been cast. I soon found out that just about anything *and* everything was arrangeable—and countable.

I was fifteen years old when I came home from Vail in February 1974. After years of worry, anxiety, and hypochondria, I had full-blown OCD. At the time, I didn't know what was wrong with me. I wouldn't discover what it was until many years later. Now it would be just a matter of developing more and more rituals, being exposed to ever more numbers I could associate with things fearful to me.

I began to avoid certain things. *Reader's Digest* became a bane to me. Almost since I could read, *Reader's Digest,* with its eclectic myriad of stories and anecdotes, had provided me with quite a worldview—that, and my other favorite, *National Geographic* magazine. As my dad was involved with medicine, I had always enjoyed reading "News from the World of Medicine," a monthly feature in *Reader's Digest*, and the oft-included medical stories involving courageous battles against diseases and disorders—some victorious, some not.

Suddenly all these stories seemed to be about cancer. Was *Reader's Digest* part of some diabolical plot to torment me? Most of the time, the ages of the stricken people were provided. These numbers immediately became bad for all time (many of them I have already listed).

Lincoln Steffens, a well-known early twentieth-century journalist, wrote a chapter in his autobiography entitled "I Create a Crime Wave." Instead of reporting on all of the happenings on his beat—good and bad—he decided for a month to report on nothing but crime, hanging out at the police station and documenting any and all violations of the law, from petty to felonious. Suddenly, patrons of the newspaper were aghast at the huge increase in crimes—except that there was no more crime than there had always been. It was merely getting noticed more.

My OCD had exactly this same effect on me. Things I would have read about, learned from, found interesting, and then moved on from now stuck in my mind—and not in a nice way. Not only was I noticing all of this horrible news, but my resultant fear and anxiety at just reading it converted the words and descriptions into the ugly wallpaper now permanently pasted into my mind's eye. No matter how much wallpaper my fears produced, there always seemed to be more inner space for its display.

My mind was expanding at a terrible rate—in all the wrong directions. In an episode of the original *Star Trek* television series, Mr. Spock finds it necessary to quickly disable the ship's computer. He gives the computer a direct order to compute, to the last digit, the value of pi. As pi has no limit, more and more of the computer's power is directed at the problem, until the entire computer is consumed by the process.

I *became* that computer. I started to notice a decline in my ability to do math at this point. Without having to study much, I had made it through eighth-grade algebra and the first semester of ninth-grade geometry with easy Bs. What prevented me from getting an A was not my test scores—it was my homework, of which I did little. Homework was for people who needed extra practice to "get it," not me. The problem was that I could no longer continuously follow the explanations. I would drift off in the middle of proofs and equations, missing the connections. What's especially ironic is that I didn't realize what had happened to me. I began to believe I didn't get math anymore.

If I had to study, I wasn't as smart. This seemed logical to me. The real issue was that I wasn't functionally smart like I'd been. But I couldn't recognize this.

And I didn't really like studying math. I liked math because I was good at it. Studying was a grind, a habit I'd never developed. I felt that if I could recall knowledge for a test, whether it be history, English, or science, that was enough. Doing projects and reports didn't really add to my knowledge base, I thought.

By being bright with an excellent memory, I hadn't needed to study at all. And now, needing to study, I had the world's worst study habits and a rapidly-diminishing ability to concentrate.

The Scout meetings were different now. At fifteen, I moved from being a patrol leader the previous year (a very active and exciting time for a Scout) to being a patrol *adviser*, a much-less hands-on consultant to patrol leaders. The story of my year as a patrol leader, especially as a non-OCD, high-functioning patrol leader, is a fun, happy, and exciting chapter of my life. It deserves to be written as a stand-alone story sometime.

Patrol advisers, however, are sort of in limbo. Having had their turn as patrol leaders, they are older Scouts of higher rank (I had my star by then, two away from Eagle), but not quite old enough to run the troop like the senior patrol leader (the young man in charge of the troop) and his assistant senior patrol leaders. These older Scouts planned and ran the meetings. Although I was allowed to help plan, my duties were limited to an occasional presentation, and being the "gopher" for the older Scouts.

I'm not complaining—it's a natural progression of duties that trains leaders—but I went from being top dog to the bottom of the pack. Sort of like going from one's senior year in high school to being a freshman in college. (Many Scouts drop out during this time, and many strategies have been attempted to remediate this. Later I found that the best remedy was a program that included *lots* of outings, especially high adventure in the summers.)

And Greg wasn't there. I thought about him a lot—many of us did—but there was little news, besides the fact that he was receiving treatment. I'll have to say the year passed in somewhat of a fog. My best recollection of it was finishing my Life Scout Badge, the last rank before Eagle. I had advanced fairly quickly—I now had three more years to make it to Eagle. And I would end up needing all of them.

Sudden impact

Near the end of the school and Scouting year, we finally began getting news about Greg. He was allowed to have visitors. Mr. Roberts, still the Scoutmaster, and Karl, had gone to see him. And it got back quickly to all of us that Greg was saying good-bye. The doctors had stopped treating him. There was nothing more they could do. It was only a matter of days, according to Mr. Roberts. We were all encouraged to visit Greg to cheer him up.

I remember the bright sun, the dense foliage bordering the parking lot, the intense, shiny green of the azalea and rhododendron leaves, the flowers in bloom, the beautiful, healthy smell in the air as I stepped out of the car, along with my parents and my younger brother, Steve. We had arrived at Children's Hospital in Laurelhurst, a well-kept suburb of Seattle, just north of the University of Washington and bordering Lake Washington, to the east.

The walk was slightly uphill. We had parked just northeast of the main entrance doors to the hospital, and I can still feel the heat of the sun, the bright light making me squint. It was as lovely a day in early June as one could expect in Seattle. We made our way to the entrance. It was cool and shady inside the hospital, and my eyes instantly appreciated the relief. Greg's room was a bit further south along the ground floor of the building, on the left-hand side, facing the parking lot.

I remember the surprising absence of color in the hospital, so drab—all whites and grays, such a contrast to the beautiful day outside. Why couldn't it have been raining, drab, and gray outside too, like it usually was this time of year? The contrast was depressing. We started counting down the room numbers on east side of the hall. We soon found Greg's room and went in.

Except Greg wasn't there. I spotted a figure in the bed, but it had to be the wrong room. The figure wasn't worth more than a glance—some emaciated old man in a hospital gown. We were in the wrong room. And then it dawned on me it was the *Children's* Hospital. The old man in the bed, sticklike, bald, waiting to die, *was* Greg. He wasn't fully awake, but we had been told it was okay to rouse him. "Greg," I called out to him. "It's us—the Dahlbergs."

And then it *was* Greg. He managed a smile, that unmistakable smile. Did I say, "Wake up, Greg," this time? I can't recall, although I think I might have said it. I do remember we had quite a chat.

"I'm going on the nine-day again this summer, Greg. Sure hope you can make it."

Greg lit up at this. "I helped plan it."

We continued to chat—all the while my eyes wandering over his poor body. My memory, perhaps due to the shock of seeing him this way, went fully photographic, solidifying images I would carry for the rest of my life. The year before, at the weigh-in for the nine-day trip, Greg had weighed 150 pounds and carried a fifty-pound pack. I remember his excited expression: "I'm carrying fifty pounds!" Most people would have complained. Did he even weigh half of his previous weight now?

And still he didn't complain. He was still friendly, optimistic Greg. Sometime during the conversation, he had a bad coughing fit. He asked me to give him a drink of water. There was a cup on his bedside table with a flexible straw. I moved the cup close to his face, and he gratefully took the end of the straw in his lips and sipped. "Thanks," he said.

Greg had always had tremendous strength, tremendous reserves, and an exceptional power to draw on them. But his strength and reserves were nearly played out. It suddenly became apparent that he had been using this power to keep up the conversation. He

94

started to drop off on us. We said our good-byes and walked back out into the brilliant sunshine. Were there birds singing? I don't remember. But years later now, OCD under control, I can finally remember this good-bye fondly.

But the remembrance—and the gladness for it—were a long way away in 1974. Had I been granted a visit to hell to view the most horrifying sights the devil could conjure, it could not have been worse to me than this fear of cancer, of disease, of getting sick, finally personified. I had thought my anxious feelings due to OCD were crippling enough – but this amplified them more than I could have imagined, adding a new dimension of worry and disfunctionality to my already short-circuited brain.

School let out a few days later, and, keeping my tradition of the last few years, that afternoon I got on a school bus and left for Shoreline Music Camp, a week of band and choir held at Warm Beach, a large resort facility on Puget Sound, west of Stanwood, Washington. We stayed in cabins with counselors, and the days were a flurry of band practices, music lessons, choir practice, and a myriad of fun activities—hikes, swimming, and group activities such as scavenger hunts on the huge, wooded grounds.

On the morning of June 20, I called home from camp to let my parents know how it was going. In the back of my mind, I had another reason as well. Mom and I chatted for a bit, and then she told me, "I have some sad news, David. Greg Brock died last night."

I had been expecting this, but it was still a shock, the final reality confirmed. Walking back to my cabin, I spotted Bob Hensey, a music student but also an older Scout in the troop. He was a camp counselor this year. I told him Greg had died. "Well, that's three," he said.

Before I had joined Troop 348, a young member had been killed in an accident. I hadn't known him, but Bob had. And a year before Greg became sick, Eric Rose, a senior Scout, a very popular young man, and a friend to all, had died while vacationing in Hawaii. He and some friends had been exploring some caves and decided to take a swim in one of the pools. He dove into a pool— no one had checked the depth—and came back up with a blank look on his face. He immediately sank back down. He'd fatally fractured his skull on a rock. I think Eric's death hit some in the troop much harder than Greg's did. I wasn't happy about it.

But I never obsessed about Eric's death. Eric had made a conscious choice to dive into that water. He controlled his own destiny, tragic as his death was. That was the difference: Greg had not asked for what had happened to him. There was no choice—only chance, it seemed to me. It had been out of his control. It was the unknown. And this is what I feared most: what I couldn't control.

Anxiety to the power of ten

Newspaper and magazine articles, movies, television—seeing illness and death in all of these media and finding out that Greg had cancer had pushed me into the stressful and dysfunctional world of OCD. But nothing could have prepared me for the effect the sight of Greg in his last days would have on me. It wasn't just another piece of wallpaper stuck on my wall of anxiety. It was an entirely *new* wall—a movie screen, really, and the horror feature on it never stopped playing.

I've always been an empathetic person. If someone is hurt or injured, I feel it too. I can't help putting myself in that person's place. I didn't just obsess about Greg in that bed; I often saw myself in it instead. This vision was even worse than the sight of Greg. Something would remind me of him, and then I would see this image of him. Or, just as often, it would pop into my head out of thin air, triggering the stress. And then I'd see myself suffering, which raised my anxiety level through the roof.

My OCD took a new and grim turn. If the image of Greg sick came into my mind, whether or not I saw myself sick as well, I would have to superimpose an image of a healthy person in place of it to cover it up. Then came an image of me healthy as well, with the first healthy person always visualized first—kind of as a shield between me and Greg. More likely than not, Greg's image would then reappear instantly, and I would have to repeat the process. Not only that, I would have to repeat the ritual a "good" number of times. I got into the habit of having "good" numbers ready—for example, the number 6. If the image came in, I just went ahead and repeated the process six times right away to try to stomp the bad thought out for good.

To do this, however, I would actually have to bring the bad thought back into my head—I didn't like to wait around for my rituals—which, combined with the counting itself, only burned the image into my mind more strongly. It was like having my mind's eye attached to a yo-yo, one that could swing for minutes or even hours. For rarely was I able to stop and satisfactorily bury a bad thought or an image with only one simple set of repetitions. My last images of Greg were so vivid, so overwhelming, that often only sheer mental fatigue was what finally stopped them. I could cycle through dozens of sets of good numbers—hundreds, even.

There were even some entirely sleepless nights over the years. Imagine sitting on the edge of your bed in a dark room, relentlessly working a yo-yo up and down, for hours, unable to stop, and forbidden to sleep until the gray light of dawn appeared. Looking at the time—even if I managed to land on a good number with a finishing good thought, if my digital clock read 3:05 a.m., a number that added up to the "bad" number 8, I would have to repeat it again. My OCD was an endless equation with infinite variables.

My first nine-day hike without Greg was spent in a state of semi-consciousness, it seemed. Greg had been so much a part of my hiking experience; we were not close friends outside of Scouting, but we were the best of hike buddies. I had done all I could not to think of Greg, to block him out of my mind, but this also blocked the grieving process. I believe that part of this process is still feeling the presence of that now-missing person—the space he occupied is still very real. And who knows if this person's spirit isn't still there, watching over us for a while longer? And by pushing all of this away, I had created a huge emptiness within myself, an emptiness I neither enjoyed nor understood.

After two consecutive nine-day hikes in previous years over some impressive terrain, we had a number of new Scouts on this particular hike, so it had to be "softened up" a bit for them, like my first long hike in 1970. We stayed more on the trails and centered on the French Creek/Stevens Pass drainage section of the

Alpine Lakes Wilderness, an area with many lakes and relatively short hops between them. We hiked relatively slowly and spent way too much time at camp—in my case, sitting around and moping, staring out at the surfaces of lakes or deeply into a campfire, sometimes numbly, at other times ritualizing internally.

There were several fifteen-year-olds on this hike, and we had all been put into a patrol together to develop camaraderie for the upcoming Scouting year. But as the old saying goes, we had too many chiefs and too few Indians. We bickered over everything, including how sufficiently cooked the freeze-dried meatballs were one night. The cooks, especially hungry that night, decided dinner was ready enough and had served it up a little underdone. We all have our own vivid memories, but the one I have of this dinner—crunching down on those underdone freeze-dried meatballs while sitting on a log in a rocky meadow—is especially visceral.

I have another memory of this hike: what happened to Matt Sirota, Greg's close friend, both inside and outside of Scouting. He very nearly joined him one afternoon.

When you hike in the Cascade Mountains in the summer, you can encounter a lot of snow. North-facing gullies shaded all round by high peaks can funnel and hold snow well past August. Some years, it never melts completely through. Our leaders trained us every year on the first snow we might hit: If you go down, roll over onto your stomach and dig in with your hands and feet. Never stay on your back. Your pack makes an excellent sled.

Jim Lansing, Mark Bradley, and I checked out a snow gully ahead of the troop one afternoon, while hiking out of Marmot Lake. Mark and I—the two lightest senior Scouts—walked carefully ahead over the middle of the snowfield. It was narrow, but the type of field prone to "bridging"—that is, being undercut by meltwater. You didn't want to walk a troop over a snowbridge, which could mean a ten-foot drop if someone fell through. Mark and I hiked out a ways, and we both felt the snow change at the same time—it didn't feel as thick, as solid under our feet. We stopped. Jim volunteered to hike up a bit and get into the gully, above the snow, and take a look at the crossing we were attempting.

He actually managed, after some scrambling, to get nearly underneath us. Obviously there *was* space below us. Then he hiked back up. "You guys are standing on about six inches of snow there."

"I guess we'd better backtrack," replied Mark.

"No, keep going," Jim said. You've actually already gone over the thinnest part—another ten feet and you'll have quite a bit more snow underneath you."

Now, of course, there's a difference between the "snow" we were on and new snow. We were actually walking on mostly ice, with a thin layer of softer stuff on top, melted by the air. But the ice had barely supported us; it would never hold the entire troop. Instead of an easy snow crossing, the troop was going to have to hike 150 feet up the hill to avoid the snowbridge and then detour back down and around. Better safe than sorry.

Mark and I finished crossing the gully, and it was easy to see the beginning of the trail again on the other side of the snow. There was about a three-foot gap like a tunnel in the forest as we neared the trail within. Looking down before the trees, we saw big rocks at the bottom (the entire gully was a rock-filled avalanche chute). However, it was more of a crevasse: the snow had split here, not melted, and went right down to the rocks. We could have easily jumped it, but decided to put our packs on the snow and sit on them. It was a hot afternoon and very comfortable waiting there on the snow. About twenty feet farther down the hill to our left, the snow had broken off and melted completely, leaving a long, steep drop to the boulders beyond.

The troop had quite a time getting above and around the snow. Clear areas are often choked with alders and vine maples, and up high there is more scree—loose, small rocks floating on dirt and sand. It was a real battle. Finally, they had to cross a patch of snow connected to ours, but at least it was not undercut. The adults crossed, kicking in steps, and the Scouts followed. They would soon be down and around.

Mark and I sat, drinking iced tea and munching trail mix, silently watching the troop proceed around this last obstacle. One or two kids slipped and quickly stopped themselves. A quick hand down from another Scout, and they were back on their feet and on the move again. Then we saw Matt slip. He had been leaning into the hill and fell onto his backside. And he didn't turn over. He started to pick up speed. Dozens of yells went up: "Turn over, Matt! Get on your stomach!"

But he wouldn't turn over. Did he panic? Forget what to do? Although he was a year older than I was, this was his first nine-day hike. He lacked the experience of some of us who had hiked across literally miles of snowfields.

Worse yet, his feet created just enough drag to turn him, so he was now heading down on his back, headfirst, still picking up speed at what seemed a tremendous rate. He headed right at Mark and me at a tremendous rate – we had to get out of the way. There was no way we would be able to stop Matt, a big kid who weighed well over two hundred pounds with his pack. He'd take us right with him.

Then I realized he was not headed right at us. He was, snow fly-ing at this point, pointed right at that boulder-filled crevasse we'd stopped at. There was no way he was not going to go in. He slid past us in a blur; by some miracle, his pack stayed just on the edge of the crack, and he flew on by.

But things didn't get any easier for Matt. The edge of the snow-field awaited, and a half second later, he launched off the lip. I'm sure he was airborne for at least a couple of seconds—and, still headfirst, he sailed a good sixty feet down that steeply-dropping hill, from an initial launch height of fifteen feet above the ground.

Ever heard the expression "being tossed like a rag doll"? When Matt landed on that boulder with a loud crash, it was absolutely like watching a rag doll land. His body and limbs just flopped. And then he was utterly still, spread-eagled, out cold—or worse, in the eyes of most of us.

"Nobody move!" yelled Mr. Roberts. Years of search-and-rescue experience kicked in as he and Mr. Lansing, Jim's dad, scrambled to the scene. Mr. Ames then slowly worked the troop down to the trail to wait. Most of us had processed our thoughts and were pretty sure he was either dead or grievously injured.

And he should have been. But Matt's freakish headfirst flight actually saved his life. Once he left the snow, his aluminum-frame backpack had swung up and around enough to interrupt his head's contact with the boulder. The remainder of the pack had cushioned the rest of his body. By some miracle, that pack full of food and clothes and camping gear had oriented itself perfectly. The frame was a twisted mess, but better that than Matt himself. He had suffered only a broken wrist, and of course the landing had knocked the wind out of him badly, paralyzing him for a couple of minutes. He was able to hike out the next day—but not before he had posed for a photo with his pack, holding up the mangled frame with a grim smile.

When I look back, this is as vivid a memory as I have. I can feel the icy spray as Matt rushes by me on the snow. I see him sailing in slow motion over the rocks, and I hear the indescribable sound of his impact on the rocks. It is an image equally intense—possibly even more intense—than that of Greg on his deathbed. I have involuntarily replayed this scene many, many times. It has its own special wallpaper on the wall of my mind's eye.

And yet it doesn't bother me one bit. Why? Is it because he lived? I don't think so. If Matt had died, it would have been quick, or at least not too prolonged. He would have suffered relatively little. Here's the difference: had it been me, *I knew I would have been in control.* Had it been me sliding, I would have turned over immediately and self-arrested—something I'd actually done before that kept me from falling. In this situation, my mind functioned like a non-OCD person's mind. I did not fear Matt's fate or what it could have been. So I didn't obsess about it.

The recall I have of my Scout hikes and outings is amazing, because *they* were amazing. Although I can remember many Scout meetings, they are a bit of a jumble; Monday nights during the school year tended to run together. Scout meetings were, by and large, training for the outdoor activities—knots, lashings, cooking, camp construction, first aid, presentations by Scouts, patrols, and guest speakers, and, of course, advancement, much of it centering on outdoorsmanship.

Scouting also promoted self-discipline. As in my next chapter, about martial arts, there were many formalities. We wore our uniforms to meetings, and the unspoken rule was that uniforms would be neat, clean, and ready for inspection at any time. We were expected to know and live by the Scout motto, oath, law, and slogan. The meetings always began the same—with the presentation of colors and the flag ceremony—and ended with the retiring of colors. In between, there were other rites as well.

Although the meetings were full of activity, the art of holding still was practiced as well. During the flag ceremonies, Scouts stood at attention by patrol file, moving only to salute the flag, lift their arms in the Scout sign, and recite the Scout oath and law. Holding still is a discipline all to itself; it is a form of meditation that calms the mind. If you want to calm a roomful of overactive Scouts, have them stand at attention for one minute. You might be surprised how calm they are afterward. It doesn't build excess energy; it dissipates it.

Patrol file was maintained after the flag ceremony, and Scouts would often stand at attention once again for patrol inspection. Everyone's uniform in the patrol would receive an inspection; Scouts might be quizzed on Scout knowledge; and the patrol would be required to display its patrol flag and perform their patrol yell. A yearly scoreboard was kept with Patrol Points based on inspections and other patrol activities, such as meetings and campouts. The winners received a prize, such as a pizza party. There was no prize for second place—at least not in my days as a young Scout.

All this was practice for the culmination of the Scouting year: the District Camporee, in which over 120 different patrols from dozens of troops would compete against each other in camping, field events (skills tests such as fire building and orienteering). A huge scoreboard kept track of all the patrol scores, which were tallied throughout the weekend of competition.

There were four divisions of thirty patrols, and the patrol with the highest score in each division was issued a red-white-and-blue Presidential Award. Our troop was notoriously resented for winning most of them. During my last year of "sanity," I was a patrol leader, and I had some pretty crack troops under me. We annoyed each other and often fought like cats and dogs, but we came together for Camporee. Before the final inspection, which often determines the outcome, the scoreboard showed we already had it won.

As I walked smartly and happily into my camp, two of my patrol members, Jim Jensen and Pat Tingel, told me they had some bad news. They had gotten into a scuffle while one of the Camporee staff members—a senior Scout—was walking by and were given five demerits for fighting. It didn't dent our score much, but there was a rule in Camporee: patrols receiving demerits are disqualified from Presidential Award contention. I was so mad at them. After an hour of watching me stew and mope around camp, dreading the awards ceremony, they finally confessed—they had made the whole thing up. We had won after all.

I am again reminded of how vivid my memory is of this incident. I can give you an exact description of our campsite and all the improvements we had made, where everything was placed, and the exact location where I was standing when they gave me the "bad news." This especially excellent recall of the details of our camp is based on looking through the intense feelings woven into this memory. It wasn't funny at the time – I was infuriated_– but hilarious things sometimes aren't. Now I can look back and see the perfect practical joke that had demanded to be played – and appreciate it.

Scouting promotes citizenship, respect, leadership—and, most importantly, leadership by the Scouts themselves. Later, as Scoutmaster, I discovered that the Scoutmaster's most important job is to prevent well-meaning parents from trying to take over the troop. The kids' mistakes are just as important to the learning process as are their successes.

Scout meetings and outings had a way of keeping me busy— learning and later teaching. Scout skills teach self reliance, out-doorsmanship, leadership, and teamwork. We spent hours over the years leaning first aid, camping skills, survival skills and orienteering – both learning, practicing, teaching, and in competition between patrols. Teaching something to others is an excellent way to drive a lot of OCD out of your thinking space.

And on the more challenging hikes, the OCD would float away at times and just disappear. Hiking ridge tops all day, exhausting myself, seeing things and places few others could or would—I'd have to say it was one place where I truly felt happy.

The nine-day hikes, in 1975 and 1977 were extra-challenging experiences that took advantage of the abilities of a disproportionate number of older Scouts and Mr. Lansing's (Jim's dad) slightly crazier hike philosophy compared to Mr. Roberts's, who was unable to go those years. In 1977, we actually found ourselves stuck on a cliff coming up on dusk—at about 10 p.m. on a July evening. By some freak chance, one of the younger Scouts had brought along a seventy-five-foot waterski line, and we were able to secure ourselves to make a tricky descent. Believe me, as I hung onto that line, making my way down a twenty-foot drop with the light quickly fading behind me, I was a long way from feeling the need to ritualize *anything.*

Scoutmaster

I was a Boy Scout for seven years. It seemed like twice that, at least. And I was a Scoutmaster for almost twenty years. And it passed in the wink of an eye.

I have my brother to thank for my reinvolvment in Scouting. He had spent his summers during college—and in medical school—running Camp Parsons, the large and historic Scout Camp on Washington's Hood Canal. It was a big job with little pay. On occasion, I would visit him for a day or two at the camp during the summers he worked there. It was always fun to attend a dinner—full of ceremony, songs, skits, and mostly good camp food. All the Scouts lined up in formation before dinner and sat by troop at long tables in the huge hall. Just visiting the camp for a few hours was invigorating and brought back many fond memories.

I'm not sure what exact combination of looking for fun and wanting to serve made me visit my old troop, but as I was living nearby, it was easy enough to drop by. It was September 1985, and I was 26 years old. . I had finished my math degree, but I had yet to complete a successful stint at student teaching and a few more math classes for a full teaching endorsement. But I couldn't wait any longer to go back and replace the memories that troubled me with new, happier Scouting experiences. It turned out to be a fortuitous time for me to walk in.

Troop 348 still held meetings on Monday evenings at 7:30. Although the troop still met at the Presbyterian church, it had moved from the basement under the main chapel to the auxiliary chapel, which was connected by a long, two-story spur containing a series of rooms across from each other, upstairs and down. The church was a lot like a medieval castle; it seemed that anywhere you went in the several-thousand-square-foot building, there were stairways leading up somewhere—some large, some narrow and half-hidden. These hallways were like secret passages, and the rooms always seemed to lead into other rooms via various doors coming in and out.

I remember simply walking into the last September meeting about fifteen minutes early. A couple of dads were hanging out, waiting for the Scoutmaster, Dave Winters, to arrive. We made introductions—Art Jameson, a tall, graying but fit surgeon, was the father of Mike Jameson, a Scout coming up on Eagle. Bob Bachman, physically much like Art but with short, curling hair, was the other; his son, Bill, had reached Eagle the previous year and was now eighteen. Both of the dads remembered my brother, Steve, who had been the boys' senior patrol leader and the junior assistant Scoutmaster for one more year—a position traditionally filled by Eagle Scouts after they had been either SPL (senior patrol leader) of ASPL (assistant senior patrol leader). They seemed very happy to meet me—Steve's older brother, who was also an Eagle Scout.

How interesting, I thought. I had attended a couple of troop meetings the year I went to Western, and I remembered Bill—a small, shy, wispy red-haired boy. I would meet him later; he is taller than me now and a gregarious young man with a great smile and a fun sense of humor. Bill's career as a Scout had spanned exactly the time I had been away. He helped out at meetings occasionally, and every time we met, I couldn't help but see that little boy in him.

By the time Dave Winters arrived about ten minutes late, the boys had already started the meeting. The troop didn't seem very large that night—two patrols and some senior Scouts, and fewer than twenty boys—half of what I was used to. The standards seemed to have loosened too. The flag ceremony was far less formal, and many of the boys were in partial uniform; some were just in street clothes. The older boys—the ones in high school—remembered my brother fondly, both from his years as a Senior Scout and from Camp Parsons. They were very talkative. Several of them were close to finishing their Eagle badges, and they had become fairly close over the years. I also found it easy to talk with the younger Scouts; they were interested in what the troop had been like in "the old days."

I got to talking with Dave Winters, whose son had finished with Scouting the previous year. Dave was still volunteering as Scoutmaster, but he made it clear he was looking for a replacement. I didn't know it at the time, but Dave was actually under some pressure to leave, both from himself and from parents who didn't see eye to eye with him. I got the full details of it later—mostly from the kids themselves.

Two weeks later, I was invited to a Troop Committee meeting. Besides having a sponsoring body (the church, in our case), the troop's critical organizational and financial needs were managed by an elected group of parents. They didn't run the meetings; they provided support for them and for the outings and camps held throughout the year. Both Art and Bob were there, as were a few other members with whom I was less familiar. They wasted no time. The troop was dying. Many members had quit, few new parents had volunteered to step in, and Dave had just resigned. They asked me if I would be willing to step in as Scoutmaster.

We all knew I was pretty green, but I had a few things in my favor. I was a "pure" volunteer—since I had no sons in the troop, I could be a disinterested party when necessary. I was an Eagle Scout and from this very troop. They knew I had a lot of pride in Troop 348 and had received training from some legendary Scouters in my years as a Scout. And they could see I related well to the kids. Somehow, when I was ready, things had come together. I was the right guy in the right place at the right time, it seemed to me. And I knew I had a great challenge to fulfill.

Reinforcing this karmic-seeming destiny was my subsequent meeting with Bill Roberts, whom I knew still kept track of the troop as a member of the Lake Forest Park Presbyterian Church. Of all my Scoutmasters, I had admired him the most, and when I finally earned my Eagle Badge, I had asked him to present my award at the ceremony.

Bill was, in his words, "tickled" that I had agreed to become Scoutmaster. We talked for a couple of hours, and, at the end of my talk, he asked me if I needed a uniform. I said I did, and he gave me his own—a very valuable uniform, in fact, with many irreplaceable, collector's item badges and insignias sewn on. I told him I was honored that he would lend it to me and promised to return it once I had purchased my own.

"No, it's yours to keep, David. I won't be wearing it anymore. Hmmm, I wonder what's in the shirt pocket?"

Bill unbuttoned it. Folded up inside was a Court of Honor program, dated June 1976. My own Eagle Court of Honor. His uniform, with the program still in it, had hung in his closet for just over nine years since that ceremony. Had it been waiting for this moment? It seemed so. We both got a chuckle out of it, after the initial disbelief.

The next twenty years deserve a book all their own. My OCD was not a huge factor during this time, and, if anything, the business of being Scoutmaster and of building so many positive memories nearly cancelled out my previously bad memories of Scouting. I quit being Scoutmaster in 2005, since my two girls were becoming very active kids and I needed the attention I had previously given to the troop.

The activities and hikes reduced my time for brooding and siphoned off much of my nervous energy. School, work, and Scouts gave me so much to do—and by then, I had developed some patterns of healthy thought processes. In a sense, I was already unknowingly performing cognitive therapy – in other words, I was forcing myself to occupy my time with constructive thoughts and activities, in a venue where it was not easy to take the time to be paralyzed by my thoughts and fears. I had to keep moving forward.

We gained some new Scouts and parents, some of whom were talented recruiters and excellent organizers for a new and improved Troop Committee. Many parents volunteered as adult leaders as well. These parents weren't afraid to challenge the kids to participate, to work on their advancements, to give fun and hard work a chance. The troop grew slowly but steadily back to healthy numbers and then maintained them.

The last older boys got their Eagle badges and moved on. It took several years for the new crop of boys to advance through the nearly emptied ranks again—but then the Eagles started coming back. Our ratio of Eagles was outstanding. It's said that only one out of fifty Scouts advance all the way to the rank of Eagle; our ratio was one in five.

If one significant thing drove me as Scoutmaster, it had to be pride. Not so much the personal pride of restoring a troop back to its rightful place, but my pride in Troop 348 itself. I had been part of the troop when it was a fantastic piece of machinery. As a youth, I had benefited from it and contributed to it, and now I had come back to give back all that I had learned and been given. I had a vested interest in Troop 348, knowing what it could do for all involved, including the community.

I remember the exact moment I realized this was a large part of my motivation. Shortly after I took over as Scoutmaster, the senior patrol leader, Scott Ottley, who was working on finishing his Eagle badge, expressed his feelings to me. It was one of those midwinter nights when the turnout was light—only about ten Scouts were present. Scott, who had seen much of the troop leave under Dave Winters, was extremely cynical that he had to be SPL of *this*.

"Why don't we just let Troop 348 *die*?" he asked me. "Scouting just isn't popular anymore."

A surge of anger hit me, and I forced myself to hold my tongue. Why did he feel this way? Then it dawned on me. What did Scott have to be proud of? I told him, "Scott, I remember what the troop was like and what it could be. Why don't we make the troop the best it can be for the rest of this year? There's so much we can do, so much *you* can do. You want to be an Eagle? Then go out in style."

Scott wasn't afraid to express himself, and he wasn't afraid to listen, either. We sat down with the other senior Scouts, and I helped them come up with ideas that would once again make the troop proud of itself—if not necessarily a whole lot larger—that year. We began with simple things: starting the meetings on time, restoring patrol competitions, requiring Scouts to be in uniform, presenting and retiring the colors properly. These were small things that would add up to larger, more important ones.

We talked about making the outings better and recruiting Scouts and their parents to participate in them. The Scouts had reached a plateau, and they had a choice: they could hike up the path toward the summit and encourage others to follow, or they could give up and begin the descent back down without ever reaching the top.

They decided to hike up.

CHAPTER 9

Martial Arts

In some ways, you could say that OCD is a lack of mental discipline. Cognitive therapy has proven successful in instilling mental discipline using physical response—or, in my case, a lack of physical response. It has helped me to refuse to engage in rituals, to taper them off, and to continue to do an action as if the disturbing thoughts or images are not there. My martial arts training gave me an additional weapon to fight OCD.

Martial arts, especially when practiced in formal, Eastern form—karate, Zen, judo, weapons—use methods, developed over centuries, very similar to modern cognitive therapy, that can help ameliorate the symptoms of OCD and its concurrent anxieties. An excellent example of such a therapy for OCD is meditation.

When my OCD was at its worst, my martial arts training helped me to hang on, to never give up. There is a saying in Japanese, *Nana korobi ya oki,* "Seven times knocked down, eight times get up." I was always able to get up, even if it meant seeking the help of others.

Ironically, my martial arts training came about as a result of yet another display of my social idiocy. At Western, Jack and Donny took me to a wrestling team party. It was in a nice apartment in Birnam Wood, the student housing section just around Sehome Hill from the actual campus.

Since it was during wrestling season, nobody was drinking too hard or getting terribly rowdy, but the young lady who lived in the apartment had set a deadline of one in the morning to clear out (pretty early by Western's standards). As that hour neared, she began encouraging people to leave. I was in line at the keg, just a few places back from the spigot, when she came up and shut the keg down. She twisted the spigot off, leaving no question about further refills.

I found this annoying, and I had drunk enough that my few social skills had disappeared, along with any ability to reason. After begging her to replace the spigot and hearing her repeatedly adamant no, I called her a bitch. The coed burst into tears, grabbed the spigot, and fled.

A few minutes later, Donny and Jack rushed up together. "Dahlberg," Donny said, "Why did you call that girl a bitch?"

"It's nothing I haven't heard *you* say before."

"This is different. She's really nice; she doesn't deserve to be called a bitch. Besides, she's DeWitt's girlfriend."

Now *that* got me concerned. I'd been to some of the wrestling matches. DeWitt was a phenomenal college wrestler, and he was bigger than me.

"It's okay, you fucked-up idiot," chimed in Jack. "We were talking with Dewitt when she came up crying. He was going to kick your ass. We recognized it was you from the description, told him you were an idiot even when you *weren't* drunk, and promised to get you out of here. All you have to do is go apologize."

"What if he tries to kill me?"

"Don't worry; Donny and I will be there to back you up."

DeWitt turned out to be remarkably civil. Donny and Jack had done their work well. I apologized to his girlfriend (by then I honestly felt badly about the insult) and shook hands with him.

"You fuck-up, Dahlberg," Jack said, on the way home (a term he used with me often). "You really have a way of pissing off the wrong people."

The next day, Saturday afternoon, I asked Jack, "Was DeWitt really going to kick my ass?"

"He was going to throw you down the stairs, Dave."

"Aw, I bet I could have handled him."

"Are you crazy?" Donny cut in. "It wouldn't even have been close. He wasn't just going to throw you down the stairs. He was going to put you in a wrestling hold, pummel you, and *then* throw you down the stairs. Come into practice and wrestle him if you don't believe me. He'd break your scrawny little neck."

Well, I had seen DeWitt wrestle. Put that way, I could easily see the outcome.

Although I felt invincible, having so many tough friends, it bothered me that none of them seemed to think I could take care of myself. I decided it was time to do something about it. Just up the street from our house was a karate school, the Bellingham Academy of Self-Defense. Another student had told me about it and that it had cheap student rates. I decided I was going to take karate.

Jack, Donny, and I shared a house just north of the campus, in a neighborhood of mostly turn-of-the-century homes. Streets were crisscrossed by alleys, and most of the homes were rented to Western students or recent graduates who chose to stay (Bellingham could be a hard place to leave). Tall, spreading chestnut trees lined the sidewalks, and there were many good-sized evergreens, plantings, and gardens in the established neighborhoods. The houses weren't all pristine, but they weren't completely rundown either. As the neighborhood was built on a hill, the west-facing houses all had large porches with stairs leading to the front doors, whereas the houses that faced the hill had single-story entrances with daylight basements. It was elegant-looking compared to the split-level houses built in newer neighborhoods.

The karate school had once been a church. It had a full basement and a good-sized main area with hardwood floors. The training hall—the main area—had the lofty ceilings of a chapel, and a small loft, originally for the choir, overlooked the main floor. Underneath the loft was the upper entrance. It was rarely used; students entered through the daylight basement, where there were men's and women's changing rooms.

Opposite the changing rooms was a long, narrow kitchen with a long, narrow table filling it. Packed with chairs, the kitchen was visited after every workout by many of the students, who were joined by the *sensei*, or "teacher." It was a relaxing time after the hard workouts and led to much camaraderie. A beer or two would be quaffed. The sensei always sat at the head of the table, closest to the refrigerator.

On the south end of the basement, an elegant, open, wooden stairway led upstairs to the *dojo* (training hall). I always found it a bit breathtaking climbing those stairs—as you emerged to the upstairs, a railing separated the stairway from the main floor, and there was no door. It was like climbing a ridge and reaching the top as surrounding ridges and mountains appear around you. North of the stairwell was a seven-foot by fifteen-foot mirror, used by students to practice their forms. It gave the already spacious hall an even bigger feeling. There was no claustrophobia in this dojo.

The dojo was open Tuesday and Thursday nights from 5:30 to 7:30 p.m., with the first half-hour dedicated to individual warm-ups and practice, and the rest of the time, the formal workout. Saturday mornings were open session, 10 a.m. until noon. There was no formal instruction, and students could work on whatever they wished.

On the last Thursday in January, 1979, I walked a few blocks up the hill to the Bellingham Academy of Self-Defense. I decided to enter through the front upper door, since I was unaware of the basement entrance. From this door, one could look down the upper (east) side of the building. Along this side, down the large, white wall, two ten-foot-long dragons—made from plywood and expertly painted a variety of colors—stood face to face. The effect was quite Eastern and not diabolical at all, as the dragons were of the Asian variety—stylized and wingless. They added a very formal appearance to the outside of the school.

I arrived about five in the evening, hoping I was early enough to talk to someone about joining. I was eager and wanted to start first thing in February. I was greeted by a stocky but strong-looking man of about thirty. He had dark hair and a mustache, and was dressed in jeans and a leather jacket. He had no shoes. "Can I help you?" he asked.

"I'm interested in joining your school."

He introduced himself. His name was Reginald Black, but he said everyone just called him Reg. He was a brown belt (one below black), and he offered to introduce me to the sensei, Duane Stevens.

Reg gave a quick intro in etiquette. "Leave your shoes by the front door. In the dojo, you should always address Duane as Mr. Stevens, or, if you're accepted as a student, Sensei."

He walked me over to a small, open office, directly across from the front entrance. A fortyish man looked up from the desk and smiled. He had a light complexion with reddish hair. He stood up to shake my hand. "I'm Duane Stevens. What can I tell you about our school?"

I returned the introduction. "I'm David Dahlberg. I'm a student at Western, and I wish to learn karate for self-defense." He seemed pleased with my interest.

We sat down, and he explained the workings of his school to me. The Bellingham Academy of Self-Defense—or BASD—was a formal Japanese karate school. Many ceremonies and routines had to be observed. Mr. Stevens was quick to emphasize these were not *religious* ceremonies; they were adapted from the Japanese culture and based on respect and discipline—not just physical discipline, but *mental* discipline as well.

I soon learned that when one is pushed physically, the real key to performance is mental—the ability to decisively act on and endure what the physical requires. The mind has a safety factor built in that listens to the body, giving into the body's call for a break long before it absolutely needs one. And, like the body, the mind can be trained. The mind controls the body. In OCD therapy, the mind ultimately controls the body as well, refusing to let the body perform compulsions.

Mr. Stevens was a true martial artist. He was not in it for the money or the glory. Unlike many other karate schools, the BASD did not "guarantee" you a black belt in three years or have you sign a yearly contract (which you would be held to financially, whether you chose to keep attending or not).

Although a highly successful tournament fighter in his twenties and thirties, Mr. Stevens had grown tired of the narrow focus and the politics and had determined to open a school that emphasized self-improvement and practical self-defense—not just scoring points in a tournament setting. Once a year, he held a loosely scored intra-dojo tournament, just to show us what the other guys did. In his eyes, tournaments were fun, but did not produce well-rounded students. It also tended to attract students with bigger egos. The students at BASD were a good mix of gender and age.

My first few sessions at the academy were spent getting used to the rigorous warm-ups before the instructional period. We would do various calisthenics, stretches, and dozens of push-ups before we did karate—a fairly fixed routine that took up about the first twenty-five minutes of class. I was sore from this alone for the first couple of weeks. And even during those warm-ups, I could see the concentration and discipline the experienced students had developed.

Besides warm-ups, the other basic—and really the most important thing—to learn was dojo etiquette. The start of class was very formal. One minute you would be stretching, practicing on your own, and suddenly, a shout: "Lining up!"

At that point, you would run—not walk—lining up in a row depending on your rank. The brown belt in charge of warm-ups would count the students and then yell out the number of rows. If there were twenty-four students present, he would shout, "Four rows!" Students would rush to line up by rank; the highest belts would be in the front row, in descending order from right to left. The next three rows would line up directly behind the first, leaving several feet of space both in front and to the sides. As the newest student, I was in the leftmost spot at the end of the back row.

From where I stood, it was a long way to the front. It could take years of study and practice to advance to the front. It was very important that all the rows were perfectly straight and lined up front to back. You had to line up exactly with the person on the right of your row, or you might find yourself doing more push-ups.

The next command, *"Yoi!"* meant stand at attention, fists at your waist, looking straight ahead to where your imaginary opponent might stand. This was the back of the person in front of you, unless you were in front.

Alex, the brown belt who usually warmed up the class, stood at the front, facing the class. Behind him was the *Shinzen*—a shrine that is the heart of all formal Japanese karate schools. It was the old pulpit space and contained a banner with the name of our style—*goju ryu*—written in Japanese characters, and various other Japanese artifacts and artworks. Again, the Shinzen was not an object of worship; it was an object of respect.

Once the class was lined up in yoi, Mr. Stevens would make his entrance, striding out of his office in his *gi*—his uniform. At the time, he was a *fourth dan*—a fourth-degree black belt. Junior ranks, or *kyus*, counted down from ten (therefore, I was a tenth kyu, or beginner). Black belts counted back up—back to ten. However, a fourth dan was considered quite high, and for a man in his forties, it was an impressive rank indeed.

Mr. Stevens would take his place beyond Alex, who would continue to stand at the front during warm-ups. Alex would reissue the command, "Yoi."

This time, it meant *sit down*. We all took the *zazen* position, a Zen meditative stance, in which you kneel down and fold your shins under your thighs. Shins and the tops of feet make contact with the floor, the upper legs make contact with the shins, and the body sits upright, hands rest lightly on the thighs. It takes time for the body to adapt to this position, especially the foot contact on the floor. Gradually the tops of your feet build up a little extra cartilage and callus, cushioning them and toughening them.

Now the command—*"Mokuso"*—meditate. Students would close their eyes, and a few minutes of calming the mind would begin. Breathing slowly—in through the nose, out through the mouth—allowed our diaphragms to push down and come back up. This produced a feedback loop that literally calms the mind.

As a beginner, it was hard for me to keep my mind off the foot discomfort, but by holding my body absolutely still, thoughts were stilled as well. It was an ancient ritual, but also Therapy 101 for OCD. I just didn't know it at the time.

Meditation also occurred at the end of class. The closing meditation always felt so different from the opening, for reasons I'll explain soon.

"*Mokuso yame!*"—stop meditation. The eyelids would open, while the rest of the body maintained its perfect stillness.

Now it was time to pay respects.

"*Shinzen ni rei!*"—Bow to the Shinzen, the heart of the dojo. You placed your left hand on the floor in front of you, followed by your right, and then bent forward at the waist, almost touching your forehead to your hands. The bow was held for about one second, and then the head came up, followed by the hands in reverse order from how they were placed.

"*Sensei ni rei!*"—Bow to Mr. Stevens, the sensei.

"*Sempai ni rei!*"—Bow to any other black belts. If there were no other black belts present, this would be skipped.

Finally, "*Otogani rei!*"—Bow to each other.

One might think the ceremony itself was some sort of obsessive-compulsive ritual invented in years long past, but to me, it was far from it. I was not allowed to repeat a bow if a bad thought flew into my head. So, it was practice in not letting such thoughts control me. After the meditation, my mind would often be much more relaxed, my eyes better attuned to my surroundings—the wood grain of the floor, the white *gis* of the other students, even the details of my fingertips that I was often too self-absorbed to see.

"Everybody up!" And the warm-up exercises would commence. Mr. Stevens was a firm believer in injury prevention. Our warm-ups were longer than a typical karate school's and incorporated many stretching and range-of-motion exercises as well as traditional strengtheners like lots of push-ups and sit-ups. They included many standing and sitting exercises, as well as some that seemed to demand everything at once. The warm-ups were always done in the same order, with the same repetitions. I often wondered how Alex could remember all of this stuff in order. I would try to duplicate the routine at home occasionally and would always leave several exercises out.

Again, the set routine and order forced me to complete activities without the interference of my OCD. It was very difficult to ritualize internally—I had enough trouble keeping up with the exercises.

Keeping busy doing normal things is a great therapy for OCD. These warm-ups were helpful to me in developing the self-control that never quite let OCD win, that kept me fighting it every step of the way.

The final exercise completed, we would once again line up to the command of "Yoi! "—be ready. Standing side by side, front to back, we were a well-oiled machine prepared to perform in unison—basic punching, kicking, and blocking.

Mr. Stevens would take the center and start the formal workout. For my first few classes, I peeled off to start a few introductory lessons with one of the senior students, to learn some of the basic stances, techniques, vocabulary, and routines. By the end of the month, I would be working out with the regular class for the entire workout—although I certainly wouldn't know everything by then; nobody ever does. One never stops progressing in the martial arts—first physically, and then mentally as well. And, being a formal Japanese School, BASD was very heavy on the mental.

I could easily write a karate textbook here, but I'll focus on some details that were the most relevant. What sort of activities took place within the dojo that mitigated the OCD thoughts and impulses in my mind?

I'll start off with the most obvious to me: why I joined. I wanted to learn to defend myself, and to practice defending oneself, one has to practice fighting. The formal techniques learned during most of the class are used—generally in modified form—during the last part of the workout: the *kumite*, or free fighting.

My first two months in the dojo was spent merely observing kumite. I was fascinated at the application of technique and at the coordination displayed by the students—especially the senior students. Although some students of the same rank were better fighters than others, any given brown belt could generally outclass a lower rank.

At this point, I should briefly describe the ranks of our dojo. Most karate schools have ten kyus, or ranks, but different schools used different-colored belts to designate them. The exception to this is a white belt for beginners and brown belts being the highest rank before black. At BASD, there were only four colors: white, green, brown, and black. But there were different levels.

White had four levels: A beginner was a tenth kyu; the belt was plain. After a promotion, you would gain a stripe on your belt. More promotions, more stripes.

There were three stripes per belt, with only white having a blank level. If you were a white belt with one or more stripes, you were called a striper. There were four levels of white, three of green, and three of brown. If you were a brown belt with all three stripes, you were a first kyu, which accorded much of the respect of a black belt and held many of the same expectations.

Depending on the rank, our particular style allowed up to moderate contact to the body, but none to the head. We did not wear protective gear. Techniques and kicks could be directed at the head, but they had to be pulled or directed to the side of the target.

To spar, the class formed two rows, facing each other. During the first part of sparring practice, all belts participated, often partnering with upper belts for coaching and tips. To start, you bowed to your partner and then assumed a formal fighting stance—in our style of goju-ryu, our starting stance was *nekoashi-dachi* (the cat stance), in which the back leg took most of the weight and the front foot was up on its toes. Once fighting commenced, most students moved into and around in a more balanced stance.

The first part of the kumite was at three-quarter speed, where you and your partner would slow down the techniques to a pace where form and variation of technique was the primary focus. Then the sensei would call out, "Speed and power!" and you would go at your best pace. Full-speed kumite could get very tiring in a hurry. You could be sweating after just one fight, which would generally last about sixty seconds.

I remember my first attempt. Gary, a twenty-five-year-old brown belt, was coaching me. We assumed our fighting stance—and I drew a blank. What should I do first?

"Punch me," Gary said.

I sort of hopped toward him and aimed a punch at his body. I missed.

"You're too far away. Move in closer, and don't be afraid to make contact a little."

As the months went by, I became more proficient with my distancing, punching, kicking, and blocking. I learned to string multiple techniques together and, most importantly for a beginner, to control my technique. There's an old saying in karate that the most dangerous person to fight is a beginner. Some beginners are so nervous and wound up they turn into Tasmanian devils. They think the green or brown belts they are sparring are going to demolish them, when actually they are in the safest of hands.

Another rule (always learned the hard way, it seemed) was that as your proficiency grew, it was unwise to take advantage of an upper belt who was not fighting his hardest—who was allowing you opportunities. I remember I threw a wild, whirling kick at Gary once; it flashed past his head, narrowly missing him. I hadn't even looked to see where it was going. He was waiting for the next one. This time, he grabbed my foot mid-kick and lifted, upending me onto the wooden floor and knocking the wind out of me. As I lay there gasping, he gave me a stern lecture on proper kicks and told me to go practice some on the bag after class. Then he reached down and helped me up.

Fights between evenly matched opponents could escalate. We weren't allowed to hit with hard contact, but once your endorphins were up, you could easily lose track of how hard you were hitting or getting hit. Often fights would escalate in this manner, causing Mr. Stevens to yell, "*Yame!*"—separate the partners, and tell them to ease off. I would wake up the next day after a class and wonder where all the bruises came from.

Kumite was truly a place where my OCD entirely disappeared. I didn't even think about OCD during a fight. In fact, I didn't really think at all if I was fighting well. And if I *did* have to think (more of a beginner's way of fighting), it was purely about attacking or defending. My body's instinct would take over, knowing that even a small hesitation put me at a tremendous disadvantage.

I noticed a funny thing about my endorphins one day after practice fighting. I was very ticklish, and a young lady named Kris (the girlfriend of another student of my age and ability) would on occasion sneak up behind me and tickle me. I'd often jump away, I was so ticklish. It was all in fun, and there was much camaraderie at the school, so I didn't mind too much. After a practice fight (the last one of the night, right before class was about to end) she sneaked up on me again and gave me another good tickle to the ribs. Only this time it didn't work. "Do that again!" I challenged her.

Try as Kris might, she could not tickle me. After giving and taking punishment for several practice fights, not only was my pain tolerance up, I was completely immune to her tickling. "Wow, that's really cool!" she said. The next practice she got me before class, and I was as ticklish as ever.

I truly stepped out of my OCD during kumite. How much was endorphins and how much was survival—being forced to pull out of "thought" mode and into reaction mode? Much has been written about "the zone" athletes achieve. From my experience, there is no room for OCD in the zone.

Proper breathing was not reserved simply for meditation. In and out of the dojo, students were encouraged to breathe in through the nose, out through the mouth. Not only does this filter the air better, it also encourages deeper and slower breathing, more rhythmic breathing. Beginning students were often told to "breathe" when they were out of breath, whereas proper breathing would alleviate this.

Often even experienced students held their breath unconsciously during kumite. This was one reason for the *kiai*—loud shout heard in karate techniques during delivery. It forces you to breathe out for maximum power. I found that immediately concentrating on good breathing could also help lessen sudden anxiety brought on by OCD—when I could remember to do it.

Various types of breathing were also taught, including soft breathing and, most notably, hard breathing where the entire body tenses up and the breath is expelled forcefully with a loud sound. This sort of breathing greatly strengthens the diaphragm and develops much better control over it as well. If you were sparring and got the wind knocked out of you, hard breathing would help you get your breath back much more quickly.

Perhaps most curious of all, I developed so much control over my diaphragm, I became immune to hiccups. Before I started karate, I would get hiccups occasionally. I'm not quite sure at what point I developed this control. But I've not had the hiccups once since then. Sometimes I can feel them coming, and I can easily stop them. This is analogous to OCD attacks and how I now deal with them.

I mentioned that meditation at the end of class was different. We often went into our closing meditation immediately after lining up from our last fight. Unlike meditation at the beginning of class, when I could feel the stress falling off, at the end of class the stress had been entirely eliminated. Ninety minutes of strenuous, regimented workout had cleared my mind, and now it was a matter of controlling my breathing to keep it deep and strong, to aid in oxygen recovery. There also was the pleasant sensation of sweat cooling my body. I could almost float off into, not a lack of consciousness, but a lack of thought itself, including intrusive thought. I was truly at peace during these times.

After three years of training, I was nearly a brown belt. But I was finished at Western and moved back to Seattle for my first real attempt at student teaching in English. During this very busy time, between working and going to school and finally completing my teaching degree—in math—it was another three years before I seriously considered getting back into karate.

I missed the discipline, the challenge, and the hard workouts. I had looked at a few karate schools near North Seattle, but they were all tournament-based schools, not formal, not artistic, but very much businesses. These schools required students to sign six-month to yearly contracts. You were required to pay whether you quit after a month. Many such schools also had more than the traditional ten Japanese ranks—the more ranks, the more promotion fees could be collected.

In fall of 1985, I finally found one right in my backyard: the Samurai Karate Academy. A small, austere dojo compared to BASD, it was actually the first school I actually visited and was indeed a traditional Japanese karate school. The *sensei*, Mr. Ian P. Harris, was very forthcoming and allowed me to work out with a class. After the class, I thanked Sensei Harris and asked him if I could join.

He thanked me but said he didn't take students from other schools. He was impressed that I had studied goju-ryu, but his style, *kyokushinkai*, had enough differences that he felt there were too many habits to be unlearned. I was welcome to drop in every month or so and visit, however.

So I looked for another school. But it seemed that Sensei Harris' was the only traditional school within seventy-five miles—the distance back to Bellingham, where BASD was located. So I took Sensei Harris up on his offer and went back and back and back.

One day, after several months of this, he finally told me he would accept me on a trial basis. My persistence had impressed him, but I knew it had to be this or nothing.

There were differences between the two schools—the formalities were virtually identical, but the Samurai Academy was a far harsher place. The practice and especially the free-fighting were much tougher. Techniques such as knee kicks and throwing were allowed. The *sensei's* son, Mark, an elite-class fighter (he also had elite-class control), would attack with blindingly fast kicks, move in with punches, grab you, and knee you a few times, and then throw you onto the floor, finishing off with a pulled strike to the head to make sure you stayed down if it had been a real conflict. Everybody aspired to and trained to fight this way.

At BASD, you were given a stern lecture if you made contact to the face; at Samurai, controlled (*not* pulled) kicks to the head were allowed. The person who *got* kicked was the one yelled at, for not covering properly. Contact to the head with a punch was frowned on, but if it happened, both parties were believed to be at fault— the puncher *and* the punchee, who again had not covered his face. At BASD, you really didn't worry about covering your face; you protected your upper body. At Samurai, you covered your head first and learned to take more lower-body punishment as a result.

A truly commercial dojo run in this fashion would have had trouble keeping the scores of students necessary for the financial solvency of the owner. Sensei Harris, however, worked as an airline mechanic and ran the dojo almost as a non-profit. He wasn't in it for the money. In fact, he expelled students if they did not train seriously or made a serious breach of etiquette.

Everything happened much faster in this new style, so it was even easier to clear my mind during the workouts. Over the years, I became much more athletic, clear minded, and focused. My physical reactions were greatly enhanced during this time—not just in karate, but in all other sports and in everyday reactions, such as catching an item knocked off a shelf before it got close to the ground.

Although different in their approaches to teaching karate, Sensei Harris and Sensei Stevens had the same goal in mind: spiritual and mental development. They were both charismatic, inspiring men whose occasional philosophic lectures during class demonstrated the logic, self-discipline, and art they were trying to teach. Like all great teachers, they inspired their students, even those they had for only a short time.

I studied under Mr. Stevens only for three years, but he taught me what karate as an art—a martial art, yes, but first and foremost an art, an expression of oneself—is about. Sensei Harris took my initial training and expanded and refined it, adding tremendous power to it over more than twenty-five years.

* * * * *

I would encourage anyone with OCD to take up a sport, especially one that requires focus and concentration. Yes, all sports do, but some provide more push and guidance, whereas others are more self-directed. I've always had a liking for sports that require speed—forcing the body and mind to clear, to react, and to be empty and ready. My daughter, a ski racer, says that when she races, she hears almost nothing—no cheering, no sounds of the snow, and only barely the cowbells at the bottom, which are deafening to spectators. After she races, she remembers *not* thinking but just skiing and reacting at a pace too fast for conscious thought, just conscious *awareness*.

And yes, human beings were made to think, but in many cases, thinking is just a means to an end. You have to think to learn a sport, but eventually you have to *stop* thinking to do it well.

Even math is this way. It's very easy to think too much when you are doing a math problem, trying to phrase an answer or even the problem itself in your head. I found math started to flow much better when I stopped thinking so hard—when I relaxed and let the picture form itself in my mind, seemingly all by itself. Of course, this took a lot of training in hard thinking to learn to do—like learning the basics in karate. But the best math solutions are elegant, even artistic—a mathematician expressing himself.

Perhaps this is best expressed by one of Sensei Harris' favorite expressions:

> We want maximum efficiency with minimum effort, not minimum efficiency with maximum effort.

Once you've controlled or beaten OCD, the former becomes the rule. I had lived so much of my life by the latter.

CHAPTER 10

The Path to Teaching

W hy did I become a math teacher? English was my declared major at Western Washington University, with a minor in journalism. I dreamed of teaching about books I loved and advising the best newspaper ever.

But I was always good at both—math *and* English. I especially enjoyed writing poems and stories. I loved American and English literature, science fiction, and good fantasy. Some of my favorite authors were Tolkien, Steinbeck, and Twain. Naturally, my love of writing led me into student journalism. I enjoyed photography as well, and developing my own photographs. I especially liked writing feature articles and the occasional editorial.

Math had been incredibly easy for me until ninth grade, when my friend became sick. My OCD had started to come on strong then, and my ability to concentrate and get through math problems began to suffer. Explanations were easy to follow, but I had a hard time breezing through the homework like before. Images that seemed to be encouraged by this manner of concentration interfered with my ability to do math.

My last year of math in high school was algebra with trigonometry; I was only a sophomore. Although I have taught trigonometry—post OCD—and now find it very easy to do (it's teaching it that's the hard part), I could not concentrate long enough in class to get a grasp on this next level of difficulty. The only thing that saved me was that I was a good test taker, but only enough to manage Cs. I literally thought I'd hit the wall on math, although my ninety-ninth-percentile aptitude test scores said otherwise.

Instead of concentrating on my textbook, I spent a lot of time studying the parking lot where the ski school buses picked us up in the winter. I suddenly had a learning disability.

Reading and writing were easier. To me, reading and writing are less abstract, so they naturally flowed. But sometimes bad thoughts could significantly interrupt my reading. Once I really had my head in a book, the flow kept the thoughts at bay. One of my favorites is *Watership Down,* a 450-page novel about rabbits—some of them very fierce and bad. For eighteen hours straight on summer, it completely obliterated my OCD. I read the entire book; I'd never before completely given up a sunny summer day to read. It felt so good to have my mind free from its prison, so absorbing was the escape.

Writing went much the same way. I took a creative writing class in high school and discovered I liked writing stories about things— like a reporter. So my teacher encouraged me to enroll in the journalism class, taught by an extremely talented woman, a master of old-school newswriting. Why are journalists so energetic? This dark-haired wisp of a woman flew about the room in her seventies polyester pantsuit. The textbook alone wasn't good enough, so she hammered in twice as much training with her own, better-written materials. Like most journalism classes, we published a Cub edition – a newspaper written just by us – at the end of the class. I was hooked.

When I entered college, I tried my hand at math again, as I was thinking about pre-med. I took a pre-calculus class, which went well enough, then tried calculus and college chemistry the following quarter. Once again, I had a terrible time concentrating on these abstract subjects, and by the end of the year I could barely manage a passing grade in chemistry. I had begun to have more trouble sleeping—it was never quiet in my dorm—and often I would put my head down and fall sleep in the back of the chemistry lecture hall. This large hall, with room for three hundred students, sloped quietly and darkly up to a dimly lit back row. It was better for sleeping than my dorm. And sleep was always an escape from OCD. I would copy the notes from a friend and read through the book, but it was no way to guarantee a good grade.

So, I went back to what was easier for me. I chose English as my major, with a journalism minor, my eye set on becoming a teacher.

I soon found that I enjoyed journalism much more than English. Much of the focus for English majors was on reading and analyzing classic English literature—books like *Watership Down* did not fit the bill. English literature had to be analyzed very intricately for meaning. I never could get over the fact that no one ever really *knew* what an author was thinking. It wasn't like math, where an abstract analysis leads to a concrete solution. It was murky, speculative—never a sure thing. I began to consider literary critics as a form of parasite, dependent on their hosts, the real writers.

The small, intimate classrooms in the hall where English majors studied often seemed like tiny prisons stuffed with too many inmates, all forced to do the same thing. I couldn't understand why so many of them *liked* it.

The journalism department, in contrast, was in an old mansion below campus. Spacious rooms for classes and news production were haphazardly strewn, sometimes spilling into each other. There were always several exits from any of them. One could never feel trapped inside. Upstairs, old bedrooms were the professors' offices. It all seemed so open and full of possibilities.

A fellow journalism student summed up the freedom of journalism for me one day by saying, "I don't want to write about *other* people's writing. I want to write my *own* writing." These words confirmed what I already knew: I wanted to write, and if I was going to teach, I wanted to teach writing.

Is there a place for writing about writing? Mark Twain did it. His critique of James Fenimore Cooper's *The Last of the Mohicans*, which he titled "Fenimore Cooper's Literary Offenses," is hilarious but accurate. To quote a bit:

> In the two-thirds of a page elsewhere referred to, wherein Cooper scored 114 literary transgressions out of a possible 115.

Twain demonstrated that even the smallest sentence can be both valuable and entertaining.

The entire piece, drawn from Twain's instructional "How to Tell a Story," shows by example and counter-example a style of critical analysis that runs absolutely counter to what my English professors espoused. But, of course, none of them was Mark Twain.

How many great writers have started out or lived their lives as reporters? What better way to learn the real art of writing than by doing your own writing? So I determined to slog my way as best I could through literature, make my way into the teaching world, and then become a journalism teacher while slipping in as much writing—*real writing*—as I could.

My first attempt at breaking into the teaching world was inauspicious. I was given my student teaching assignment at Sehome High School, very close to Western's campus, along a road where I frequently ran. I had an appointment one afternoon to meet with a teacher there, and I decided to kill two birds with one stone. I would run the three miles to the school, have my meeting, and run back to my apartment.

I ended up killing three birds, not two.

I arrived at Sehome right on time when the day came. I went to the English teacher's room, and we talked. He seemed a bit aloof to me, but I was sure it would get easier once we got to know each other. I was eager and looking forward to the assignment.

The next day I got a call from my adviser, asking me to meet with her. She told me the English teacher had been gravely insulted by my showing up in running clothes and without further deliberation had called Western and told them I was unsuitable—no pun intended. That was my introduction to some of the egos in the world of teaching.

Everybody has family friends. One of ours was a man who had spent years as a PE teacher, gone into administration, and then found he missed teaching more than he enjoyed managing. So, he went back to the classroom.

I called him and told him my sorry fate. "It isn't fair," I lamented.

"Dave," he said, "*life* isn't fair." For the first time in my life, this statement really meant something. We discussed the future and other possibilities. When someone is depressed—and I was depressed over this—nothing helps better than to have someone to talk to who is knowledgeable and who truly cares. John had had his own struggles over the years, and each time he had overcome them. With his help, I could as well.

I had been scheduled to student teach at the start of winter quarter 1982 and to finish by spring quarter. I had twelve credits of literature to take that summer, to complete my English degree. I was set to apply for jobs the following fall. Now I had to I hastily register for three literature classes instead. My student teaching would have to wait until spring quarter and would not finish until after fall—far too late to apply for a teaching job for the year. My neatly planned finish to my college career had completely unraveled.

To complete the unraveling, my girlfriend of the past year had left town to become an intern in Olympia, as part of her political science degree. We knew that, at least for the present, our relationship was on hold.

It was a dark day in January when I trudged to my first of three literature classes for the day. It was rainy and cold—in other words, typical Bellingham winter weather. To make it worse, I was now living in a dim apartment in the woods instead of on the sunny south side of Sehome Hill, where I had shared houses for many a quarter with fun-loving, if not always scrupulous, roommates.

I had chosen this apartment because it was close to Sehome High School. It would have been a perfect location for my student teaching, but now it just served to remind me of the harsh unfairness of life. To top it off, my new roommate was an incredibly pessimistic and cynical fellow journalism student. I had found him through the notice board in the *Western Front*'s newsroom.

We quickly grew to dislike one another, once we discovered how incompatible we were. He was a morning person; I was a night person. He was hypersensitive; I was hyposensitive. He complained that the light in my room kept him awake at night, even though both our doors were closed. He complained if I left a glass in the kitchen sink; he complained if I left a light on when I went to class in the morning. I began to wonder if he'd ever had a roommate before.

We stopped talking to each other. I soon found snotty notes slipped under my door when I woke up in the morning, and he would invariably be gone by the time I was up. "You left the bathroom window unlocked," one note said. "Haven't you heard the Spider-Man burglar is in the neighborhood?"

Another protested my leaving my toothbrush out on the counter. Eventually the notes took on a grim, angry tone. They began to include profanity. Somehow this triggered the only outlet for enjoyment I seemed to have left—writing notes back with even greater profanity. He conjugated the F word five times in one note. I sent one back with twelve.

I was pissed off, depressed, and ready for a fight. It seemed all I had left to defend was this small bit of dignity. We finally became shadows to each other, ignoring what we could, dismissing what we could not.

All my best friends had graduated or left town. The only thing I had to look forward to was a call from my distant girlfriend, who was going to phone me with her new number. But she didn't call.

Well, she didn't call for a week, that is. I still consider it the longest week of my life.

In times past, I would have enjoyed the moral support of roommates who would have told me to move on or at least would have to get drunk with me. But I felt truly abandoned. I spent several days trying to track her down; nobody knew her number in Olympia— or nobody was telling me. But she knew mine.

I felt very depressed. My OCD had spiraled to include my "missing" girlfriend. Like many OCD sufferers, I became convinced that my bad thoughts somehow affected the well-being of others. I knew every bad thought and every counting ritual affected her as well. My OCD sent out emanations that affected her feelings for me in a negative way, even though she was 150 miles distant. My rituals grew lengthier to neutralize fears not only about my health, but also about my relationship with her.

How many nights did I spend doing continuous rituals before bed—putting my toothbrush under the faucet over and over, taking my feet off the floor, putting socks on and taking them off, writing and erasing words and sentences, all the while feeling that something horrible was going to happen to me soon—to my health or to my relationship?

And I was alone. Sometime during that quarter, I think my roommate moved into a friend's wardrobe. I'm not sure I ever saw him again.

Now, looking back, that period in my life seems almost comical to me, and certainly pathetic. My girlfriend, sensing my depression at the upcoming quarter and finding herself in a vibrant environment with exciting people, was loath to leave it to rescue me. She needed to be rescued *from* me.

My last date with her, around Christmas, resonated with OCD. We had gone to a bar in North Seattle for a little drinking and dancing. Worried about never seeing her again—and about dying young without her—I began to obsess. I knew these thoughts weren't reasonable, but they were powerful. The more I tried to stop them, the stronger they became. So terrible was this internal battle, I could not break free. Of course, she had no idea what was going on—that a war was being fought inside me. To her, it simply seemed like I was throwing the most enormous pouting fit she had ever seen. In her mind, I was acting like a child. She couldn't understand why I was giving her the silent treatment, and so she became upset and we went home.

I was lucky she only waited a week to call. A week after that, she broke up with me completely.

Back to the trudging. The first of many days of living hell—if, for nothing else, the prospect of three literature classes in a row for three months. My first class of the day was with a professor I liked. He was an older, kindly, white-haired Southern gentleman with a gorgeous accent. (I often wondered how he'd ended up in

Bellingham.) I'd had him for a previous literature class, which he had made tolerable. But not even this talented professor could make a class on American playwrights sing for me.

Don't get me wrong. When it comes to song and dance, no one beats the Americans. To me, Rogers and Hammerstein alone outshine all else foreign. But American plays—*Death of a Salesman, The Emperor Jones, The Crucible,* to name a few—are the absolute darkest and most depressing pieces ever written. And these were what started off my day for the entire quarter.

We started *The Emperor Jones* the first day. The play, written by Eugene O'Neill, concerns mysticism. A corrupt African warlord has been deposed by British colonialists, and military officials are trying to hunt him down for his various crimes against humanity. They have little luck finding him in the dense jungle; he has many hideouts known only to him.

The primitive tribal natives assure the British that "We cotch 'im" and proceed to ceremonially invoke spells and spirits to hunt him down, accompanied by loud drumming and singing. The laws of physics state that no sound travels further than low-frequency sound; therefore, the former emperor feels and hears the distant drumbeats, even in his faraway hideout. Soon he starts to see apparitions. He is eventually apprehended when the spirits send him screaming back to the British for safety—better the British Army than the "hai'nts," as he calls them.

Here a fan of J. R. R. Tolkien, Frank Herbert, or even Robert E. Heinlein might conjecture that some actual spiritual power could have been involved. However, this sort of modern literature is apparently more oriented along Freudian lines—perhaps the id or some sort of underlying sexual theme.

I found this out the hard way, after writing a paper on the play. I had argued my case along the more magical bent, writing that Western society has lost or rejected the power to communicate with the ancient spiritual world and that in its native element, it is still a force to be reckoned with.

This earned me a surprising D+ grade and comments from the kindly Southern gentleman of, "How dare you!" Although I'd thought my argument was sound, according to him, it couldn't even be considered. Couldn't I see what this play was all about? Hallucinations brought on by repressed guilt, no doubt. I thought I might just as well have suggested that the emperor masturbated too much, or not enough, and it would have gone over better. So my aversion to the analysis of literature was furthered.

Fast-forward to September 1982, the date I had set to start a real teaching career. Instead, I was simply starting my first of two quarters of student teaching. I had a new student teaching assignment, a new girlfriend, a new dog. But I still had the one constant in my life: OCD. After my winter quarter literature ordeal, I was finished with my requisites for my internship. I had gone back to Seattle and found a job as a busboy, waiting for the fall, living with my parents. That May, I met Christina, a vivacious young woman waitressing her way through college. By the end of summer, I had moved in with her, and my parents had generously agreed to pay my tuition through my student teaching. Things were looking up.

My assignment was at Meadowdale High School in Edmonds, not far from the North Seattle area Christina and I lived in. Her mother and two friends had found a beautiful rental house overlooking Lake Washington, and Christina sublet the mother-in-law basement from them.

This time, I made sure I dressed well for my meeting with John Eastman, a man in his late forties who taught junior literature and journalism. John reminded me of a professor, in a coat and tie that loosened quickly as first period and his high energy progressed. Often the coat would spend the better part of its day draped over his chair. Balding, with dark, close-cropped hair, he was the epitome of an experienced teacher in the prime of his career.

John taught in three rooms, all with adjoining doors. His English classroom was classic fifties school architecture, set in a rambling, single-story building. The many windows, mounted in cold, aluminum frames, looked out onto faint green grass and spindly deciduous cherry trees. I remember the sky always seemed gray and cloudy. Was there ever a sunny day here? I honestly don't remember. The room had hard, asbestos floor tiles and white asbestos ceiling tiles; the walls were nondescript, faded white.

Occasional posters—pictures of literary settings or authors—were tacked to the walls. One-piece desks easily slid about the room.

My first quarter was part observation, part teaching, and part classes at a nearby converted elementary school, what was originally Brookside Elementary School, near where I had grown up and had many a Little League baseball practice. Western had leased this now rather run-down, chipped-blue painted facility for students in the Seattle area.

On Tuesdays and Thursdays, I left Meadowdale early to receive instruction in how to teach—educational theory classes at the old Brookside school location.

And I thought literature was tough. At least literature has a fixed context. In my mind, educational theory is too often the business of experimenting on children—and those who teach them. The fad at the time, which I and the others in my class were subjected to, was ITIP—Instructional Theory Into Practice.

It was team-taught by two young ladies who looked like they belonged in high school themselves. Now, the concept of ITIP seemed good: observing the planning and teaching styles of good teachers and implementing these concepts into one's own teaching. But to me it was too abstract. It lacked the *in the trenches* instruction I needed. What if students don't pay attention, or talk, or become disruptive? Good teachers have this down also, but I don't recall any of that being mentioned.

Who hasn't heard the saying "Those who can't do, teach?" I wondered about this. How does this all work? What couldn't my teachers in these classes do?"

Years later, an Australian fellow, long ago a teacher, told me the complete saying:

> Those who can't do, teach.
> Those who can't teach, teach the teachers.
> Those who can't teach the teachers, administer.

And those with OCD... Ironically, I saw a lot of my own brightness manifested in my new girlfriend. Except for her hatred of math, Christina was a good example of a very high-functioning person unencumbered by mental dysfunction. Her brightness attracted me.

She knew I was bright like her, and she was attracted to this. She also liked the way I looked. The feelings were mutual. She was seventeen and in her second year of community college, getting ready to enter the University of Washington as a junior in Criminal Science. She had already taken a few classes in criminal science and law enforcement. She was a talented waitress as well, very outgoing and charming. She always made more in tips than the other waitresses.

Christina worked hard, no question about it. She also played hard. And she was very observant. It didn't take her long to notice a peculiar habit I'd started to develop. I would hold my breath and let it out, little by little, staccato-like. It made a soft, rhythmical sound. It was faint but could be noticed by somebody nearby.

She asked me about it once, and I told her I was keeping time to music in my head, which was sometimes true. Inevitably I'd start counting the beats, get stuck in the "shoelace cycle," and be unable to stop. I hadn't realized she'd noticed. After that, I was careful to do it softly enough so she wouldn't hear.

Christina had also noticed my ability to go into outer space at will and my need for more sleep than she required. Of course, it was because I often lay awake at night unable to sleep, but I wouldn't confess this to her any more than I would confess my hidden rituals.

Student teaching required rising early, and I often had to scramble in the morning to get to Meadowdale, sometimes barely on time—forty-five minutes before school was due to start. An hour or more early would have been better looked upon, but I considered it a major victory to make it when I did.

It was easier to hide my OCD at Meadowdale, because I knew what was expected. I had to show energy, enthusiasm, and a lack of eccentricity to obtain a good rating, which was crucial to an eventual teaching job. At least I *thought* I was exhibiting energy and enthusiasm. This came at the cost of a certain reserve, a fear that I was going to reveal myself inadvertently. I lacked much spontaneity due to this. John noticed my reserve and encouraged me to take more initiative by introducing myself to and helping students.

My first potential bit of trouble occurred the second week of school. John had been telling me to try to talk with the students more, so I made it a point to really mix in during study times. One of the students, a junior named Teresa, asked me to meet for a cup of coffee after school. I was completely naïve. My lack of innate social skills once again caused potential trouble. It never occurred to me that a high school student might be attracted to a teacher. I certainly felt no real attraction toward her. We had a nice talk, after which I went home and told Christina about my progress.

"So, how was your blowjob?" asked Christina, angrily.

"What are you talking about? We just had a conversation."

"I can tell you she had a lot more than that on her mind."

"She's a junior."

"Yes, that's exactly what she is. And what if she goes and tells her friends she gave you a blowjob?"

"Why would she do that?"

"The point isn't whether she does it. The point is she *could*. And then you'd never see the inside of a classroom again."

Christina was every bit as street-smart as I was street-dumb. Plus, she had studied molestation cases in her criminal justice classes. She was only a few months older than the girl I'd just had coffee with and a lot more mature than I was at the time, as she had just demonstrated. She certainly would have done a better job student teaching in my stead.

She was a morning and a night person. She could sustain late nights and early mornings indefinitely. We'd go to bed late, and I'd drag myself out of bed at 5:30 the next morning. It was hard not to stay up with her.

Gradually, through the quarter, I began to get more and more fatigued. Apparently, student teaching is supposed to be a bit like medical school. After working, planning, grading, and university classes and classwork, there is plenty of leftover time—as long as you don't need to sleep.

The time came for me to take over a class. I was expected to teach the same curriculum as John's other literature classes, but with my own lesson plans. Gradually, I would slide into the English classes and work into the journalism classes the second quarter. I was to teach *The Crucible*.

Before you can begin to analyze literature, you have to remember the important literary points. It's common when teaching literature to have students answer questions on the key points of the story and to learn the vocabulary used in it. As a teacher, it's very easy to go through a story and write questions, pick out vocabulary words, and hand them to the students to answer.

It seemed logical to me as a student teacher—a bright, college-educated young man—that all the students would already know the expectations, and, wanting to succeed, would answer the questions, just like I would have. I questioned John's style of discussing the questions out loud for much of the study period. I would have preferred silence. I didn't realize that John was doing more than involving the students in the material—he was involving them with *each other*.

John was good at encouraging discussions. He would often have students arrange themselves in a circle, give them some time to read, and have them share answers and thoughts. Lather, rinse, repeat. His style was effective. He made it look easy.

Although I had read *The Crucible* long before, I had to go through it again carefully to pick out the questions and themes. I wasn't good at analyzing them. And it seemed the more tired I got, the more difficult it became to deal with the constant images and fears that still tormented me. On more than one occasion, I had become briefly paralyzed during a study period when Jack was in charge. It interfered with my mixing in with the students; both John and the students noticed that I would occasionally fade out. The energy it took to shake myself from these internal struggles contributed to my constant fatigue.

I also found the material boring. In sort of a personal coup, John had integrated Frank Herbert's classic sci-fi novel, *Dune*, into his curriculum, but it would not be taught until later in the year. First I would have to show I could succeed with the present material. (Now, if you are a lover of literature and the study of literature, I apologize for the apparent insults I have thrown your way.

Literature and its study are important and should be taught by someone who possesses that love.)

The journalism kids and I got along great. My excellent training from Western allowed me to augment their work and focus myself, but John told me he would not let me take over that class until I showed him I could teach literature up to his standards.

He stood back and let me try my own style. Trying to emulate John, I would open a discussion by asking questions straight from the play and would ask for volunteers to raise their hands. The same students always answered; most others did not. I would use a tactic one of my professors had used, asking a student directly if I felt he wasn't participating to my satisfaction. But I never seemed to get John's results.

Looking back, I see now that John was an energetic man. I was not afraid to get up in front of a crowd, but I did not project his aura and enthusiasm. He had a knack for following up on a question or answer, where I would often move on to the next one. I was a novice, and in my tired state I did not project the necessary energy.

I had one successful discussion. It was a follow-up on a special assignment I had given them: "Write down your thoughts and suggestions on my teaching progress so far."

I found out how two—or really thirty—heads are better than one. When you are standing up in front of thirty people, between them all, they see everything. They'd noticed my thousand-yard stare. They'd noticed my at-times disjointed thinking. One girl, especially observant, noticed that I had a habit of continually touching my face, somewhat covering it. I thought it would be viewed as a mannerism conveying thoughtfulness, but I had not kept track of its increasing frequency or actual effect—that is, disconnecting myself from the kids.

Unfortunately, this happened near the end of my first student teaching assignment, and John thought I was simply not ready to teach. He had seen me have a hard time leading discussions; unbeknownst to him, there were times when a distasteful image would flash into my head, and I would momentarily freeze, lost in thought. I could not make my discussions flow.

This had also led to classroom management issues. When students don't feel the flow, they naturally socialize with each other, creating noise and distraction. I was reluctant to correct kids quickly, hoping the problem would resolve itself if I brought the discussion back on track. Too often I would let things build to a point of no return, when it would be a major interruption to stop what had become a loud discussion of its own. When we discussed my teaching, the kids were very emphatic to me on this point. Don't wait, and follow through.

I decided one day to let the kids suggest an activity to get them excited, to warm up for the discussion. One of the boys, Larry, asked matter-of-factly: "Can we have an all out paper fight?"

Why not? I thought. "As long as you pick it up afterwards."

In less that two minutes, all of the students had torn several pieces of paper out of their notebooks and had them tightly crumpled up on their desks.

"Go!" yelled Larry. In an instant, scores of paper projectiles were hurling and bouncing around the room. It was like a blinding hailstorm.

Right then, John walked in. We had a very unhappy talk at lunch.

John probably did me the biggest favor of my life. He told me to come back when I was ready, which certainly I was not. And he told me something that has stuck with me my entire life: "As a new teacher, you come into the class with a certain amount of respect. You either build on it, or you lose it."

He didn't think I'd built, that's for sure. But he also went to bat for me, because he could see my desire to teach and my love for working with young people. I confessed to him that literature was not a great love of mine. "What interests you besides journalism?" he asked. I told him I had always wanted to teach math, to make it easier and more enjoyable for students. John thought this was a good idea, especially since math jobs were easier to come by.

He convinced Western that I deserved another chance and made sure they agreed I would have another opportunity once I finished my math degree.

At the end, he told me, "I hope you make one hell of a math teacher."

CHAPTER 11

A More Successful Battle

I decided to pursue my math degree at the University of Washington. I had no further taste for Bellingham. I managed to register for winter quarter 1983, immediately after my one quarter of student teaching.

I remember walking into the UW admissions office. Everywhere I looked, the signs said, "Wait." Wait weeks for admission or maybe even months. There were wooden bars everywhere, like teller stalls in a bank, warding off would-be freshmen. "Oh, you're a transfer student from Western," the admissions lady observed. "Use that door."

Inside, friendly and sympathetic people awaited. I was admitted the next day.

I would graduate from the UW with a math degree. There was still some hell to go through, but this time I would step out of it merely into purgatory.

My first year at the UW was a frenzy of college physics and first-year calculus. Fighting my OCD all the way, I still had trouble concentrating. But I had the advantage of more maturity and fewer distractions. I was able to maintain a B minus average and focused better during lectures.

I began to realize that if I spent long enough on a problem, I could probably work it out. If not, collaborating with other students often provided final explanations and the solution. But I truly struggled my first year as a math major. A wall of images and anxiety always compromised my full concentration. I could follow explanations, but the intricate little twists that led to clever solutions, the thought patterns of someone who simply got math, stayed mostly out of reach.

I attended classes for the next two years, taking a partial load, as well as working part time as a landscaper and a tutor. I also had some assistance from my parents. They could see I wanted desperately to succeed, and their continued support showed their approval of my desire.

I graduated in June of 1985 with a Bachelor of Arts in mathematics, including a year of physics with calculus. I did not attend my graduation. I was busy finishing a landscaping job. I was a long way from my initial plan of becoming a teacher by fall of 1982.

I had originally student-taught English. Therefore, I had taken English pedagogy classes at Western. It made sense to take math pedagogy while I was studying at the UW. My adviser at Western had, in fact, suggested this. The only problem was limited space; UW students took priority as far as getting access to math teaching classes. One education professor told me flat out he didn't take students from other programs. "Torment him," my brother advised me. "He talked to you once, didn't he? Keep calling him."

I have found out over the years that persistence *does* pay off. Teachers and instructors are impressed by prospective students who don't give up. And, in this case, obsessive-compulsiveness was my friend. I could not get the thought of failing at teaching out of my head. I *did* torment the fellow—in a polite sort of way—and eventually he agreed to let me enroll in his class if I finished the prerequisite math classes by the time it was to start.

The Prerequisite Class

Nearly two years of calculus was required, among other types of math, for a math degree from the UW. First-year calculus was mostly two-dimensional calculus, with some volume thrown in; second-year calculus concentrated intensely on all three or more dimensions, such as a path through space including the component of time. Much of it was centered on the study of vectors, mathematical descriptions combining both speed and direction. One might call it beginning rocket science.

My math degree had required me to complete the first two quarters of second-year calculus, Math 325, and Math 326. To qualify for the UW teaching program, I needed to take the third quarter, Math 327, as well as an extra linear algebra class.

I had once again timed things to the last minute; this calculus class would allow me to enroll in the math education courses the very next quarter. If I missed this deadline, I would have to wait another full year to enroll—if ever. I was fully confident I could grind another quarter out. I never seemed to see obstacles coming.

The class began with twenty-seven students—all but seven would drop it. The most nerve-wracking portion of my life was about to begin.

The class was on the ground floor of Smith Hall, just off the UW's Red Square. Although Western and the UW both had "Red Squares" in the middle of campus, Western's was a postage stamp compared to the University of Washington's. The two obelisks in the UW's Red Square had more bricks in them than Western's entire square. The classroom had inner and outer entrance doors; the latter looked out on one of the many cherry-tree-lined walkways that snaked everywhere on campus.

Back then, solving calculus problems with vectors usually meant a lot of brute-force equation writing on tons of paper. But my professor completely disregarded the book's and the curriculum's methods that used vectors. He was a genius with differential equations. He could take long, time-consuming vector problems and reduce them to a handful of differential equations quickly and effortlessly. It was like watching a magic show; he amazed his students by producing solutions that matched the answers in the back of the book, solutions that vector calculus would take hours to solve, and not always properly.

The difficulty was with the professor—having recently emigrated from Poland—possessed the Slavic/Russian discipline and talent for math but lacked the ability to speak understandable English. He could understand English fairly well, but his inability to communicate well reduced the class to basically learning vector calculus by pantomime. And he refused to use vectors at all, ever. "Differentials are better. You can see this, yes?"

Apparently, but *explain* how you're doing this, sir!

By the middle of the quarter, I was barely making a 2.0 grade, so I was in danger of slipping below the minimum mark necessary to get into the next quarter's introductory math education class. It was almost time to give up and walk away. But I stayed. I had to. And then the point came when it was too late for me to drop the class. I could only pass it or fail it. Seven of twenty-seven were left. Why were the others still in? I was too busy worrying about myself to ask.

I had never failed a college class in my life. But I began to fear I would fail this one. More than that, I began to obsess I would fail it. I had thought there was no more room in my mind to obsess about *any more* bad things, but I was wrong. I now discovered I was able to *multi-task* obsess. I lost more and more sleep, as my bedtime counting rituals now began to include how the wrong thoughts or number of repetitions would affect my math scores. While attempting to do math problems, I worried about the problems themselves. My rituals took my standard worries to an extreme level as I tried to make sense of my notes, comparing differential equations (which I had not yet had a class in) to the vector explanations in the book.

Coming up on the final exam, I had several nights with little sleep and then several more with none at all. I began to shut down physically and mentally. I couldn't think; I could barely move. I thought I had hit bottom at Western. I was wrong. At least I could still function. *This* was rock bottom.

I did something I had vowed never to do. I called my parents and asked them for help. Not financial help. Psychological help.

"Do you need someone to come get you?" Mom asked.

"No, I can make it. I just have to pack a few things."

It had been agreed that they would put me up for a few days while I saw Dr. Dale, our family doctor. I hadn't told them the OCD details, but had related my situation with school and the tremendous stress I was under. I felt like I was under a full-strength adrenaline charge.

Now I had somewhere to run to. I was actually surprised at the support my parents provided. I finally opened up a bit to tell them I was worried about failing—and they both supported my desire to succeed, realizing finally something had been in my way all of these years. It's amazing what opening up about problems—even what you think are crazy problems—will garner you in the way of support. My father, not discounting my issues this time, nevertheless realized he was out of his league. He insisted I see Dr. Dale *immediately*.

In a few hours, I was back in my parents' basement; conveniently, the house had a furnished downstairs. Nearly a decade later, my wife, Judy, and I would live there for a year while we built a house of our own. What is it that makes the old family home so reassuring and comfortable? When a college roommate had troubles of his own during my second year at Western, his father sent him a letter, saying, "Your family will always be there when everyone else is gone." I'd had my share of struggles and disagreements with my own family, but they were definitely there for me.

Dr. Dale was a genius—a family doctor by profession, but so much more than that. He was one of those gifted people who needed little or no sleep, so he lived two lives—doctor by day, sculptor, mechanic, architect, and many other things by the night. He was in his fifties then, kind and infinitely patient. He projected a gentle energy that was itself therapeutic. And back in the 1980s, doctors could still take time with their patients.

In the examining room, he pulled up a chair and asked me to describe the nature of my stress. I told him about my problems in math, and then I confessed—for the first time ever to anyone—the horrible images of dead and sick people that would not leave my mind and my own morbid worries of getting sick and dying. I told him about all the years I had kept this bottled up. The only thing I did not share with him was my ritualizations. But I told him more than I had thought I could.

He looked me in the eye and did not say what I feared he would—that I was crazy. He said, "Well, it's simply not true."

I described specific thoughts I'd had to him. And he said again, "Well, it's simply not true."

We did this again and again, a number of times. We agreed that my fears were irrational and untrue. "But how do I get the obsessions to go away?" I asked.

Although talking helped greatly—Dr. Dale would counsel me further and check my progress almost daily for a week—he also decided to prescribe a fairly new antianxiety drug called Xanax. Even though very little was known about OCD in 1986—in fact, the International OCD Foundation was not even founded until 1986—Dr. Dale knew me and he knew my family. Our families went to church together. We had dinners together (during which time I'd admire all the fabulous artwork he had crafted at his home). We even vacationed together occasionally. And Dr. Dale knew I wasn't psychotic—I was anxious, and he knew how to treat anxiety. He knew me and my family better than any shrink could ever have hoped to—and with no preconceived psychoanalytical presumptions. If I'd needed a psychiatrist, he would have referred me to one.

In fact, I have never seen a psychiatrist about my OCD—unless you'd like to count Dr. Dale or my own brother, a family practitioner who would eventually find support from me when he himself was hit by powerful obsessions a few years later during medical school. And, in return, Steve would provide me with the tools to defeat my OCD another twelve years down the line—mainly by handing me a copy of *Brain Lock* by Dr. Jeffrey Schwartz.

OCD was essentially quite unknown at this time. But I was not alone at all!

The National Institute of Mental Health estimates that more than 2 percent of the U.S. population, or nearly one out of every 40 people, will be diagnosed with OCD at some point in their lives. The disorder is two to three times more common than schizophrenia and bipolar disorder.

OCD is often described as "a disease of doubt." Individuals living with OCD experience "pathological doubt" because they are unable to distinguish between what is possible, what is probable and what is unlikely to happen.

Who gets OCD?

People from all walks of life can get OCD. It strikes people of all social and ethnic groups and both males and females. Symptoms typically begin during childhood, the teenage years or young adulthood. The sudden appearance of OCD symptoms later in life merits a thorough medical evaluation to ensure that another illness is not the cause of these symptoms.

What causes OCD?

People with OCD can often say "why" they have obsessive thoughts or "why" they behave compulsively, but the thoughts and the behavior continue. A large body of scientific evidence suggests that OCD results from a chemical imbalance in the brain. For years, mental health professionals incorrectly assumed OCD resulted from bad parenting or personality defects. This theory has been disproven over the last few decades. People whose brains are injured sometimes develop OCD, which suggests it is a medical condition. If a placebo pill is given to people who are depressed or who experience panic attacks, nearly 40 percent will say they feel better. If a placebo is given to people who experience obsessive-compulsive disorder, only about two percent say they feel better. This also suggests that OCD is a biological condition as opposed to a "personality problem."

Genetics are thought to be very important in OCD. If you, or your parent or sibling, have OCD, there's close to a 25 percent chance that another of your immediate family members will have it. *(More of this website excerpt to follow shortly.)*

I waited until I arrive home to take the Xanax. Dr. Dale had advised me not to drive until I had built up a tolerance. I had never tried a psychoactive drug before, only alcohol, which helped my OCD very little. I had no idea what was going to happen.

I remember taking one of the little white pills and joining my parents in our family room, where they were watching a television program. I remember lying on the couch, head up on some pillows. And suddenly I started laughing, quietly, but belly laughing—real laughter, from the gut. The anxiety, worry, and adrenaline I had lived with for ages were suddenly gone. I felt an incredible, relaxing, happy sense of well-being I had forgotten had existed. Or perhaps it had never existed for me.

I remember going downstairs, and for the first time that I could recall, falling into a deep, real sleep.

What I liked about sleep was that it obliterated my OCD. It almost never entered my dreams. Sleep kept me sane. And the best *and worst* part of sleep was waking up. Every day I woke up OCD–free. For a few moments, I would be happy, relaxed, and wide awake. Super-conscious, even. Then a worry would hit me like a ton of bricks. Internal springs would wind up to tremendous tensions in milliseconds, and my mind would be off and running again, never escaping the images and thoughts until I fell back to sleep.

Between Dr. Dale's counseling and the Xanax, even if I was not completely able to dodge the irrationality of my faulty instincts, I could at least stop much of the repetitions and let the bad thoughts slide off my new armor of non-anxiety. However, the effects of Xanax are short-lived, four to six hours per dose. And when it started to wear off I *knew*. My anxiety still allowed my OCD to take control. I became dependent on taking Xanax every few hours. There were no withdrawal effects—just the absence of the anti-anxiety effect. I would often wake up halfway through the night and have to take another dose to finish my sleep. I was dependent on the drug, no doubt.

But it seemed a small price to pay.

The biggest advantage of reduced anxiety was my ability to string complex analytical thoughts together long enough to let them form connections. The Jacobian vectors started to look more doable, although the book itself was still not terribly helpful. Calculus books typically *assume* so much, but at least I had a *chance* of getting problems partially correct now.

I understood enough to plow through the final exam and receive a B minus in the class. I honestly don't know if I actually passed or not. To this day, I suspect the professor knew the seven of us had to stay and rewarded us in the only fashion he knew how.

Will OCD symptoms go away completely with medication and behavior therapy?

Response to treatment varies from person to person. Several studies suggest that medication and behavior therapy are equally effective in alleviating symptoms of OCD. Furthermore, the combination of medications and therapy has been found in many cases to be superior to either treatment on its own.

A small percentage of people with OCD find that neither medication nor behavioral treatment produces any significant change. Most people who receive effective treatments find their symptoms reduced by about 40 percent to 50 percent. That can often be enough to change their lives, to transform them into individuals who can go back to school, work and their families. Another percentage of people are fortunate to have a complete remission of their symptoms when treated with effective medication and/or behavior therapy.

Reviewed by Ken Duckworth, M.D. and Jacob L. Freedman, M.D., April 2012

From The National Institute of Mental Health: "Obsessive-Compulsive Disorder" http://www.nami.org/Template. cfm?Section=OCD2&Template=/ContentManagement/ ContentDisplay.cfm&ContentID=138432

In my case, I would see that Dr. Dale had helped me achieve that 50 percent improvement.

College on Xanax

Winter quarter arrived. I had moved back to my house in Northgate. I had come to notice the daylight in every day versus the darkness in everything I was used to observing. I started to enjoy the world outside my mind's eye again. I was more awake than I'd been in years. And although I can and will go into detail about my everyday life later, the measure of the greatest impact had to be the class I took in differential equations—Math 238.

This class was a degree of difficulty above any math class I had yet taken. My professor was the same gentleman from whom I'd struggled to obtain a 2.8 in Math 127, second-quarter beginning calculus. A tall, intense fellow in his late thirties, with dark curling hair and a commanding yet friendly voice, he had the attitude that "being clever" was great, but one did not have to be clever at mathematics to succeed, if one was willing to work hard.

I'm always nervous the first day of a new math class. Some professors hit the ground running, filling chalkboard after chalkboard with equations and theorems faster than I could write them down. No time for questions or example problems. Others encouraged students to work together in small groups or with a partner to figure out examples in class. I knew this fellow was a straight-down-the middle lecturer; he would answer questions from the previous day's assignment, and then proceed to give instructions and notes, and assign the next day's homework to finish the class.

The classroom was in Gowen Hall, again near Red Square, medium-sized with a twenty-five-foot ceiling. Windows let light filter in from far above. It felt very academic. I sat down in my chair, comp book ready, completely relaxed. Yes, relaxed! I was not ritualizing internally or externally, I was completely focused, and I was able to remain so during the lecture. How much more sense my professor made this time! Why couldn't he have explained calculus so well the first time around? I took notes easily, following every detail, not constantly tuning in and out, able to concentrate and absorb everything during the entire hour. And when I started my assignment later that afternoon, it was like being back in third grade when math was so *easy*.

I realized very quickly that my inability to think and make analytical connections had gone the way of my anxiety. I did have talent at math after all. Day after day I went to class, understood the lessons, and flew through my assignments. Tests came and went, and I scored in the high nineties. The professor always posted test scores on his door to show the grading curve and handed back tests in class, a usual courtesy provided by instructors at the competitive UW. My scores had always been in the middle of the curve. Now, against these same students, I was at the top.

This class was known to be difficult to get an A in. A 3.6 was considered great. I pulled a perfect 4.0, and, at the end of the quarter, the professor thanked me for enrolling in his class and being a good student. The warm glow from this has never faded, and to this day I still have my notebook from Math 238 displayed on a shelf in my study.

In my spare time (of which I now had more), I went back and looked in my old, first-year calculus book, the one with which I had struggled so. Looking through it again, it all seemed so clear. When it came to math, I had attained even better than a 50 percent comeback.

Although I was better able to function, especially analytically, my OCD hadn't really been defeated. It was still there, it still bothered me, but the tremendous anxiety I had lived with was under control. It would be years before it reared its ugly head high again, forcing a final, major confrontation.

I had expected student teaching to be easier the second time around. But it really seemed like a whole lot more work. Was it because I was actually able to plan lessons and thoroughly study a complete unit beforehand to see the whole picture, instead of a fuzzy day at a time? Was it because my cooperating teacher actually let me teach the class this time. And was this because I actually seemed like a living, breathing, aware human being to him?

So many people had seen the potential in me. Most of all, and unmentioned so far, was Dr. Chuck Pearson, a professor of education at Western. He didn't know about my problems; at least I never told him. But he stuck up for me and saw me through my unsuccessful first attempt and my successful second attempt at student teaching. He was one of those people who must have seen something in me. He let me back in. Why?

When I look back on my life, I sometimes feel I had a mentor, someone who understood my real condition, who lobbied for me, who explained and fought for me, who kept the door open for me and allowed opportunities to occur that my past actions should have long shut me out of. Was there such a person? Is there still? Are there such things as guardian angels, or was God himself whispering into the ears of important and relevant people? Logically, only a real person would make any sense.

And if that person was real, was it just me? Could the same obsessiveness that crippled me for so many years be one and the same with the perseverance that simply would not let me quit? I kept coming back. I kept tormenting people with an intensity that only a person with OCD could generate. Can a person get where he wants to go by being so unrelenting that others simply feel sorry for him?

CHAPTER 12

Making a Living

After receiving my teaching degree, I applied for jobs for the fall of 1986. I called up nearby districts and asked their personnel departments how full their substitute pools were. It turned out that the schools in Everett were eager to have me apply, given that math substitutes were difficult to find. Everett was only a twenty-minute drive north from where I was living.

And so began my life as a substitute teacher. I would usually receive a call by 6:00 a.m. I wouldn't bother to set my alarm—the phone took care of that. The first year, I ended up substituting about 140 out of 180 school days. These were decent enough numbers to support myself, even though the pay wasn't spectacular—about seventy dollars per day, with no benefits. My house payment wasn't much, my other expenses were minimal, and I had taken on a roommate—Eugene Zamperion, a student at the John Bastyr Naturopathic College in Seattle.

Most of my calls came from Everett High School's math department. I was able to go into any math class and provide better help than most substitutes in a math classroom, who could usually only give the assignment, monitor students for progress, and hope for the best. I was even able to introduce new topics, as needed. In fact, I became valuable enough that, when Fred Pinney, an older math teacher, needed gall bladder surgery, I was hired to fill in for him on a long-term basis—the next-best thing to a real teaching job. He would be gone for six weeks.

Fred was a very interesting fellow indeed, very much an old-school type—he'd begun teaching back in the 1950s. Balding, with short-cropped gray hair, he wore a suit every day and, with it, a fierce demeanor. I was paid to assist him in his classroom for a few days before I took over, both to learn the routines and to demonstrate to him I was a satisfactory fill-in.

That year, Fred was teaching two sections of sophomore world history, two sections of algebra, and one section of calculus. We had all agreed that Dale Sanders, the math department head, would take over the calculus class in the interim, switching me to an algebra class he taught that same period.

I soon found out that Fred had no patience for underclassmen. He always spoke with a stern, often loud tone, and in his algebra classes he strictly insisted that students do the work his way. A student who did not comply would receive an F on whatever assignment or test was given. Since this wasn't my style of teaching, even before Fred took his leave, the students appeared to like me more than him. But I remembered John Eastman's advice to me: I was in there to build on my respect, not make friends.

I remember one day Fred was teaching an algorithm for factoring—and he insisted all students do it exactly the same way, showing the exact same work. There *is* an argument for highly structured teaching. In Fred's mind, it built discipline, attention span, and attention to detail. But he was merciless with students' complaints. On one occasion, a young lady complained she didn't understand an explanation he had given. Fred replied, "If you don't get it, then you're stupid."

Fred was really telling her she wasn't stupid, she just needed to try harder. But he liked to challenge his students emotionally as well as mentally—again, he was an old-school man. He believed in teaching mental toughness as well as problem-solving skills.

In retrospect, many of his students thanked him. I was quite surprised when several of his calculus students, mostly seniors, came to his room for lunch that first day. They hadn't come in for help; they had come in to enjoy his company. I think Fred must have attended or taught at a military school. His demeanor with the accomplished upperclassmen—many of whom had despised him in their earlier classes—created an atmosphere of good humor and appreciation. They knew how to play the game now and would laugh at the underclassmen when they complained about "Mean Mr. Pinney."

Another favorite phrase of Fred's was "If you don't like it in here, there's the door," often used when a student expressed his displeasure or objections to Fred's teaching methods. It was a phrase that worked for him, because the students knew he meant it.

I realized quickly that I could never be Fred Pinney. Although I admired him in many ways, and he got results, I could not belittle my students. Heck, I *looked* like a student—albeit a senior student. But I had come into the classroom with respect attached, and I was determined to build on it in my own way.

The first day I took over, there was a palpable lack of tension in the classroom. I realized the students had largely lived in fear of Fred, and I was going to have to establish my own controls, routines, and procedures. One commonality was that Everett High School's math department all used the same tests, versus the older method of having individual teachers write their own. Although I was good at writing my own tests, I was glad for a level playing field. It made my planning much more directed and coherent.

The history classes were easy. Fred believed in teaching from the textbook, so he had given me the chapters to cover and had provided some tests and quizzes. All I had to do was briefly cover the day's assignment, assign the reading and questions, and help the kids during what was mostly a study period. I would read ahead the night before and be ready the next morning, the information fresh in my mind. Occasionally I would supplement with current news, relating the contexts of newspaper articles to historic events, establishing an extra connection between past and present.

A change slowly came over the classes, especially the math classes, as I began to stretch my teaching legs. We got along. My student teaching had prepared me for classroom issues, and I was determined to never need to say, "There's the door." The students soon found out I was willing to explain problems in more than one way, and I soon found out something as well: I had a knack for dealing with "problem students"—kids who acted out. I was able to talk things over with them, and most found me easy to talk to. I had patience, and I was willing to provide help during study time to fit their learning styles. And I knew what it was like to be emotionally screwed up. I could relate to them from experience.

Every day, students asked me the same question: "Is Mr. Pinney coming back?" And I would tell them it was out of my hands.

The day before Fred came back, I found out my students had collaborated behind my back. All of my classes threw parties for me. They brought in cake, cookies, and thank-you cards. I can still see the pink frosting on one of the cakes. It was truly one of the most touching moments of my life.

I substituted at the district's other schools as well—middle school and high school. I like the fact that, as a substitute, I didn't have to plan, and I didn't have to correct tests or assignments. My day was done when the bell rang. But if I didn't work, I didn't get paid. I remember covering one day for a teacher who had called in sick. I had a horrible cold and was probably sicker than the teacher, but I needed the money. I went through about two boxes of Kleenex that day.

Like any large school district, Everett had noticeable demographics. The south end was more affluent, with nicer schools and a higher percentage of kids with family support. The north end had more poor, often single-parent families. For example, Evergreen Middle School, on the north end, was the epitome of a school in a demographically poor neighborhood. It was a mishmash rambler of old, leaky buildings and portables. I guess the school board figured, What the heck, the kids are going to trash the place anyway.

At Evergreen Middle School that winter I landed another long-term substitute math job, this time for two months. I had "benefited" from the misfortune of one Mr. Hutchins, an older fellow who, between burnout and classes full of rowdies, had simply decided to stop teaching. One day, he came into class with a book, sat down at his desk, and started reading. "What are we doing today?" a student asked him.

"I don't care" came his reply. "Do whatever you want."

So the students trashed the classroom—that is those, who didn't leave and start causing trouble in the rest of the school, running around the halls, yelling, knocking over garbage cans, and flooding the bathrooms. It was truly a free-for-all.

I was called in because I was a math teacher. The interim substitutes had been driven crazy, not knowing how to teach math and being put into a setting where the kids felt they could run wild. And I was given little warning by the school's administration about what I was getting into.

Fortunately, Bob Donnelly, a younger but experienced math teacher at Evergreen, filled me in: "You'll be teaching classes of sixth-graders, seventh-graders, and eighth-graders. The sixth-graders are energetic, but fun. The seventh-graders are probably the most level-headed, but there's some characters in there as well. You might have heard eighth-graders are the toughest to teach, and you heard right. They're exploding with hormones and think they know more than you do. Don't ever turn your back on them."

His advice seemed sound.

He continued: "If a kid acts out, give him a detention. If he acts out twice, give him two detentions. Anything after that, send him to the office—but don't send him to the vice principal, Mr. Danson. I call him Mr. Wet Noodle. If you do, he'll probably send him back and tell you it's your problem. Send him to one of the counselors instead; they can assign consequences, and they will. And if you ever need help right away, I'm right next door."

I had been assigned six classes. There were two sixth-, two seventh-, and two eighth-grade classes, in no particular order, throughout the day. I had thirty-five minutes for lunch, with no planning period for correcting papers or preparation. The day rolled by practically nonstop.

I was isolated in a portable as well. There was no phone or intercom (in those days, there were no computers or e-mail). If something came up, my nearest help was indeed Bob next door. Bob had already helped me in other ways—he had filled me in on where we were in the curriculum and had gone over the materials and textbooks with me. So I was not completely unprepared when I walked up the stairs into my room.

The inside of the portable was as ancient-looking as the outside. Wood paneling covered the walls four-feet high. The desks were one-piece—wooden seats and scratched, pale-yellow Formica tops. My desk was directly across from the door I had entered. I went around and straightened the desks into rows. Every one of them was decorated in written and/or carved graffiti. I don't think a single desk had escaped having the F word carved into it—some several times, others incorporating other expletives as well. Full sentences had also been imprinted, many incorporating various obscenities along with Mr. Hutchins's name.

In the morning, my classes were seventh, sixth, and eighth, in that order. And I would soon find out there is no greater difference in demeanor than between these three grade levels.

The first morning, I was standing by my desk when the 7:25 bell rang. Class began at the 7:30 bell, also called the "tardy bell." When the first bell rang, the seventh-graders started filing in. I could hear them clump, clump, clumping up the steps. They entered quietly, some not quite awake yet. Often students who would transform into terrors later in the day would be very subdued during the first couple of periods; they were not at full alertness. This group of kids seemed reasonably awake and well behaved.

"Are you the sub?" many of them asked me.

"Yes, I'm going to be here for a while, to steady things out for you guys."

Determined to learn their names, I made up a seating chart by walking around the class and writing down names to match the seats and rows in the room. My plan was to let them sit where they wanted the first few days; once I'd noted certain kids that shouldn't be seated next to each other, I would assign seats to ameliorate the issue. Quickly introducing myself, I handed out an evaluative worksheet to check the class's general skill level and continued filling in my chart.

Overall, things were starting out pretty well. Once I'd finished the chart, most of the kids still seemed to be working, so I decided to introduce myself to them more thoroughly and then go over a few of the problems for the day. I walked up to the front chalkboard. "May I have your attention, please!"

It was then I noticed I hadn't written my name on the board. "Excuse me, just a moment, ladies and gentlemen."

I wrote my name on the board and made a huge, rookie mistake—while doing so, I turned my back on them, on a class that was used to this room being a place of unmitigated chaos. Just as I finished and was turning back, a huge spit wad flew inches past my face and exploded on the board just underneath my name. But the kid who'd done it had made a mistake of his own: he'd waited just a bit too long to throw the projectile, and my peripheral vision caught sight of the end of his throwing motion. I had him cold.

Ignoring the drool and chewed-up pieces of paper flowing down my board, I walked up to him. He was sitting in the back of the second row, by the door. He looked back and rolled his eyes in resignation. There wasn't much to say. I looked down at my seating chart. Andrew Mullins. Dark-haired, somewhat heavy-set—he didn't look like a particularly bad or mean kid.

"You have two choices, Andrew. You can walk to the bathroom and bring back some wet and dry paper towels, and clean the board *now*. Or you can stay forty-five minutes after school tomorrow."

Andrew got up and went to the bathroom for the towels. We finished up the day's lesson uneventfully.

The bell rang. The seventh graders left quietly. And all of the sudden a zoo piled into my room, cheering and laughing and bouncing around like kangaroos.

The sixth-graders were the friendliest group of kids I had ever met. It's been said that many kids learn to hate school when they get to middle school because it's more challenging and kids are much more on their own. Elementary school is a big family that lasts forever in kids' minds. And then comes middle school, and the time starts rushing by faster than they can keep track.

But these kids were not jaded. They were glad to have someone there who could teach them. And they were so small. I largely repeated my routine from first period, and the kids were eager and asked many questions; they were motivated about their work. Then I walked up to my desk and noticed numerous small spitballs clustered around it and on the wall behind. The old spitball-shot-from-a-straw trick.

Pretending not to notice, I resumed walking about the room, helping students with their questions, but keeping my head up just a little better. And soon enough, at a desk next to the far wall by the door, I saw a small, blonde boy with a bowl-cut hairdo slip a straw out, place it into his mouth, and fire another small, arcing spit wad at my desk.

I glanced at my seating chart again. John Meyers. As I looked up again, he fired another round, which bounced off the wall behind my desk. Then he realized I was watching him. He made no effort to hide the straw and patiently watched me approach. He wasn't disrespectful, but when offered the choices I offered Andrew, he quietly refused.

"It's that or the office, John."

"I'll take the office."

Great, I thought. *Was Donnelly right? Would Mr. Danson just send him right back?*

But John didn't come back, and when I checked at lunch, he hadn't reported to the office either. Mr. Danson's secretary had me write out a full disciplinary referral and leave it with her. I would hear more about John the next day.

The sixth-graders bounded out much as they had come in. The classroom so silent, I wondered for a moment if I was the last man in the world. Then, heavy steps on the stairs. Someone big. Or two of them? What now—elephants?

The door opened, and a young woman the size of three sixth-graders entered. She was a head taller than the tallest sixth-grader and may have outweighed me—she was solid and strongly-built.

She glanced at me, then walked over to the third desk next to the wall and sat down. She wore a dark, hooded sweatshirt and gray sweatpants. Her dark, curly, medium-long hair was pulled back in a ponytail. Two more eighth-grade girls followed her in and sat in front and behind her. One was dressed in jeans and a denim jacket; the other had on a red sweatshirt and jeans. They all wore tennis shoes.

As the rest of the class filed in, I realized I would never be a fan of mixing sixth-graders with eighth-graders. The sixth-graders were just so—tiny, while these older students, especially the girls, were really almost young adults. The first girl who had entered deigned to notice me. "Are you the sub?"

(Quick note on this—"Are you the sub?"—a question asked frequently during my substitute career, four words that seem to be hardwired into students' brains. *Substitute* is always contracted into *sub.* You get used to hearing it.)

"Yes."

The bell rang. I'd been warned again and again that eighth-graders are the toughest students to deal with. Now I was going to find out.

My first impression was how calm they were compared to even seventh-graders. They liked to lounge back in their chairs or rest their bodies on their desks, arms tucked underneath their chests. They were attentive during my initial introduction—I was something new and temporary, after all—a good diversion.

I then began the assignment. Some paid better attention than others. The three girls who first came in felt it was a good time to talk among themselves. I decided to start my seating chart with them and to get them working as I did so. As I walked up to them, I could hear them discussing a party one of their older siblings had thrown that weekend.

Courtney, the first to come in, gave me her name and waited for me to add her two friends—Julia and Sam—to my chart. As soon as they knew I had their names, they began talking again. I paused, using body language to hint that I wasn't done with them. They stopped talking. Courtney asked, "Aren't you done now, Mr. Dahlberg?"

"I'm done getting your names. But I'd like to see you get your books out and get going."

"Get going on what?"

"Well, I did write an assignment on the board."

"Oh, that board. I'm sorry, Mr. Dahlberg, nobody's written on that board for so long, I never look up there anymore."

"Do your other teachers write on their boards?"

"Yes."

"Well, consider me just another teacher who writes on his board."

I developed a different style with the eighth-graders. I could approach sixth- or seventh-graders and get them going quickly. The eighth-graders often would delay, taking their time. I found that repeated, patient, calm nagging served my purposes best, rather than saying something to Courtney like, "Get your work out now, or I'm giving you a detention."

Staying calm with students was easy. Having dealt with the anxieties of OCD, I found the reality of a real classroom much less nerve-wracking. As a result, I was always able to maintain an even keel with my students. They knew I wouldn't yell, and I knew they would respect my requests and reactions.

John the spitballer wasn't to be seen the next day. He had skipped the rest of school the day when I sent him to the office. That afternoon, while playing soccer in someone's front lawn, he had chased the ball into the street and been struck by a car. His skull was badly fractured and he died on the spot. I heard about it from a seventh-grade friend of his, about five minutes into first period. He was discussing the event with his neighbors as if it were a sporting event rather than a grieving event.

I'd taken roll and hadn't quite started class yet. There was quite a bit of noise in the middle back of the room. I walked up to this piece of conversation:

"There was blood *everywhere!*"

"Did he really run into that car head first?"

They noticed me. "Mr. Dahlberg, did you know that John Meyers got killed yesterday?"

"I saw it," said Mike Powers, a now former friend of John's. He was a dark-haired kid not much bigger than John himself. "He didn't have a chance. There were police cars, firemen, lights, and sirens *everywhere!*"

"And blood," another boy reminded him.

"I already said that."

Strange, I thought. Here a kid made a first impression on me and then died. I can't say I felt too upset—I'm being honest here—but

I was disturbed that I hadn't been told by an administrator before school. Being out in a portable does tend to cut one off.

That morning, my students didn't seem to be affected by John's sudden demise at all. Apparently he didn't come to school much, and he didn't seem to have had many friends. I'd seen more emotion expressed over a lost dog. By lunchtime I was wondering if anyone cared about John at all. Did no one feel sorry about this?

Actually, someone did.

"Too bad it wasn't his brother," said Ken Simpson, a dark-haired history teacher with a brown mustache, while at lunch that day in the staffroom.

There was general assent among the other teachers, male and female.

I suddenly realized what a hardened lot this school's teachers were.

Taking a drag off her cigarette—it was legal and quite common for teachers to smoke at school back then—Barbara Tompkins told me about John's older brother, Josh. "He's the most cynical kid I've ever seen. Mean, disrespectful. Don't ever leave your car keys out if you get him for a student."

"Am I getting him? Is there something I don't know?"

"He goes through teachers on nearly a weekly basis. Danson believes nearly nothing is a discipline issue—it's a teacher issue, as far as he's concerned. Several teachers have threatened to go to the union to get Josh removed from their classes. It's one of our legal rights, you know. Danson doesn't want union trouble—like he doesn't want any trouble—so he signs the transfer papers. Josh is running out of teachers, so don't be surprised if you end up with him sometime."

Josh was what teachers call a game-changer. Sometimes a combination of the wrong kids—kids who build off each other—can disrupt a class on a regular basis. Such kids can be like an OCD trigger—sudden and unrelenting.

But Josh was eminently capable all by himself. He could anger his teachers with disruptive remarks. There's a first rule of engagement for disruptive students—*don't engage.* Josh could be so smoothly insulting with his remarks that you'd engage him without thinking. And if you did try to reason with him, he was very crafty at fooling you into thinking you *were* reasoning with him—until you found out he was only pretending to listen to you. Then he would step right back into arguing or furthering his original disruptive comment. When all was said and done, when you'd managed to get him to shut up or send him out, you may very well have lost ten minutes of class time. About this time, there was a popular movie called *The Time Bandits.* Josh was a time bandit.

By the way, I'm able to describe Josh so well because I did end up with him. I was warned in advance by one of the counselors that Josh would be appearing in my third-period class the next day. And so I began to mentally prepare myself to not let him get to me, to never get angry with him.

Josh was surly right off the bat. He waited until I had started to explain the day's material, and then, without raising his hand, he began to question the relevance of education in general. I told him he could stay after class if he wanted to, and we could discuss it at lunch. Generally, I refused to let him sidetrack me. If I could get him past the lesson, he was much less trouble, having lost his opportunity to be the center of attention. He would even help other students during study time.

But a day never went by when Josh didn't try to get under my skin. He was relentless. Still, by not losing my temper with him and generally refusing to engage, I disarmed the worst of him.

Josh would overtly disrupt with loud running commentary. But most disruptive students don't work this way. They're more passive-aggressive. They carry on quiet—or not so quiet—conversations, either distracting themselves and those they talk to, or slowly building up the noise level to where a teacher has to teach over it—that is, raise the volume to compensate.

It's very tempting to teach over noisy students. In fact, I know some teachers who are good at it. As a rule, however, raising your voice to accommodate these students' "needs" shows a lack of classroom management on the part of the teacher and leads to disrespect from all students—both from the disruptors and from those who *want* to learn. And most of the students do want to learn.

The first line of defense is to ask the students to quiet down. Many such students will. Or they will—for a while. I might warn such students a second time, and then if they don't stay quiet, I move one or more of them to different seats. Some will move without complaint. In all such cases, a minimum of class time is wasted.

On the other hand, some of these young people want to argue. Various levels of argument might include:

"I wasn't talking."

"We were talking about the problem you were explaining."

"Julie talked to me first."

"You let everyone else talk. Why are you picking on me?"

"I can never understand the way you explain it, so why should I listen?"

"I'm not moving."

Again, there is a general rule: *don't engage*. Engaging takes time. It validates the student's argument and wastes the time of others. My usual response would be "Please be quiet, or I'm going to have to move you." Or I might make the offer to argue off the clock: "If you'd like to come in before or after school, or at lunch, I'll be glad to discuss the matter with you."

How like OCD a disruptive student is! He will take all the time you will give him, while you accomplish absolutely nothing. And, if you put him off until a later time, he will often stop being a nuisance, much like delay therapy. I can count on one hand the number of occasions when a student had taken a minute out of his time to argue issues, such as coming in at lunch, instead of my class time.

You might notice that I made every effort to keep the student in the classroom. Sending a kid out of class was a last resort. And there was more than one way to send a kid out of class. The first option would be to ask the student to step outside for a minute or two to cool off, and then let him back in. But, if a student flat refuses to stop arguing or to move or continues to disrupt after a move, the greater good has to be considered. The student must be sent to the office to talk with an administrator.

An effective administrator will take time to talk with the student and to administer appropriate consequences if necessary. It is a two-way street, however. If a teacher sends too many kids to the office for perhaps minor disruptions, the administrator starts to assume the teacher can't handle his classroom. It's best to send kids few and far between, and only when absolutely necessary.

I had students who were used to entering an out-of-control setting and used to acting in a manner that would get them sent to the office. And, according to Bob Donnelly, I had an administrator who would send the kids right back to class, sometimes without even talking to them.

It's amazing how much in-class discipline a teacher can supply. An administrator I knew once told me he ran his own discipline completely when he was a classroom teacher. He kept a file on each student and had measured, documented steps of responses to student behavior. His biggest weapon was parent phone calls. Most parents are willing to do a lot to help out with their children's behavior—if they are kept in the loop. Parents can issue consequences that administrators cannot, and misbehaving kids hate being nagged by their parents. If the parent is called whenever a student misbehaves, the nagging becomes so annoying that a student will modify his behavior on this basis alone. I've had students beg me not to call their parents; sometimes even the threat is enough.

On Bob's advice, I began calling parents. It was more trouble in the mid-1980s. Nowadays, you can pull student info directly from the district's network and dial on your own phone. Or you can e-mail, which is very effective as well. Plus, most households have multiple phone numbers due to family members having cell phones. In 1986, I had to go to the office to get student info, use a phone in the office, have no answering machine leave return messages on, and often found the number to be no longer in service. I would have to call emergency contact numbers to get current numbers.

Josh was an example of a student with no parent number. He lived with an aunt who was rarely home. I finally made contact with her. After giving her condolences for his younger brother, I told her about Josh. Through the earpiece, I could almost see her eyes rolling. "Yes, Jack has had trouble with all of his teachers. I'll speak to him about it, though. He just never seems to listen."

But Josh did not like the fact I had called. "Why did you call my aunt?"

"Because she's responsible for your behavior."

"*I'm* responsible for my behavior. Whatever you have to say, you can say it to my face."

"I *have* been saying it to your face. It just seems like you need someone to repeat it to you. I'm going to call her every time you won't listen to me from now on."

I walked away to the sound of muttered expletives. But he did control his speech a bit better after that.

* * * * *

With OCD, the anxiety includes not just responses to bad thoughts but also anxiety over thoughts to come. I knew something was going to trigger it—another cancer article in the newspaper, a news report on some awful new disease. I would often avoid the situation altogether if I could. If there was a bad headline, I'd turn the page. A radio or TV report—I'd change the channel. Every source of news contained a possible dreaded event. But I read and listened to most of the news anyway; I had to stay informed on the world. I would not let the OCD debilitate me completely.

I faced the same kind of dread when I started this job. I would come to school dreading all the disruptions some of the students would come up with. I felt like I was fighting a war sometimes, like I was constantly under attack. But as my experience grew and I became more adept at methods of discipline—and, most importantly, became aware that most of the students in any given class supported me and disliked the behavior of the problem students just as much as I did—I stopped feeling apprehensive. I actually started to look forward to dealing with the problem students, because I began to realize that I had the upper hand. It was they (with Josh as a prime example) who were going to change their behavior; I had the ultimate say. This gave me more power to reason with them and to make a positive difference in their lives.

It was this attitude about my OCD—that it was no longer going to affect me, that I was going to affect *it* instead—that eventually restored my control of my life.

I will have to say that "Mr. Wet Noodle," as Bob had put it, did expel a student of mine on one occasion. He was one of a set of identical twins, and his name was James. Not big for a seventh-grader, darkish-blonde, and always wearing dark-rimmed glasses, he specialized in passive-aggressive sarcasm. We had some interesting discussions on him using his class time efficiently.

James had been sent to the office from another class one day. And, with his particular style of communication, he had managed to get thoroughly under Mr. Danson's skin. He'd gotten Danson hopping mad, and during a pause in this exchange, the boy had quietly, confidently, and levelly told him, "If I had a gun, I'd blow you away."

I honestly think James would have done no such thing, but he couldn't resist this ultimate opening at Mr. Danson. I hope he tempered his speech at whatever new school he ended up at.

Mr. Hutchins had left at Thanksgiving, never to return. My long-term substitution had lasted from this point until the end of the semester, which was the last week of January. A permanent replacement teacher—a "real" teacher—was to be hired to teach second semester and to continue the assignment into the years to come. I assumed I was going to be granted an interview. However, I never received a call or letter regarding interviews, so I finally called personnel to confirm an interview date.

"You're not on the interview list," the woman at personnel informed me in a kind voice.

"Didn't you get my application?"

"Yes, but you didn't make the list."

I was infuriated. Here I had busted my tail to put these classes back into shape, and they couldn't even offer me a shot. There was a saying among the substitutes in the Everett district: "Everett doesn't hire subs." I was never sure if this was because they liked having familiar subs or because subs were by their very nature beneath consideration. Either way, life wasn't being fair again. But that's life, I told myself this time, determined not to show my anger in this conversation.

"You know, I've done a lot with this class. Don't you think I at least deserve an interview in return?"

The woman to whom I was speaking must have had some clout. "You have a good point there. I'll see to it you get your interview."

I got my interview. But I still didn't get the job. Instead, an experienced teacher with a master's degree, recently moved up from California, was hired. Her credentials were much more extensive, and her husband added a nice touch—he had recently been hired as a professor at the University of Washington. I had no such impressive spouse, at least not yet.

I met Vicki Martin on the staff day between semesters, with the instructions and intent to catch her up on student progress and with the students themselves—their quirks, what sort of approach worked with whom, and some of the little tricks I had figured out for dealing with these North Everett kids. But Vicki was aloof. She really wasn't interested in what I had to say, of what I knew. I think she figured she knew a lot more about teaching than a lowly substitute did, and she basically told me she'd figure it out. It was quite patronizing, and I went home early, hoping she'd treat the kids with more respect than she'd treated me.

A month later I received a substitute call—for Vicki Martin. A surge of adrenalin hit me, yanking me out of my usual early-morning funk. A chance to see my kids again!

It seemed like I had never left as I climbed the stairs to the portable and opened the door. The desks were still in the same arrangement. Then I turned on the light. Oh, the irony.

On nearly every desk and on numerous other surfaces about the room—walls, shelves, books—was scrawled "Mrs. Martin is a bitch." Many were accompanied by what seemed to be a stan-dardized picture—a scrawny stick figure of a woman with long, unkempt hair. Why hadn't she erased this stuff? One of the first things I had done when I started my job was to eliminate the com-ments and pictures regarding Mr. Hutchins. Was this some new discipline strategy?

As the kids entered the room, a look of disbelief hit them.

"Mr. Dahlberg?"

"Have you come back?"

"Is she finally gone?"

"Please, please stay this time!"

All day long, this theme recurred; every class begged me to come back and replace Mrs. Martin. Apparently her classroom management differed greatly from mine and did not include smil-ing. She had given the kids the impression of a "mean" teacher. She put them down as being lazy and undisciplined—not the way to treat this particular demographic of children.

They had rebelled and made life hell for her.

Many asked why I had not landed the job. I simply told the kids she was more experienced and that there had been a lot of quali-fied applicants.

One eighth-grade girl was curious. "How can new teachers ever get experience if schools don't hire them?"

"That's a good question," I replied, trying to hide the bitter-ness in my voice. "New teachers have to try longer and harder, and they may have to substitute for a while to get noticed, to build up a reputation."

What I didn't tell her was that new teachers were hired all the time, but they had high grade-point averages compared to my mediocre one, and they had great student teaching reviews instead of my reasonably good one. My OCD had held me back—and yet it had also given me a frame of reference of always having to struggle, an outlook that gave me the ability to relate to the troubled kids both emotionally and academically. I was good with tough kids, and yet this never showed on my resume, at least not at this point. I wasn't good enough on paper. The sharp, creden-tialed Mrs. Martin had carried the day.

Apparently the kids made an extra effort against Mrs. Martin the rest of the week in retaliation for her "stealing my job." She quit at the end of the semester.

The rest of the year, I bounced around to every middle and high school in the Everett district and managed to work over 130 days, receiving about eight-five dollars per day, working out to approximately eleven thousand for the school year. I could have substituted more days, but when spring came, I started to receive calls from landscaping clients. I gradually shifted my work hours over to installing and repairing sprinkler systems. It paid better. Not much, but better.

I also applied to teach summer school for a six-week term back at Evergreen Middle School. I wondered if I would see any of my former students. This short term would begin the week after school let out and finish at the end of July. I would teach two math classes, from eight to noon, which were designed to reestablish credit for students who had failed a semester. It was quite possible this job would lead back into another interview and a real teaching job at Evergreen. The pay wouldn't be much, but between the fifty dollars per day and part-time landscaping, I should make it through the summer with my head still above water.

I did get the job, and Bob Lapoint, the administrator I interviewed with, expressed optimism that is could lead to something full time. It was exciting to think I might finally have my opening.

The week before the job was supposed to start, I received a call from Mr. Lapoint. Most of the kids had signed up for the later class, and there were fewer kids than had been predicted. The job had changed from a half-day job to a job that paid half as much and still went until noon every day. If I took this job, I would have much less income than I needed for most of the summer. I was finally making an independent living, and I wasn't going to ask anyone for any more money. I told Mr. Lapoint I could not support myself on what the district would offer and would have to decline the job.

"This is very short notice you're giving," Bob said.

"I have to support myself."

"You know, declining this opportunity may not look very good when it comes time for you to apply for the full-time job in the fall."

Perhaps I should have taken the job and borrowed money from my parents to live on. But they had been generous enough to me. I could not ask for more at that point. I was going to make a living on my own from now on. "I hope when that time comes, Mr. Lapoint, that you will consider the fact that I needed to support myself."

I did apply for the job again and did not obtain an interview. In the fall, I noticed my substitute calls were fewer. I was no longer in good standing with the Everett School District. Far closer to home, the Shoreline School District, in a North Seattle suburb, needed substitutes as well. So I went to the district office and put myself on their list. But everyone wanted to work for Shoreline, a well-to-do district with a distinctly higher standard of living than that in North Everett. Between Everett and Shoreline, I was still getting far fewer calls than I needed.

On the other hand, my landscaping calls were really picking up.

The deciding factor in my leaving teaching was a call from a nightclub I used to DJ at during college. A DJ had recently quit, and Brad Jones, the manager, asked me if I could come back and fill in for a while. I could DJ for nine hours per week and take home six hundred dollars per month as well as work my landscaping business.

Between my three-days-per-week, 10:00 p. m to 1:00 a.m. gig spinning records for the dance floor and a steady stream of landscape and sprinkler system installation and maintenance, I was making a better living than substitute teaching—and with the satisfaction of being my own boss. I knew I had the potential to grow a business and make more than I ever could as a teacher.

It was September 1987. I called up Everett and Shoreline and had them remove me from their sub lists. After starting college in 1977, finishing my classes in 1986, and substitute teaching for one year, I figured I was through with teaching forever. I wondered why I ever attended college. And I was alone when most of my friends were married, except for my constant companion—my OCD.

Like many careers, my landscaping business started with a Boy Scout project. To complete my Eagle Scout badge, I had to put together a major community service project, which included finding a project, organizing labor, finding and paying for supplies, and keeping charge and hands-on the entire time. My church, Northlake Lutheran in Kenmore, Washington, has extensive landscaped grounds and was considering a landscape sprinkler system. Since the cost was great, the church asked me if I would be willing to put the project together, as a volunteer effort would save much money.

I did such a good job that members of the church started calling me about their own lawns. During summers in high school and college, I did several jobs per summer, making decent money—all by word of mouth. After I finished my teaching certificate, I applied for a contractor's license and became licensed, bonded, and insured, thinking I had a good second job. Little did I know it would become a career for several years.

Life as a contractor

Contracting was much different from teaching. The hours were a lot longer and year-round. Although many contractors did pretty well, I had one problem most of them didn't. Although I was willing to put in the hours, I spent many of them nonproductively. Not being in the spotlight in front of a class, my OCD started making a comeback. As I worked alone much of the time, I had more time to ponder and was freer to perform my compulsions, so images and repetitions became more pronounced. And, the images and thoughts had never stopped—I had been partially treated, after all. I was now thrust into a situation where my partial treatment was less effective. And my financial success was being severely compromised.

Repetitive behavior again became my worst enemy. It cost me a lot of time and money during the seven years I worked full time as a landscape business proprietor. Sprinkler systems required quite a bit of intricate manual labor. Certainly digging trenches was not terribly complicated, but pipefitting and electrical work provided me with many opportunities to manifest time- and money-consuming behavior.

The perfect OCD example

Connecting wires contained nearly endless possibilities. Let's say I was going to connect a hot wire and a ground wire to a sprinkler valve, the typical voltage being 24 volts, quite a bit less than a 120-volt household current. Such a voltage was considered safe to work with. And sprinkler cable, which carried bundles of wires for multiple valves, could be directly buried alongside the sprinkler pipe without hard conduit.

When two wires in a bundle were selected to connect to a valve, they had to be cut to length. The ends had to be stripped to bare wire for about half an inch from the end. This was to allow the wires to be crimped into a connector and then snapped into a waterproof housing.

Stripping the wire was done with a pliers-like wire stripper. Normally half an inch of insulation could be stripped off in about three seconds, with time to spare. But not if a bad thought went through an OCD sufferer's head—my head—at the instant the wire was stripped. If this occurred—and more often than not, it did—I would have to strip an additional piece from the wire to make it right.

Now the wire's stripped end would be too long. I would have to cut *it* back. Another bad thought at this point? Another strip, another bad thought, another cut, another strip. In a worst-case scenario, I could (and did, numerous times) cut the wire so far down that I'd literally have to splice another piece of wire back on to get it to reach again. Later I just got into the habit of cutting the wire about a foot too long in the first place.

So many painful things—wasting time, wasting money, wasting life—and all the while under compulsion, compelled by fear of something bad happening, tense, sometimes teeth clenched, knowing I was a slave, feeling even worse for not being able to break free. Sometimes it seemed an observer part of me would let the process take place, waiting, fretting the entire time. Obsessive-compulsive disorder is not a pleasant experience at any level of consciousness. So many feelings and thoughts to the point of overload, all of the time—how could one not have a nervous breakdown?

It's amazing to me that in twenty-five years of suffering from it I had only two. Both times I was unable to function for days.

And yet, if you were to tally up all of the "mini" nervous breakdowns—all the wire-cutting episodes, all the broken concentration over my years of schooling, all the lost sleep, all the worrying when I could have been productive on thousands of different occasions over those years—it had to have added up to tens of thousands, perhaps even hundreds of thousands of dollars in lost time, money, and potential. And the living I wasted was beyond price.

The real irony of it all is that I never realized my potential as a contractor. I moved back into teaching, where I could concentrate and teach successfully—especially with an audience to watch my every move. Now, having defeated my OCD, when I do mechanical work around the house, I am always amazed at how a former two-hour task—such as replacing a pump controller in our well house—can take less than fifteen minutes.

And yet I miss my contracting days too. The variety of clients, young and old, and the travel to every borough of Seattle gave me a sense of freedom and a knowledge of the city matched by few. I loved the variety of my students, but I miss my travels and my being outside among the incredible variety of the neighborhoods, new and old, near and far.

CHAPTER 13

Grown-up Life

June 1987. Ten years since high school graduation. When I graduated from high school, I had thought in vague terms of perhaps going to dental school, following after my father, or perhaps some similar health profession. My plans had changed to teaching English, then math. I had struggled the entire way, never quite sure what I wanted to do.

I had had a few relationships by 1987, but nothing that had lasted, and I had found no one I considered a potential mate. A long-term relationship of three years, from 1982 to 1985 had ended badly, but it had never felt right anyway. I hadn't really seen anyone during the two years after that breakup, as I was busy finishing my schooling and partially reigning in my OCD.

But my desire to do something with myself had not abated. I had restarted my martial arts. I was a new Scoutmaster. I was working an interesting part-time job three evenings a week, never knowing what was going to happen any given night. And I was a full-time landscaper.

During my first full-time year of landscaping, I did small jobs, working alone. It could be very serene—when my OCD wasn't making me cut wires ever shorter. During those times, rain or shine, alone with my thoughts and my work at hand, I often reflected on the past ten years and how I might as well have just landscaped all along. And yet I valued my education and my experiences. I just didn't feel successful.

I felt like my life was on hold. I was waiting for something to happen. I was busy, but not very fulfilled. I was not alone, however. I had my two big, young dogs, and I had taken on a boarder to help pay my house expenses. Eugene was a charismatic fellow from Long Island, a worldly and well-traveled young man who had enrolled at John Bastyr Naturopathic University. He loved my dogs, and, unlike me, he loved to cook. He would cook up tomato stock by the quart and stuff the pans into the freezer. I quickly and permanently began calling his cooking efforts swill, which he took with good humor, and I did appreciate some of his very good—albeit messy—cuisine. Dino and Tasman, the dogs, also grew to be great friends of Eugene's, as he would often let them lick his cooking pans.

Eugene had partly paid his way through college by working as a radio host and had an excellent speaking voice. He had entire monologues memorized, including Eddie Murphy's first and quite graphic comedy album, and he would perform on cue, whether spontaneously or as requested. His vocal talents would serve him well later as the host of several successful naturopathic radio shows.

Between Eugene, my animals, Scouts, karate, DJ'ing, and running a business, I rarely lacked company. In my small neighborhood, I was also surrounded by many interesting neighbors.

Some years go by faster than others. I had established patterns and activities I would maintain for years. I would go on to spend nineteen years as Scoutmaster and would have done more, save for the fact that my two future daughters would need this time from me. And I still teach karate. (I still miss Scouting terribly.)

Looking back, the year from the fall of 1986 to the fall of 1987 seems like an entire decade. I have so many vivid details and individual memories of this period—so much had come before and so much would come after—and yet here I was, caught in an eddy in the flow of my life, static.

I began to have many regrets about my OCD. I still didn't know what it was; I just knew it had wasted years of my life and had possibly cost me as the girl of my dreams. I dated some women during this time, and none of them met my standards like the girl from Western had—although most of them were nicer, which I can just as well attribute to not getting to know them long-term.

There were exceptions. One woman I saw for a few weeks had a penchant for fighting and making up. The making up was nice, but the fighting wasn't worth it.

I also met a woman at a wedding reception. We hit it off, and I got her phone number from a friend of mine who knew her. I called her a week later, and we dated for about a month. She was one of the nicest ladies I've ever met, and we had many interests in common. Looking back, maybe she would have been very good for me. But she lacked my level of education. I held back, and eventually we tapered back to friends. She reconnected with and married her boyfriend from the last year.

I met quite a few women while I was a DJ. Some were just friends; a few I went on a date or two with. One woman, a statuesque Norwegian girl, would occasionally have a beer with me after the dance floor closed. I asked her out a couple of times; she thanked me with a smile and said maybe one of these days. Perhaps she was dating someone; I didn't pry.

I met a very intelligent blonde name Katie. We dated for a while, but after the first date we found we enjoyed each other's company but not a whole lot more. We had little in common: I loved the outdoors, for instance, and she could not spend a night away from a shower. Occasionally she would sit up with me in my DJ booth to keep me company, enjoy the ambience, and not have to deal with men trying to pick her up. I knew Katie was seeing other people, and one night she told me she had found someone she thought she could be serious about. We said a friendly good-bye, and I never saw her again.

At twenty-eight, I felt like an old man. I was apparently a some-what established bachelor, but I didn't like being one. I needed the companionship and I wanted to have a family. The women I dated were mostly younger. The ones my age were largely married off—at my tenth high school reunion, I found that most of them had children as well. And, of course, many of the men had fol-lowed the same path. I have to say I related to younger women bet-ter; they were closer to my maturity level. The ones my age seemed so grown up.

The week after Katie disappeared, what appeared to be a sev-enteen-year-old girl came up to my booth, and said, "Would you like to dance?" (Of course she had to be at least twenty-one to get in the door. If she had really been seventeen—well, I would have probably danced with her anyway.

"Sure," I replied. I never turned down a dance offer; it was a chance to stretch my legs for a couple of minutes. And this young lady was very appealing. Petite and slim and athletic-looking, she was wearing well-fitting blue jeans along with a shirt that together revealed very nice outlines from top to bottom. I put on a long single, and we danced for a few minutes before I had to run back up to work. I had never seen her before. Usually the regulars asked me to dance. Who was she?

By the time I got off work, she was gone. Would I see her again? All the next day I wondered about her. Was she interested in me? I usually didn't hang around the Keg when I wasn't working, but since this day was a Saturday and I wouldn't have to get up and get to work early Sunday, I decided to visit the place a little after ten, when the dance floor music started. Would she be there?

The Keg was on the southeast corner of a large shopping cen-ter with groceries and retail stores accessible from a huge, flat parking lot with little landscaping and lots of open, paved space. The only other outlier besides the Keg was a bank with a drive-through attached. The Keg itself was the newest building on the site, a wood-and-brick structure surrounded by a landscaping of shrubs and trees. It was a contrast to the rest of the retail cen-ter, which was mostly finished in stucco, with a landscaping of tall poles holding mercury-vapor lights.

The Keg's main entrance was on the building's northeast corner. You went up a short flight of steps, took a hard left into the dance floor/bar or straight ahead into the restaurant, or a hard right into the restrooms. You had to pass a podium staffed by the hosts and hostesses to enter the restaurant. A few padded benches lay beyond the host, to accommodate patrons waiting for a table on busier nights. Hardwood or tile flooring combined with dark woodwork gave the interior a dark, romantic, relaxed feel.

A line had already formed at the entrance to the door when I arrived at about 10:30, but the bouncer waved me right by. Every job has its perks. I stepped in with a good vantage point. The north and south areas of the bar were elevated; from there, you could step down to the lower level, which contained a long bar on the west side, the dance floor on the east, and more seating in between. A railing surrounded the dance floor, and another railing separated the upper area from the lower.

The dance floor had—or I should say, had had—some pretty fancy lighting. It had been constructed during the height of the disco area, the late 1970s, when the restaurant, originally named Baxter's, had been built. (I had visited Baxter's a few years back—ironically, Tina worked there when I first met her.) Many switches on the DJ panel were dead—colored floodlights, what once had been a large hanging disco ball and its spotlights, and a box of narrow lighting surrounding the floor, just inside the perimeter were—the one bit of gaiety that still completely worked.

Between the bar, the tables, and the dance floor, the place could hold well over two hundred people—people who generally drank a lot. Two or three bartenders plus several cocktail waitresses were kept very busy serving martinis, shots, draft beers, and wine. Between the crowd, the noise, the music, the colored lights, and the then-legal clouds of cigarette smoke, it was easy to become overloaded. There was a steady stream of people constantly coming and going for fresh air outside or a bathroom break.

One of the most recurrent memories of the old days, when indoor smoking was legal, was the plethora of cigarette butts thrown in the urinals. It was more convenient and safer than throwing them into the paper-towel-filled trash. These cigarette butts, often with much of the cigarette remaining, afforded amusing target practice while relieving oneself. If you really had to go, you might be able to destroy several of them before you were finished. Of course the filters remained. I always felt sorry for the janitors who had to clean the men's restroom.

Inside the surreal atmosphere of the bar, I was looking the place over, trying to see if that young lady had shown up again. It turns out she wasn't far away, in the sunken area by the bar, directly between the counter and me. We spotted each other almost immediately. I think she had been watching the door, and she had certainly chosen a good place to stand. Obviously, this woman had some intelligence about her. From a distance, she looked even more attractive; I could see all of her. She was wearing form-fitting pink cotton pants and a light button-down shirt.

It was magnetic. I could have said we gravitated to each other, but magnetism is a much stronger force at close range. We immediately struck up a conversation. By the time I had made it down the steps, she was there waiting there for me. We exchanged hellos. Without stopping to introduce myself first, I asked her for her name.

"Judy Utter."

For a few seconds I was amazed. I had gone to junior high school with Jenny and Jeff Utter, apparently her brother and sister. We had attended different high schools, however—I had gone to Shorecrest High, whereas Jenny and Jeff had gone to the more westward Shoreline High School. (Later, Jeff would be extremely appalled when he found out Judy and I were planning to marry. "You're engaged to *Dahlberg?*")

I was not a friend of either of them, but we knew each other from band and orchestra, and had attended Shoreline Summer Music Camp together several times over the years. Jeff and I had talked a little at music camp. He wrote a column for the camp newspaper called "Dear Irving," dispensing helpful, amusing, and quite cynical advice. I had expressed my admiration for his writing style more than once.

Years later, I was looking at a woman who had a beyond coincidental family resemblance to Jenny and Jeff. The most striking resemblance was in her eyes—large and brown.

"You're Jenny and Jeff's sister, aren't you?"

We talked and talked, standing across from and close to each other. Although our height differential is nearly a foot (five foot two and six one), it seemed natural and comfortable. Much of our talk seemed to center around mutual interests. If I could have pulled out a written checklist of everything I was looking for in a woman, I would have been checking every box right down the line. I was especially impressed how physically active she was and how she loved the outdoors and participating in sports. And she was sharp—a graduate student at the University of Washington. Most of all, there was a distinct magnetism. Both of us had tuned out the outside world.

But someone had not tuned Judy out. She had come in with a bunch of friends from her alma mater, Shoreline High School. After receiving her BA in nutrition from Western Washington University, she was a first-year graduate student at the University of Washington in the food sciences program.

Suddenly, a fellow came up, gave Judy a beer, retreated quickly. "Oh thanks, Nick," she said and turned right back to me without pause.

Later I found out that that Nick had driven Judy and a friend of hers to the Keg that night. She had been having a friendly conversation with him, and he had bought her the beer. He was starting to feel a little lucky (who wouldn't?). But she had spotted me and immediately forgotten him. The beer arrived. Nick waited. Judy and I talked. Nick waited some more. Judy and I talked some more. Nick had finally brought her the beer in disgust.

We'd been talking nonstop for at least thirty minutes, with a few beers thrown in. The physical attraction was really starting to kick in. "Would you like to dance?" It seemed a good time to ask.

"Last call!" announced the DJ. Where had the time gone? This was too soon! There was a Denny's down the street. I asked Judy if she would like to stop by the Denny's, and then I would gladly drop her off at her residence. The bar closed soon after, and I found myself at Denny's, across a table from her, drinking coffee.

I really don't remember in what order I found out about Judy and her interests. Although we had grown up geographically close,

Judy was six and a half years younger than I was. We had followed a somewhat similar path, however—Western, then the UW—too far apart in years to have met and become attracted. At twenty-two and twenty-eight, our age spread was ideal for both of us.

Judy lived a few miles south of me in a boarding house uphill and west of the UW. I drove to the front of her house, let her out, and we exchanged phone numbers.

I called her and we talked, and still had that rapport we'd felt the other night. We agreed to meet for coffee and went to a little tea shop that was a favorite of hers just north of the U District, really at the beginning of Capitol Hill. I've always loved the setting of old Seattle, its many, varied, and beautiful neighborhoods and boroughs (I knew the area well, having many landscape clients there). We had muffins and tea.

By then, we knew quite a bit about each other. We loved animals, hiking, skiing, waterskiing, running, and were proud of our educations. We shared stories of camping, skiing, and other family outings we'd had, and we agreed those things were very important. In light of our interests, we decided to have a real date: we would go for a run at Magnuson Park on Lake Washington and then go out for dinner at a restaurant I liked. We set the time for the following Friday. Being mid-November, the entire late-afternoon's outing would be in the dark. But the park was reasonably well-lit, and after dark in November we would probably have the place to ourselves.

I brought Dino and Tasman, my Doberman-Shepherd mixes, along with me, as Judy liked dogs. I had a canopy on my Nissan, and they would ride in the bed, stick their heads out the back window, and bark nonstop. As I put on my cold-weather running outfit, I informed them we were "going to the park," which sent them into a berserk frenzy, tearing around the house, whining ,and barking, and knocking over pieces of furniture.

Ironically, Dino seemed to have canine OCD. He had the habit of biting the fur on his paws, which had earned him "The Cone of Shame" on more than one occasion. There was no way to train him out of it. Nowadays, Prozac can help with such behavior. Dino had his crutch, the cone, I had mine, Xanax. As hyper as he could be, I often wonder why I never thought to give him some.

Magnuson Park is a former naval base on the northwest side of Lake Washington that had included a long runway for planes. When the base was closed and the runway was torn up for park space, the perimeter runway road was left mostly intact. You could walk (or run) about two miles from the south end of the park to the north end on a very nice concrete road that closely paralleled the lake. Closer to the lake, adjacent to the shoreline, weaving in and out of trees and shrubs was a footpath more rugged than the road but more scenic as well. I preferred the path, as it was more secluded, challenging, and actually easier on my body, the dirt of the path being less jarring than the concrete.

As we left Judy's, the dogs started their usual barking. Why did it suddenly sound louder than usual? "They won't stop," I told Judy.

They did bark, all the way to the park. Dino would bark continuously; Tasman would join in on occasion. I've never had a dog before or since that could bark like Dino. He truly was an obsessive barker.

By the time we arrived, we had an unwelcome companion: rain. "Do you still want to run?" I asked her. She was all for it.

"How fast would you like to go?"

"Whatever pace you'd like will be fine," she replied with a straight face.

So we took off, staying on the paved trail in the rain, the dogs running ahead, crisscrossing and backtracking and covering twice the distance of the humans, as dogs will do. I like to warm up slowly when I run. Judy ran right beside me, the rain hitting our faces. *Well, why not speed up a little,* I thought? Judy sped right up. I opened my stride. Somehow Judy matched it. It was like her legs had grown.

So I finally kicked it into a pretty decent gear, one that felt good and flew me along at a wonderful, stretched-out pace. I was seeing how long Judy could match it. Obviously, she was trying to impress me (or was I trying to impress her?). Although the pace felt great, it was not one I could hold indefinitely. However, it was one that Judy could. Damn! "How's the pace?" I sort of panted out.

"It's great," she replied easily.

Somehow I gutted the pace out, splashing hard through puddles as rain whizzed into our faces. Dino and Tasman were thrilled at the speed and the rain and the mud. All four of us were thoroughly soaked and covered in sand and mud when we made it back to my truck, the rain pouring even harder.

"You know," Judy said, "I don't think it's going to work going right to dinner. I need a shower."

My house was on the way, so we agreed that we could stop off there, clean up, and go to dinner.

Judy really enjoyed Mediterranean Pizza and Pasta, the place I had chosen for dinner. The owner, Gary, was visibly happy seeing me with such an impressive prospect, especially in light of my previous girlfriend, who had worked for him for years and always cut into his profits by mixing in house wine with her Sprite during her shift. However, her charm had always brought extra customers in, and he probably profited in the end.

The Med's specialty was pizza topped with whole-milk mozzarella cheese. If you've never had this kind of mozzarella, it makes the part-skim stuff taste like stringy cardboard. The Hawaiian pizza was always excellent, as was the vegetarian Italian special. We ordered a half-and-half, accompanied by dinner salads topped with more of the same excellent mozzarella sprinkled with sunflower seeds.

By the time dinner was finished, it had become a very late dinner. The topic of running had come up during the meal. Judy had been a star runner in high school, and, although she did not run competitively in college, she had kept her fitness up. But more than that, she possessed natural talent. As I drove Judy back to her room, I noticed it was almost eleven. The evening had passed quickly.

I was thinking I was going to steal a nice kiss as we pulled up into her driveway. Instead, she looked over at me and said, without hesitation, "Would you like to see my frogs?"

Did she even have frogs? I decided she must have frogs. "Okay." The next night, when she came to visit me, she brought a bag.

We went Christmas tree shopping. Although I preferred Noble firs, I let her pick out a "Christmas Bush," as I called it. It's amazing how Christmas trees vary from family to family. I was crummy at decorating; Judy apparently had professional skills. My house had never looked better, Christmastime or not.

Judy came to my dad's office Christmas party, held at my parents' house. She wore a tight-fitting blue dress with heels; her sharp appearance and equally sharp mind in conversation impressed my dad's staff, especially my matchmaking Aunt Helen, who worked for him at the time. And Judy was one hell of a pool player; we traditionally had games in my parents' basement, and no one could touch her. And, being petite, she looked good doing gymnastics to get the cue to the ball.

My parents were very pleased with Judy. Initially my mother had asked if I'd met her at "that place" (the bar where I worked) and had grimaced when I said yes. Judy was invited to a nice dinner "with the parents" and almost burst into tears at the grilling my dad gave her. She had passed the test, however, and my father never asked her a harsh question again.

A short time before Christmas, we turned off the lights and sat by the Christmas tree, its tiny lamps glittering. Judy, sitting next to me, got up and climbed onto my lap, facing me, her arms around my neck. The Christmas tree lights threw sparkles to the wall that reflected back into Judy's eyes. Everything felt so perfect. I knew she was the one for me and I the one for her.

Suddenly I heard my own voice. "Will you marry me?"

Complete shock and surprise. Eyes wide. Speechless. I probably looked the same way. What the hell had I just done? What kind of a proposal was this?

Finally she started to speak. She hesitated. Then "Uh…yes!"

From dance to proposal: three weeks. We tied the knot the next September, although Judy moved in as soon as we announced our engagement.

Fred and Nancy Utter, Judy's parents, deserve a quick mention here. Nancy was a UW grad in speech therapy; her father was a PhD in genetics. Nancy was twenty and Fred was twenty-six when they met at Nancy's sorority. They have practically the same age difference as Judy and I. Fred had graduated, gone into the service, gotten out, and was working as a sorority houseboy to help pay his way through a graduate program at the UW.

Fred was running a small brewery in the basement of the sorority, which would cost him his job. Knowing Fred had a supply of corks, Nancy asked him for one to help polish the wax on her skis. While assisting her, Fred acutely noticed Nancy's derriere as she was bent over, waxing her skis. It was love at first sight.

They spent their honeymoon tagging fish.

On the way to meet her parents, Judy warned me about their dog, Meg, a Cocker spaniel. Apparently, Meg loved attention and would run up to be petted, even by strangers. Then she would squat and pee. I told Judy this would not bother me; I had raised two large dogs from puppies and had dealt with many an accident.

Judy lived in a wooded neighborhood in Shoreline. After driving up through some evergreens and turning right into a small driveway, we were at her parent's front door. We rang the bell. Barking, lots of barking. The door opened, and a golden Cocker spaniel rushed out, jumping at my knees. Instinctively I reached down to pet her, and Judy's warning was fulfilled. Nancy kept a roll of paper towels next to the doorway, and the puddle was quickly gone.

Nancy and I gave each other wide-eyed looks. They say that a man should look at the mother if he wants to see his future wife. I saw a silver-haired, slim, very attractive lady who obviously kept herself fit. She was actually training for a marathon at the time and had already run several. It was pretty clear to me that Nancy approved of the way I looked; she started beaming. If only she had known about the dark companion I carried with me. Would it have made any difference?

We pleasantly chatted in the living room, finding out about each other, me petting Meg, until Fred came home from his work. He met me with an enthusiastic grin and a handshake.

During dinner, it became clear again that Judy and I shared many interests: the outdoors, reading, music, her petiteness complementing my tallness. At the time I was mostly running a landscaping business, but everyone knew I was looking to get back into teaching. No one knew at the time that it would take over five years, however.

Fred and I met for lunch later, man to man. He told me he didn't really care who I was—he'd never seen Judy so happy. He expressed thanks for my education as a bonus.

Fred is a famous figure in the world of genetics, both through his deeds and his extraordinary editing skills. His credentials often brought him invitations to reside as a guest at universities around the world. In fact, Fred had accepted a guest position at the University of Girona, and he and Nancy would be departing in January, not to return until August. Therefore Judy's and my engagement would be significantly longer than our courtship.

We looked at several locations for the ceremony and found that Saturday, September 17, was open at the beautiful Lake Forest Park Civic Club, a semi-private facility on the very north tip of Lake Washington. The grounds, clubhouse, and dock were first rate, and I had many splendid memories of growing up, playing, boating, and celebrating at this popular facility.

During the months before the wedding, Judy and I kept busy, me with my business and she with her graduate studies. She was finding the lab work a bit dry but enjoyed her teaching assistant work. The summer after we were married, she worked as a nutrition tech at Stevens Hospital, a possible precursor to her future career. She hated it. It was demanding yet boring, unrewarding, and draining, especially after the youth and vitality in the educational environment where she had always excelled. She so enjoyed working with students, expanding their minds and her own mind, and helping them to reach their potential. She came to the realization that she was born to be a teacher.

Judy did not return to her graduate studies. Instead, she enrolled at a community college to take prerequisite classes that would allow her to reenroll in the UW secondary teaching program. She was going to become a science teacher.

The wedding itself was inexpensive, mainly because Judy catered it. She had worked at Larry's Market for many years, helping with catering, and was experienced in all aspects. She also recruited family and friends as servers. She even commissioned a friend to build a trellis, which he built at no cost and Judy painted. All this was occurring while I was working overtime, trying to finish a sprinkler system at the Garfield Library grounds in South Seattle in the late summer heat.

Statistically, September is a month of good weather in the Northwest, and the wedding had been planned as an outdoor event just feet from the Lake. But it clouded up and started thundering the night before. Although the club building had plenty of space in contingency, it would be so much better outdoors. I remember Judy wiping away tears that evening.

But the next day was clear; in fact, a washed-away clear, free of dust and haze. Rushing to finish my job that morning, I was finally done by mid-afternoon and on my way. I remember cleaning up fast and slipping into my tux. Then there were some pictures. As I suppose many weddings are, it was a blur of events.

The afternoon sky was a deep blue, as was the lake that day, surrounded by the still-summer greenery of grass, trees, and rhododendrons. Boats sported on the lake; the occasional seagull floated overhead.

The ceremony was very musical. Fred, also a semi-professional cellist, performed in a quartet, while my mother and a close family friend sang a duet. Judy's brother, Jeff, accompanied them on guitar. We had no control over the Kenmore Air Harbor, however, and part of mom's singing was drowned out by a loud seaplane takeoff. In the video, the camera zooms in on Mom, standing by the windowed clubhouse. Then she is drowned out. In the windows behind her, the reflection of the seaplane flows by. These memories are the type I had before OCD; my tormentor had faded away temporarily in all the excitement, activity, and nonstop presence of an audience. What a remedy—just get married every day!

That night we left for the Puyallup Fair, where we had rented a suite in the Red Lion. We saw the Beach Boys the next day. Judy had a small headdress of flowers she had worn during the ceremony that she wore all day long. I couldn't stop looking at it. It was a cheerful and pleasant day, sunny and warm once again.

From there we proceeded to Curlew Lake, a remote lake half a mile high in the Colville Range, popular during the summer. After Labor Day, there is a brief window of time—days, weeks sometime—when the weather can be sunny and perfect, the nights a little chilly, yes, but the summer crowds have fled. Is heaven crowded? We had the place practically to ourselves. The weather was sunny—not quite perfect, as the wind came up in the afternoons and rendered the lake unskiable—but there were plenty of sightseeing and hiking activities nearby to fill the gap.

We would return the following fall, our first anniversary, to an equally pleasant time. The year after, either Judy and I, or both, were teaching, so the September window closed—we could visit only during the busy season. We went less often until the arrival of our first daughter. Once both children had arrived, we went nearly every summer—sometimes twice. It was, and still is, a place to forget about our troubles. Even better, it's a place that has changed very little, an eddy in the backwaters of time, where childhood memories are undiminished.

But life is about troubles, just as much as it is about happiness. Can you have one without the other? Can you have the appreciation and perspective on one without the other? My happiness with Judy was tempered by the secret of my OCD that I hid from her. Sharing my house in close quarters with my housemate, Eugene, had conditioned me well to keep my symptoms mostly out of sight. Additionally, one tends to overlook, or even be blinded to, another person's peculiarities and struggles when you first fall in love.

Eventually, Judy noticed some quirks. I had developed a small tic: I looked to the side quickly to move bad thoughts out of my line of sight and leave them on the outside of my vision. And of course it had to be redone a "good" number of times—never just once. By the time I reached a "good" number, a bad image would reappear again, straight ahead, right where I had originally been looking. And then it was back to square zero.

If I was alone, my head could look like a weather vane in a crazy wind. Around Judy I would dampen the motion, but I could not always stop it. She asked me about this more than once, and I passed it off as a habit of cracking a chronically sore neck. Boy, was it chronically sore! I would eventually seek chiropractic treatment for my constantly abused neck.

I was never a light-switcher or a hand-washer, but I was a doorknob turner. Our house, built in the 1940s, had old, rickety, round, stylized doorknobs. They had seen better days and rattled a bit. When opening or closing a door, I would often give them an extra turn or three. I never got into counting the turns much—it was more an OCD manifestation in which, if I didn't wiggle the handle, it just didn't feel right. It felt as if something bad was going to happen if the door wasn't shut "just so."

When a man gets married, domestic life becomes much more important. Suddenly the house needs to be cleaned more often. The garage needs to be kept more organized. Projects appear and must be done—from fixing items in the house to remodeling, from weeding to new landscaping. There's more laundry to do, dishes to clean, cars to maintain. Many men don't take as well to the extra domestic duties, but they make up for it by performing projects that improve the house and yard as a whole. Before Judy and I eventually sold the house, we had remodeled the kitchen, bathroom, and laundry room, repainted the house, installed new electric and plumbing, and had completely landscaped the front and back yards, including installing irrigation systems.

This occurred over five years, from about fall of 1988 to the fall of 1993, when we sold the house. During this time, Judy noticed my lack of speed when it came to completing projects. My quality of work was very good, but it seemed to Judy I progressed far too slowly. If only she'd known all the times I had to take things apart and put them back together "properly" when I was rewiring and replumbing the house, for example. Even getting started could be dreadful, meaning the beginning of a tedious OCD-filled task. I could have redone the plumbing in a few days, but it took me weeks.

In contrast, Judy was a monster worker. She could perform hard labor twelve to sixteen hours a day when she really got rolling. I remember she repainted the house in a weekend, staying up late and finishing a job in two days that would have taken me two weeks. Her ability to focus on her work plus her phenomenal physical condition put her into the mechanical category. Yes, Judy was a machine. And it frustrated her that her smart, talented husband seemed to have defective gearing when it came to completing projects in a timely fashion.

And yet, when it came to planning for long Scout hikes or embarking on other recreational activities or practicing my karate, I *could* be a machine. Over the years, Judy came to the firm conclusion that I could selfishly knock out projects I liked in a hurry, whereas jobs such as tiling the bathroom were way back on my list of other priorities, such as sleep and leisure. Technically, she was right. And at times I would agree with her. I didn't want to spend my life tiling the bathroom—I would rather go waterskiing. And I didn't understand why she didn't share these priorities. I would think that the girl I proposed to had shared them. We'd had so much fun together early on, taking trips, hiking, camping, waterskiing, or just sitting down and reading together.

Where had this girl gone? She was still there—it's just that we now lived together and had set some goals to progress through life, both vocationally and financially. My inability to work well was in direct contrast to Judy's ability to put things into overdrive. She *enjoyed* work—maybe a little too much at times, I thought. I felt it was called "work" for a reason. It never completely occurred to me that work could be a pleasure. I would blame the boredom of work for inducing OCD attacks, never using the more subtle reasoning that I could enjoy the work if there hadn't been the OCD.

What I failed to realize was that a job well done and *quickly* done can be a pleasure to perform. Scouting was a place where my OCD was subordinate to the pleasure it gave me, whereas tiling the bathroom (which we had ripped out down to the water-logged joists), provided me with the most intricate opportunities for OCD attacks. It was bad enough putting the tiles up—and taking them back down sometimes, if a bad thought came into my head while setting them—but I am also a perfectionist. If the tiles weren't perfectly in place, if there was the slightest misalignment, I would have to do them over. I figured if the job didn't look professional, I had no business doing it. We were looking to sell the house eventually, after all.

Most every job that involved manual labor also involved OCD. Simply starting a job involved OCD. I was not fully conscious of this at the time; I merely hated such work and felt I was wasting my life when I could be doing other things, such as beachcombing.

Later—much later—I found that any job done efficiently (without rituals, my mind focused on the task at hand) could provide a focused, accomplished feeling.

Once I was "cured," the after-effects persisted. I was still slow to start jobs. I believe that the physical part of me remembered the bad feelings that used to accompany such work, and at times it still slows me down.

The reason I could perform jobs I liked or activities I loved efficiently is that they kept my mind occupied and focused, and that the OCD was largely out of the picture. It wasn't just an escape from doing work; it was an escape from my OCD.

Although Judy and I had accomplished a lot together, we had also in many ways grown apart. I wanted the affection she had given me early in our marriage, but she always seemed too busy to have much time for it. In my mind it seemed she had plenty of time and that she simply didn't want to, or she was upset at my expressed desires. In Judy's mind, I think, she was taking up the slack I couldn't fill in—and she was right. At the time, I couldn't. And in the classic OCD pattern, I didn't feel I could tell her why. It's frustrating but true that you can never adequately perceive another person's mind.

Something kept us together, however. An unspoken depth of feeling always seemed to be present, which inevitably led to us getting along splendidly at times. We were never completely happy with the other, but we both felt strongly enough about our commitment and the apparent strength of our bond to want children. We had finished our schooling, obtained jobs in the Snohomish School District—I had renewed my credentials and was now a full-time teacher as well—and built a new house to live in. This process had been slow but steady, and after eight years of marriage we became parents of a very cute little girl.

Callie was a "good" baby. She slept reasonably well, and, per Judy's wishes, co-slept with us. A crib with an open side was attached to Judy's side of the bed, where she could reach over and feed Callie during the night as well as hold her close in our bed. It was extremely convenient, and, as Judy had hoped, and a bonding time for her and Callie. Since Judy still worked full-time as a teacher, Callie spent time with a sitter during the day. Although our sitter was kind, nurturing, and experienced with infants, Judy missed Callie greatly during the day, and this nighttime bonding opportunity meant a great deal to her—and to Callie, I am sure.

Judy *had* to work. Our large house had strained our financial limits, and there was no question we both had to work full time to afford it. We had painted ourselves into a financial corner. What made this especially hard on Judy was that she had been able to stay at home with Callie for the first six months. Callie had been born in April, and Judy had enough family leave time accumulated to last her until summer break—at which time she was free anyway. Judy found it extremely difficult to return to work. In hindsight, she was a great teacher following a higher calling, so she has had no long-term regrets about her decision, but that does not remedy the tearing away she felt at the time.

The stress was great on both of us. And when it came to helping with new chores, baby changing, and so on, my OCD made no distinction on the type of chores it made me underperform in. Judy felt she had less and less time for me, and at times I felt she had no time at all. And there is one very important point to remember as we passed these critical months: *I still didn't even know what OCD was.*

Still, we managed to keep ourselves entertained and rejuvenated at times. Before Callie's birth, we had made many trips to the San Juan Islands (where Judy's parents had a cabin with a breathtaking view), Desolation Sound (my parents had a large motor yacht), and hiked and camped extensively.

Judy enjoyed going on my nine-day, high-adventure hikes with me and the Scouts, although this was tempered after her third nine-day hike. We had camped in heavy rain one night, and every mouse in the forest seemed to find the shelter of our tarp preferable to that of flooded burrows. Mice were squeaking and skittering everywhere; quite often they would run right over your face or hair. The Scouts hatched plots to dispose of the mice that very evening. Snares, knifings, pits filled with gasoline to be lit after mice fell into them, smashing with rocks and beheadings were just a few of the options extensively discussed. Judy, a great lover of all animals, actually burst into tears and swore she would participate further on hikes with me only if we slept separately from these young savages.

A great athlete, Judy enjoyed skiing and waterskiing with me, and quickly caught up to me skill-wise. She was the only woman I'd ever had a relationship with that enjoyed such things—and could keep up with me.

Callie became part of our outdoor lifestyle. Although Judy could no longer go on the extended hikes with me, Callie was present at nearly all outings, even riding along in the boat (in her car seat, life vest included) when we waterskied. There were very few activities we did where Callie couldn't come along. Not only was her presence important, but we hoped to condition her to the great outdoors, instilling a joy of being active. And, over the years, she has become quite a participant and contestant in many sports and activities. Judy and I take great pride in being a part of Callie's outdoor education.

One of the main factors in raising Callie was our gift of time. Both being schoolteachers, we had extra time together with her during some parts of the year. On the other hand, during the school year itself, time was limited—we had grading and planning to do on weekends, and school days could be hectic with caring for Callie, my Scouting and karate, and Judy's running.

As Judy recovered from her pregnancy, she entered the most competitive running phase of her life, training extensively and running many 10Ks and half marathons, competing very success-fully. Her goal was to run the Portland Marathon in less than three hours, and a coach she worked with thought she might even have a shot at the Olympic trials. Judy ran extensively—seventy to eighty miles a week. Her fitness level was becoming incredible; she was running half marathons at a 2:48 marathon pace, and it seemed assured she would reach her goal of a sub-three-hour marathon easily when the time came. She worked her tail off and ran and ran and ran.

During the school year, especially with our respective training and activity levels, it seemed like we had almost no spare time at all. This was a period when Judy and I found it easy to grow apart.

Our common denominator was Callie, and she took a lot of time—worthwhile time, of course—but it cut that much more into the time Judy and I had once spent together on our own. Even though Judy's running consumed much of her time and I resented her putting it before me at times, I have to confess that race days were very exciting. I was Judy's support man, and I drove her, cheered for her, and found it exciting that she was so competitive.

In October 1998, Judy ran the Portland Marathon. Although she had developed a mild case of plantar fasciitis, it seemed to be under control and responded well to icing and ibuprofen. It was an exciting time for everyone. In many of Judy's longer races, I was able to watch her go by three or four times, moving and reparking my car, leapfrogging ahead of her to cheer her on. During this race, I cheered her on at the 10K point; she ran the first 10K in about 38 minutes—a perfect pace. I saw her again at the halfway point: her first half was around 1:25. She looked strong. What I didn't know was that her plantar fascia was starting to bother her. At the twenty-mile mark, I held out an energy bar to her, but she felt so strong, she waved me off.

Past twenty miles at a race pace, a runner's reserves of blood sugar can run out within a matter of seconds. This is the "wall" marathoners have to contend with. In hindsight, Judy regretted not grabbing that bar—she "hit the wall" at about twenty-one miles. She also was in severe pain; her plantar fascia had either torn or become severely inflamed. She had to walk for about a mile to recover enough to run the rest of the race.

I was at the finish line. I had been waiting since the 2:45 mark, expecting her to come in sometime soon after 2:50. The minutes came and went. Where was she? The three-hour mark passed. Something was wrong. At 3:07, Judy jogged in, crossed the finish, and started limping badly. Still an impressive performance.

Judy had injured herself badly. She was unable to run for six months afterward. To go from such a high level of training to a forced little or none is extremely frustrating, both physically and mentally. Judy needed to run to stay happy; she needed an outlet for her tremendous drive. And now her life of the past eighteen months had abruptly stopped. This put further stress on both of us, as I could not provide Judy with what she was now missing—her running and the camaraderie she had developed with so many of her running friends. Fortunately, Callie was developing into a toddler and gave Judy many opportunities to expend her energy and time as Callie became more active, fun, and demanding. In fact, our lives seemed busier than ever.

I began to feel constantly fatigued. In years past, I could do reasonably well on less sleep than I liked, but something changed when Callie was born. Many people have more trouble sleeping as they enter their forties, and I had always had trouble since I was a child. Largely unknowingly, I was losing my ability to sleep at all.

I have to confess that in one way the co-sleeping worked in my favor, since I did not have to go retrieve a crying baby from a nursery—certainly an exercise in sleep deprivation for many fathers. But Callie's presence in the bed, especially as she passed one year of age, became a space and activity issue. I was constantly being woken up and was unable to fully go back to sleep. Sometimes when this happened, I would lie in bed, often obsessing quietly to myself about just how few hours were left until the alarm was now going to ring. If I woke up at 2:00 a.m., I knew that alarm was going to ring at 5:30, and it would set my mind flying about, me lying awake the entire time, knowing how exhausted I would be the next day.

More often I'd fall asleep—or think I had. Then I would hover at the edge of dreams, never quite dropping into restful sleep, half dozing the night away, semiconscious that the least movement or cry from Callie would wake me up again.

CHAPTER 14

Treating It, Beating It

As Callie approached two years old, she still shared the bed with us, disrupting my sleep even more. I went through a period of about three months when I lost the ability to sleep effectively at all. I remember week after week of dozing, dragging myself out of bed, working, not being able to rest on weekends, stuck into a mode where I made myself function. Inwardly, however, my reserves were nearly gone. During this time, only my martial arts training allowed me to continue on; I relied on the ability to draw my reserves down to the last drop, not listening to my body, using my mind to override all signals of distress.

What Judy saw was a man gradually becoming a zombie at home. I was less and less effective at helping out and was distant, having expended all my energy at work. I remember receiving the occasional comment at my late Monday-night Scout meetings that I looked tired. No wonder. On Mondays I would work, then run down to Seattle for my karate workout, then speed over to my Scout meeting, which went from 7:30 until 9:00 p.m. Then, I had a forty-five-minute drive to get home, at which time Judy and Callie would likely be in bed asleep. And, finally, I took sixty minutes or so to drop off, which in my case meant dozing off, not really resting at all.

In January 1999 I had a bout of bronchitis. It lasted several weeks and pushed me deeper into fatigue. Due to chronic allergies and a "sick" workplace, I'd had great trouble kicking it. The science building I worked in was later found to have a saturated, leaky roof infested with mold.

To top things off, I had been weight training in our home gym four hours a week, working to get stronger, trying to fatigue myself to the point of forcing sleep to come naturally. The strength was increasing more gradually than it should have been; I was in fact overtraining, unable to recover properly. My fuel supply was leaking from all points imaginable.

Somehow, on the morning of Saturday, February 27, 1999, I had dropped into a deep sleep for the first in quite some time. I remember this because our co-sleeping girl needed changing, and it was my turn. It was about six in the morning. Judy roused me, and I started to come up from the beautiful depths I had visited. And I briefly realized I could return to them if I just refused to respond. But it was my turn and my duty. I could not tell Judy how I was feeling—again, I hid the effects of my mental state from her.

Dragging myself into consciousness from this state was one of the most painful and difficult things I have ever done physically; it would not have been possible without my martial arts training. Little did I know it was my body's last warning to do something. I was swimming up through molasses. I slowly got up, took Callie into the bathroom, and changed her. I put her back with Judy and dropped back onto the bed.

But the moment had passed. I could not return to the place I had been. I was floating on top of the molasses, stuck to it, back in my restless dozing. I remember no other detailed aspects of that weekend, other than a half-aware state of mind that stretched into the dread of returning to work Monday.

On Monday, March 1, I came out of my doze and could not move. I literally could not get up out of the bed. Invisible bonds seemed to be holding me down; I could barely raise my head. I'd never had such a sensation before. It was like one of those dreams where you feel awake but are completely paralyzed. The alarm clock radio was giving its talk-show chatter. It was time to get up.

Unlike the previous Saturday, my body was through trying to convince me. It had thrown a last-resort safety switch. And yet I've always believed the mind has the final say. I'd always been able to function at the survival level one way or another. I wondered if—deep down, at the uttermost depths—my soul itself had finally taken over and said, "Enough."

"Dave!" came Judy's voice from downstairs. She would usually get up half an hour earlier than I to get herself ready for the day. Other days she would rise earlier still and work out before everyone else was up. Often Callie would be awake at this point, and Judy would need help changing and feeding and dressing her—or merely keeping track of her. Judy always took Callie to the sitter in the morning, as she had first-period prep; she didn't have to jump right into a class first thing in the morning. Plus, this added to her morning "Mommy time."

"Dave, are you up?" Louder this time, in case I was still dozing.

I couldn't answer. I made an effort to move again. Nothing doing. Apparently I was going to conserve my energy, no matter what I wished to do. The problem was, I couldn't really rest. I felt anxious, panicky, my mind racing. Is this what bound human sacrifices felt like? At least their troubles would soon be over. I could feel a thought racing around and around in my head: somehow, I had become some sort of invalid. I was going to lose my job and never be able to support my family, much less myself, for the rest of what could become a long, tortuous life.

I could hear Judy walking up the stairs to our bedroom. If she found me still in the bed, wasting precious before-school time, she was not going to be happy. But I just lay there at this point, without even the strength to struggle.

Not a happy voice: "I really need some help here." Then, seeing my condition (I must have looked quite ill), "Are you OK?"

I'll have to admit my usually clear memory continues its fogginess at this point. I know Judy was concerned—both about me and about the consequences of my nonfunctionality. I think she helped me to get out of bed and walk to the bathroom to relieve myself. Then she assisted me back to collapse on the covers.

I did not know what was wrong. Neither did Judy. But she did know I couldn't work if I couldn't move. She called in a substitute for me. And she had to get Callie to the sitter and herself to work. "I'll check on you later," she said, flustered.

"Better leave the phone by the bed," I muttered.

I suppose you could call what I was experiencing a nervous breakdown. My body seemed incapable of functioning, of responding to my will. The involuntary had overridden the voluntary, but my mind was intact—unfortunately.

There's an old saying about being caught between the hammer and the anvil. Both with my lesser breakdown back in college and this completely incapacitating one, imaginary and real fears stacked on each other, working with each other to spiral my OCD out of control.

In both cases there was an underlying fear of getting sick or images having to do with sickness projected my mind. In my earlier years of OCD, I had learned to live with it, to coexist with it, to function with it. In college, the real fear of failure had put me into a repetitious state, counting images of failing and passing—a rational fear placed into the realm of irrationality by my OCD. I remember an all-nighter pulled on this one.

But this wasn't college anymore. And though I thought I had been cured of the worst of the OCD anxieties, they suddenly rushed back in full force, my mental shield from them broken down by an obsession that I was going to lose my job.

My OCD kicked itself into a gear I had not thought possible anymore, rivaling if not surpassing the episode during my calculus class back in college. The anxiety was tremendous. I'd forgotten just how anxious I could be. In that past case, a threat to my future had triggered the overwhelming anxiety. In this case, I was living that future—and about to lose it all, from what it seemed. Back in college, I could still move, call my parents, drive, feed myself. Now I was totally helpless.

The fear of losing my job would not stop banging around the inside of my skull. What was really wrong with me? Had I come down with a horrible disease? I tried to think optimistic thoughts, but as quickly as I pushed one through, a bad one would follow. I found myself counting good thoughts and bad thoughts in my head, lapsing back into the tortuous internal rituals I had experienced in years past, using small movements of my eyes to provide the physical sensation of keeping track of good and bad numbers.

I couldn't move, couldn't sleep, couldn't stop. I was resting, but this was only a stopgap. I really needed to sleep.

All that Monday I lay in bed, physically resting as I had not done in quite some time. No work, no kid, no workout—a sense of resignation, but of relief too. I was able to doze off some, a time free from my obsessions. About midday I felt well enough to call and make an appointment with my family doctor for the next day. *This is great,* I thought cynically. *All I have to do is sleep all day instead of working, and my life might be really good.* I knew this wouldn't fly for me, my wife, or my growing family. *If I could just sleep,* I thought

The next day, Tuesday March 2, I saw my family doctor. The office was only a fifteen-minute drive from home—doable even in my exhausted state. A medium-sized one-story clinic, it contained a full complement of medical resources with many doctors, nurses, and assistants who maintained a cheerful atmosphere.

Dr. Owens listened to my story. I concentrated mostly on my inability to sleep and also mentioned my obsessions, which I felt had been mostly under control since my first course of treatment. I asked him what he thought I needed.

"I think you need a good night's sleep," he replied.

Again, at this point I had never heard of obsessive-compulsive disorder, and had no idea I suffered from it; if I had, I would have had little clue how many others suffered from it too. The Obsessive Compulsive Disorder Foundation had been created a relatively short time before, in 1986, and much information about the disease, including effective treatments, had only recently been discovered. Jeffrey M. Schwarz's groundbreaking OCD treatment book, "Brain Lock," had been published merely three years before. It was a book I would soon become familiar with.

Here is an extract from Dr. Owen's notes from that appointment:

He complains of persistent fatigue and malaise. This flared up when he had an episode of bronchitis in early January. Those symptoms have essentially resolved. He has had a chronic sleep disturbance for a number of months. This relates to his two-year-old daughter generally sleeping with Dave and his wife, nursing during the night. Dave wakes up frequently and has a hard time getting back to sleep. Prolonged sleep latency has actually been a lifelong issue for him.

Usually he does well with seven or eight hours of sleep at night. He estimates recently he is sleeping about four hours per night consistently and does not feel rested in the morning. He remains quite active, works out two to four days per week, which might include running for seven miles or so. Recently his workouts have not felt good and he feels less restored. He is still having a number of rest days in his schedule.

He does not feel he is depressed. He has recognized a tendency toward obsessive-compulsive behavior for a long time, but feels he manages with that okay. He is not seeking specific treatment for that. He does not feel sick in other respects.... He appears tired, otherwise well. Affect somewhat anxious.

Of particular note is the term *obsessive compulsive.* I knew I was a person who often became obsessed, but I had not gone into the details of my ritualizations with the doctor. I only related my chronic worries and the images and thoughts that often would not leave my mind—most of those pertained to me losing my job.

Dr. Owens prescribed me some Restoril, a powerful sleep medication to help me sleep in the short term. I was to check back in two weeks after I had got some rest.

On March 3 I went to school, having not worked for two days. Although the Restoril didn't seem to put me to sleep very well, my fatigue had somewhat diminished. But by the end of the day I was once again exhausted. I left a plan for a substitute on my desk just in case and headed home to crash on the bed.

Once again, that night I slept poorly. The Restoril seemed to have little effect on me. During the night, realizing I was going to be lucky to sleep at all, I called in sick and determined to see Dr. Owens again as soon as possible.

On March 4 (a far cry from two weeks), Dr. Owens was unavailable, but Dr. Jacobs, my other main doctor, familiar with my history, was present. My blood tests had come back normal, and this time we talked in depth about what had been occurring in my mind all those years. Once again, the doctor's notes are informative:

> Several week history of increased anxiety, fatigue and insomnia. Long history of intermittent insomnia. Probable history of OCD and anxiety disorder. Course of Alprazolam (Xanax) about 10 years ago but no regularly scheduled anxiolytics in the intervening time. Factors include job stress and 2-year-old daughter who sleeps in bed with he and his wife. Recent evaluation by Dr. Owens including labs which were within normal limits.

> Anxious male sitting without difficulty. He easily carries on a conversation without difficulty. No atypical thought content, homicidal or suicidal ideation presented.

> 1. INSOMNIA.
> 2. ANXIETY DISORDER.
> 3. PROBABLE OBSESSIVE-COMPULSIVE DISORDER.

> (Prescribed) Paxil 20mg …alprazolam .25mg for short-term use while Paxil begins working for him. Handout on sleep disorders and children. I strongly recommend that the child be moved out of their bedroom into her own bedroom in the immediate future. Follow up with Dr. Owens for a recheck, sooner p.r.n. any problems.

For the first time in my life, I had heard the term obsessive-compulsive disorder!

Newer drugs like Prozac, Paxil, and Celexa were useful against the symptoms of OCD, suppressing both the impulses and anxieties that accompanied them. After a few days, I could literally feel the Paxil slowing down my "busy mind" in the background—that wild, tossing sea at the edge of my consciousness.

Since the Restoril wasn't working, the doctors re-attacked the anxiety, putting me back on the Xanax, which did help considerably. It once again helped me sleep and function with less anxiety during the day. I was also prescribed rest for an additional day—Friday. With the weekend, I was expected to be able to catch up on my rest. In the long term, my finally identified disorder would probably require long-term treatment, I was informed.

Callie was able to understand her need for separate sleeping arrangements, but wasn't happy about it. Our bedroom has a large walk-in closet where we put down a mattress and some bedding for her. She would sleep about five feet from us, but behind a wall. It took several nights for her to settle into sleeping without crying herself to sleep, but, when she realized crying wasn't going to work, she settled into a craftier pattern. She waited until we were asleep and then quietly push the folding closet door open; soon she would be snuggled up against Mommy again. Callie would gradually pressure herself further into the bed, and this would wake me up. My kind wife, to help me sleep, would wake up and quietly put Callie back into her bed, sometimes even snuggling with her on the floor.

Preventive measures were attempted. I tried putting a forty-five-pound dumbbell at the fulcrum of the folding door, but she soon learned to brace herself against shelves and quietly push the door open with her legs. I thought about cutting a board to brace the door, but then I thought that might be going a bit too far. Fortunately, Callie developed a sleep pattern in her little room, and everyone was able to sleep.

The next week I was able to teach on Monday and Tuesday. Although I was sleeping better, I would often wake up during the night to take more Xanax. Although the drug acted quickly, it also wore off quickly—in about four hours. With very low on energy again, I left sub plans for Wednesday, planning to consult with the doctor on my prescription again.

On Wednesday, Dr. Owens read my file and prescribed Clonapen, an antianxiety/antidepressant with a longer action than Xanax. He hoped this prescription would allow me to sleep through the night.

About this time I turned to my brother, Dr. Steve Dahlberg. Steve was a family practitioner who had suffered debilitating severe depressive and obsessive thoughts himself, and he had been through counseling and treatment. Steve approved of the treatment I was receiving and lent me a copy of a book that had greatly helped him—Dr. Jeffrey Schwartz's *Brain Lock*. I only skimmed the book at first, reading with amazement the various manifestations of OCD. But I did not spend much time going through the cognitive therapy sessions. At the moment, I was glad to know I was not alone and I was receiving reasonably effective treatment.

I taught Thursday and took Friday off on the doctor's advice, to build up a three-day reserve of rest. Although I had taken four days off the previous week and two more that week, I was gaining strength, no longer losing it. I would not take another sick day for the next two months—and that day off was due to a virus, not sleep deprivation.

On Tuesday, March 16, I went in after school for a follow-up. Here are the doctor's notes:

PROBLEM: Followup sleep problems and OCD.

He returns for plan followup. Overall he is feeling considerably better. I started him at one mg at h.s. and he is also taking Xanax .25 mg at h.s. and Paxil has been increased again to 20 mg daily. He is tolerating this well and symptoms are somewhat improved as well. He has been sleeping away from his daughter and she is starting to sleep through the night pretty consistently also.

He appears comfortable, more relaxed. Affect still moderately anxious.

Improved.

Continue current medications. Recheck in one month, consider dose-adjustment of the Paxil at that time. He may be able to stop the alprazolam and he can experiment with that. Both alprazolam and Klonopin (alternate spelling) are refilled to 30 tablets. He has also quit caffeine which is good.

One month later, I was sleeping better than I ever had in my life. It felt very strange to be able to drop off to sleep relatively quickly and to wake up feeling rested. One small problem had started to supplant my sleeping and OCD issues, however. Doctor Owens noted at the March 16 appointment:

He returns for a planned followup. He is continuing Paxil 20mg daily and Klonopin 1 mg and Xanax during the night. He sleeps well with these medicines and is not sleeping during the daytime. Paxil seems considerably helpful with his depression and OCD symptoms. He is bothered by persistent delayed ejaculation, often simply unable to complete intercourse.

DEPRESSION AND OBSESSIVE COMPULSIVE DISORDER. Klonopin is refilled 1 mg #30. I told him I would speak with one of the specialists about alternate medication to Paxil which would minimize sexual side effect; I have now done so, and will switch from Paxil to Celexa (Citolapram) 20 mg daily with recheck in one month.

The sexual side effects disappeared, and with the new medication I continued to improve in my day-to-day living and in my sleeping at night. Although the OCD thoughts and images still appeared in my mind, they did not affect me nearly as much— although I still shunned projects that gave me alone time.

I finished the school year with good energy and sleeping well, yet with frustration that my OCD symptoms and my anxieties were subdued but still present. Doctor Owens noted on June 15:

FOLLOWUP OCD

He returns for a medication review. He is on Celexa, Xanax and Klonopin per the flow sheet. Overall he is considerably better. His chronic obsessive symptoms are improved, although not resolved. He feels he is functioning well, sleep is much better with the benzodiazepines in the evening. He notes no significant side effects of the medication, in particular, no sexual disfunction on the Celexa.

He appears well. Affect is still fairly anxious.

OBSESSIVE COMPULSIVE DISORDER. We talked again about how these medications worked and long-term treatment actions. I think he should plan on some form of treatment long-term. He may be able to gradually come down on the benzodiazepines, for example he might be able to use Klonopin alone and stop the Xanax. For the time being, however, his prescriptions are refilled and continued. Also suggested increasing Celexa to 40 mg daily and he will do so, and report results by phone or in person in about a month.

As the year progressed, I found medicines that work in the short term do not always pan out. You develop a tolerance to them, or your OCD finds a way around; it could be different manifestations, or undesirable side effects, such as one I had already experienced. Dr. Owens noted on November 10,

Is concerned about his psychotropic medicine and ongoing sleep trouble. Celexa 20 mg has given reasonable but not terrific control of his OCD symptoms. At a higher dose he had delayed erections which was a problem. With Klonopin at 1 mg plus Xanax at .25 mg he has started to have more fragmented sleep again. He suspects he has become tolerant to the Klonopin. His brother, who is a physician, mentioned trazodone or amitriptylene as possibilities. Other medicines reviewed per flow sheet.

He appears well,...Affect is mildly anxious. Not depressed....

OCD with ongoing sleep problems. We discussed options and agreed to add trazodone 50 mg (at night) titrating for effectiveness without daytime sedation. Ideally this would allow tapering of his benzodiazepines. He will report results by phone or in person in about a month.

Steve told me one advantage of Trazadone is that you don't build a tolerance to it; I had definitely built a resistance to the Klonopin and the Xanax. Indeed, once we had worked into an effective dose of Trazadone, it became permanently effective. I was able to stop taking the Xanax except on occasions when I woke up in the middle of the night, which was not often anymore.

My conundrum was with the Celexa. I had built a tolerance toward its control on my OCD. Higher doses were required, which disrupted my sexual function.

At this point I took another look at *Brain Lock*. Obsessive-compulsive disorder can be treated using three different combinations: drugs alone, drugs in combination with cognitive therapy, or cognitive therapy alone. In many cases, including mine, anxiety is OCD's main weapon. My cognitive therapy involved tackling this anxiety head-on.

Ironically, effectively dealing with OCD on a cognitive basis involves *increasing* the anxiety. A bad thought comes, but instead of performing a ritual as an immediate response, I delayed it, and during the delay, my anxiety increased. I was not "protecting" myself by giving in to the compulsion right away. I started out with delays of one minute, and these small delays were a big step in the right direction.

This is how I began. One of the worst places for OCD to hit was on the drive to my job at school. It seemed that every twist and turn in the rural road would somehow generate a new thought. As soon as I had ritualized one away, a change of scenery would trigger another. My rituals in the car were limited to tapping fingers, turning my head slightly, moving my eyes back and forth—all to a count of good and bad numbers to "count in" good thoughts. I could spend the entire drive exhausting myself mentally.

Although my car was a bad place for OCD, it became a good place for defeating it. When a bad thought, feeling, or image came in, I would make myself wait one minute, using the clock on my car, before I would give in to the compulsion. At first, even a one-minute delay would spike my anxiety greatly, as the fear of something bad happening if I didn't perform my ritual tormented me. But even at first I found great satisfaction in putting off the compulsion. After a few days, I was able to double my wait time—two minutes. Again my anxiety spiked with the extra time, but so did the relief and satisfaction on the defeat—though temporary—of my OCD compulsions.

Two minutes, five minutes, ten—as the weeks went by, I was able to increase the delay. As the anxiety decreased per new time interval, I would increase my delays further.

There came a day when I delayed a compulsion for ten minutes. I became distracted by the news on my car radio, and fifteen minutes later I realized I had forgotten to do a ritual entirely. I did not use delay therapy strictly in the car, by the way. It soon branched out to include all times, all situations, from home to the many activities in which I participated.

Minutes stretched into hours—I would now wait until lunch until I would allow myself to ritualize, and I allow myself just a few minutes to do so. If a few minutes wasn't enough, it would be put off yet another hour or two.

I got to the point where my obsessions seemed to separate from my rituals. I would perform a ritual two hours later and it would seem silly and unnecessary. At times, I would even force myself to perform them. By this point, I was performing only a single ritual; they were no longer spiraling out of control. Once I had reached this point, I progressed to rescheduling my rituals indefinitely.

Eventually, I had conditioned my body out of nearly all the anxiety response to my OCD and out of reacting to it. And, "nearly" is where I stayed. Obsessive-compulsive disorder never goes away; there are always nagging thoughts and fears. But with its energy source—the rituals—cut off, it no longer had power over me. It could be ignored. Yes, I still have thoughts and images that whirl around my head, but they come and go now; they have no staying power.

Cognitive therapy is not merely a conditioning of your mind or spirit; it is literally reprogramming your brain to stop its unnecessary fight-or-flight response to OCD impulses. Performing compulsions only reinforces fight-or-flight chemistry. Once the rituals are stopped, the disproportionate fight-or flight reactions stop too. You have literally changed your brain chemistry back to a more normal pattern.

Usually with the help of antianxiety drugs, people can find good success with cognitive therapy—even stopping drug use entirely after a time. Others need the combination. Statistically, the combination of cognitive therapy and some medication provides the greatest success.

My own case is interesting. I have ended up taking very little of the Celexa, dropping back to 5 mg, technically not a significant dose. But it seems to take just enough of the edge off. My OCD has essentially been eliminated. My real issue is that I simply cannot sleep without medication. In one sense, I cope with OCD largely with my cognitive training alone. But I'll never be able to sleep without help.

Occasionally, I will sit down with my doctor and review my medications, but they have been unchanged for years now. In this memo, Dr. Owens notes the pattern I have settled into comfortably for years, noting both my physical and mental condition:

CMR ENTRY followup anxiety disorder

Here for planned follow-up and review and renewal of his medications. Overall he feels that he is doing well. He is on Citolapram (Celexa) 10mg daily (5 mg for years now), clonazepam (Klonopin) 10 mg daily, trazadone 150 mg (all medications taken at bedtime), and uses alprazolam very rarely. He has occasional mild OCD symptoms, which he can manage successfully. Higher doses of citalopram have caused unacceptable sexual side effects. He sleeps well with the current regimen, but usually can't sleep without the clonazepam and trazodone. He has adhered to recommended dosing. Overall he is satisfied with the current treatment. Functioning well at home and at work. He exercises vigorously. Can sustain a heart rate of 180 without any chest discomfort.

Healthy-appearing. Weight is stable at 179. CMR blood pressure 128/78. Mood neutral. Doesn't appear anxious or drowsy.

OCD, doing fairly well with this regimen and it's reasonable to continue with phone refill of 3 months and office review at 6 months.

At his request we discussed pros and cons of routine cardiovascular screening such as treadmill test. Since his first profile is very low and he is fit and exercising intensively without symptoms, I think the likelihood of false positives doesn't really warrant testing in this case [I was forty-seven at this time, and continue to exercise to this day], although some would disagree. He seems to understand the risks and benefits and is satisfied with our current approach.

* * * * *

Nothing comes without a price, however. Dependence on sleep medication is a willing price I pay at this point. I have tried to stop taking it a few times over the years – and the result is always the same. The first time I attempted to get off of my medications was quite inadvertent – and quite cold turkey.

Coming into camp, deep in the Cascade Mountains on the first day of a five-day Scout hike in 2002, I realized I had forgotten to pack my sleep medication. There was no going back to get it. Although the hard exercise of the backpacking would help make me tired, I dozed fitfully the first night and woke up with a dizzy headache. I knew it wasn't going to be an easy day. By the time we made our next camp, I felt like I'd drunk twenty-three cups of coffee—twenty-two too many. Again, due to the hard workout and swallowing several Advil, I was able to doze somewhat.

Fortunately, the next day, it poured like hell. Lucky for me, we had built in some contingency time, and nobody minded waiting it out, staying dry, and playing cards under our tarps. I spent the day seeing and feeling fireworks go off inside my head, the aftershocks traveling down to my toes and back up again. I couldn't eat—I just lay there. I explained my situation to my other adult leader, Owen Oldfield, a senior Scout just turned adult, and he told the boys I had a touch of the flu. By evening, the worst of it was over. Another night of barely dozing and I was ready to move on.

By the end of the hike, I was completely free of the effects of the withdrawal. I knew my cognitive therapy could control my OCD at this point, so I thought, What the hell, I'll go without the medication and see what happens. My first night at home, I left it in a bathroom drawer—and spent the next three hours staring at the ceiling. No sleep. It might as well have been the middle of the day. Not good. I hadn't really slept in several days, and although I could tolerate a week or two of this insomnia, eventually it would debilitate me again. Resigned, I got up, took my medication, and went back to bed—easily falling into a restful, peaceful sleep.

CHAPTER 15

Beating the Compulsions

Compulsions are performed to force bad images and thoughts from the mind, to force away the accompanying anxiety.

Notice the term *force*. It took me a long time to realize that images *never forced* their way in. They just appeared, popping in vividly out of thin air. There was never a door I could hold shut, knowing an image was right behind. They came in like phantoms, sometimes there before I even realized it.

And yet the rituals were an attempt to use force to throw the images out. I used both mental and physical effort to perform them, often for extended periods and often exhausting myself.

And here's the key: The original thought or image did not force its way in; it just happened. Any attempt to use force—ritual or compulsion—reinforced the image.

Any attempt at forcing out an image *gives it more force to stay*. It's like pushing on a brick wall: the harder you push it, the harder it pushes back. It is immovable. You can lean ritual after ritual onto that wall, and it will never give way. You will only pile up more rituals, more anxiety, more frustration. The only way to lessen the image is to do nothing in return.

Any action of any kind directed at a bad thought or image will cause the thought to reinforce.

Cognitive therapy trains you to lessen your response—letting the images come without reacting to them. Not ritualizing, or not stopping what you are doing. *Bit by bit*—until the thoughts no longer control *you.*

Here's another example of delaying: I could take me feet off the floor to get into bed at 9:03 p.m. A bad thought or image comes into my head. Therefore the feet count back down and up, and hopefully the clock doesn't get to 9:04 during this time, which adds up to unlucky 13. I might not finish a proper count again until 9:12—12 being a good number.

What I started doing—*and it was hard at first, very hard*—was to tell myself I would get into bed without regard to the time or to bad thoughts. Then I would wait at least one minute—more as I became better at delaying—and then allow myself only half a minute of ritualizing before forcing myself back into bed. I was so sick of being a complete slave. But I had partially disrupted the feedback mechanism, and the break would lead to a smaller ritualization, or even (rarely at first) a cessation of the desire to ritualize at all.

This is the mind controlling the body and thus controlling the brain, where the conscious, nervous anxiety occurs. I could—the "I" that is the cold, detached observer in all of us—make myself not do something for at least a few minutes, no matter how jittery my body might feel.

In uncontrolled OCD, the emotional part of the mind gives in to the anxiety, *and the body has controlled the mind.* The decision to ritualize and the act of ritualizing are ultimately voluntary functions.

But the observer mind has ultimate control and can create delay after delay until delay becomes a habit. Then the delays can start to get longer. *The mind controls the body.*

There's an old saying in Zen: "The mind controls the body controls the mind." The mind steps out, recognizes it is separate from the body, and no longer allows the body to control its actions. The mind identifies itself as *separate* from OCD. Better yet, the OCD itself becomes identified as a separate object.

For me, stepping out was key. I eventually could step out far enough to say, "Well, that was silly," but the initial stepping out—starting with the first delays—was like casting off heavy chains. Pulling the mind away at first is exhausting, like extracting yourself from molasses. A martial arts analogy could be judo; at first it is very difficult to throw your opponent, but after a while it becomes easy and natural.

It became easy and natural for me to neutralize an OCD attack rather than easy and natural to have one.

Good thoughts, bad thoughts

I was once walking around Greenlake, a beautiful park in Seattle, and a tree with cascading orange blooms caught my eye. This generated a surge of pleasure and admiration, and I was flooded with a good feeling. And then something awful popped into my mind's eye, straight ahead—something I would have to look straight through to still see that tree. I don't remember what the image was. A surge of fear and adrenaline knocked the pleasure from my mind and body. And my eyes looked away from that image and that tree, the picture of the blossoms permanently tainted.

A nice thought or image, such as that beautiful tree, was often a strong enough stimulus to knock my ever-present fear and tension out of my system for a few moments, leaving a vacuum. There's an old saying that nature abhors a vacuum. Nature doesn't hold a candle to OCD. If there's a space for it to rush into, it will.

I would try to look back at the tree, but even if I saw it clearly, it would be only briefly and soon marred again by another image. And I would never recapture that initial good feeling that itself seemed to bring on the attack. Sadly, I would have to leave that tree behind.

But now I don't look away. This was my key. Look at the tree and act normally, even if the bad feelings come. Yes, I was looking through the bad image. But I did not let my eyes veer or my body participate in the OCD event. I do not concentrate hard on the tree, as that is another use of force that reinforces the OCD. I relax and enjoy the fact that I was not pushed around this time. Maybe I don't regain the initial good feeling, but I am one step closer. A big step closer.

The mind is a huge place; infinitely huge, some believe. It is not possible to block off or insulate every space in the mind from the effects of OCD. When you try to bury one image, the space next to it is still limitless. Infinity minus any number is still infinity.

But I had to realize that no matter how many bad images can pop into my mind, there are infinitely more images that are good. The problem is trying to concentrate on these good images. For me, diverting my thoughts to a good image took energy—required force—which further reinforced the feedback loop ingrained into my brain and nervous system.

I had to ignore the bad images, developing the confidence that the good ones would come.

CHAPTER 16

Moving Forward

CD runs in families. It and other depressive issues run both in my family and in my wife's. Callie, born in 1997, had some aggression and withdrawal issues as a young girl, but she did well with a few school accommodations. It is difficult to say whether she inherited much of anything.

When we had our second daughter, Elise, I was aware that she might inherit what her older sister had not. If OCD were not treatable, I'm not sure I would have wanted another child. As it was, I determined to watch her carefully for any signs of what I had presented early on—anxiety, depression, compulsions.

Many colicky babies like Elise do not manifest OCD later in life, but we could quickly tell a difference between Elise and Callie. Callie had been a good sleeper from the start. Elise spent her first thirty-six hours of life emitting high-pitched cries that drove my wife to the point of insanity. At two on the second sleepless night, Judy woke up my brother with a desperate phone call for help. Of course, Steve was the only physician we could reach on immediate notice. He immediately sympathized with Judy's late-night sleeplessness. I think he said something like, "Yes, Judy, babies do cry a lot."

Later that day, Elise finally stopped crying, allowing Judy to get some rest. The break was all too short. In just a few hours, Elise was rested enough to produce her sounds again.

Possibly the worst part about Elise's colic it seemed to come from a distance. First she would start to move. Then she would make intermittent, small growling noises. It was like a creaking door, slowly opening to admit a storm. Within two minutes she would be fully warmed up and shrieking again. There was no stopping her once the process began. Judy would offer to nurse her, and we would try rocking her and holding her, but to no avail. Just hearing the first peep would induce full stress, as the end result was inevitable. We had an automated baby swing that had always calmed Callie right down and stopped an oncoming fuss. It seemed only to amplify Elise's. When Elise was a month or two old, we got rid of the swing; clearly, no mechanical device was a match for her.

Judy would take Elise to get groceries, and Elise would cry, and people would come up to her and tell her "something is wrong with your baby" or "I think your baby is in pain." Judy has often speculated that Elise simply wanted to communicate better, and part of the tone of her crying was frustration at being unable to. Given her substantial vocal talent, we've also speculated she was just warming up for a future Broadway career.

Late that summer, the stress, the thought of going back to work, and her family history meant Judy developed post-partum depression. The descent was slow and gradual, but after a period of eighteen months it clearly hadn't tapered off—it was out of control. Judy lived inside a continuous black cloud. Once she received counseling and medication, she recovered her functionality and spirits over a matter of weeks. It was another positive statement that treatment can make such a difference. This meant that the two of us—Judy and me—could have provided depressive genes to our new offspring. And yet we both had been successfully treated.

As a toddler, Elise was a happy, well-adjusted child. Perhaps Judy's communication theory had some truth to it. Elise learned to talk early, and although she did not start reading earlier than normal, once she began, her skills shot up in a dramatic, well-above-normal rate. Elise tested with very high aptitudes.

Elise has insatiable curiosity. When she reads a book, be it picture or chapter, she constantly calls on us to explain the nuances of meaning. She is not satisfied with face value. One of her favorites was (and still is) Gary Larson's *The Far Side*, which exhibits both silliness and humor but also more subtle analogy. Reading *The Far Side* with Elise was an exercise in explaining every last scrap of humor present. She enjoyed adult-level humor and quickly learned the meaning of the word *irony*. By first grade, *irony* was one of her favorite words. As you can imagine, reading an entire Far Side book and dissecting each joke is an exhausting process. Recently Judy's mom made a request in regard to this: "Next time Elise spends the night at our house, could you not send a Far Side book along with her?"

She also enjoyed movies and shows with overt and subtle humor. Judy had bought me the entire *Monty Python Flying Circus* series as a Christmas present, and Elise soon grew to enjoy the finer points of British humor. She absorbed everything, but did not always understand the deeper meanings. She knew the meanings were there, however, and watching shows with her meant providing exact interpretations of the script. She had to know everything: where it was made, the plot, who wrote the lines, the actors' names and ages. We finally had to institute a rule that she could ask only ten questions per movie.

This didn't stop Elise, however. She has a phenomenal memory and can quote long passages of the shows we watched—sometimes weeks, months, and even years (yes, years) after watching. She also would bombard us with questions while we were trapped in the car. Once she was done with movies, she would question us about the lyrics of songs. Again, she had to know the depths of the meaning, the names and ages of the musicians, and later the names of every single instrument in the arrangement. You could say she was obsessive in her attention to detail.

Elise was very lucky to have her older sister's kindergarten teacher, who by then was teaching the children of her former students. Mrs. Hathaway was an energetic teacher who was a master at working with kindergartners. Elise enjoyed her kindergarten experience.

In first grade, Elise began her three Rs. She was an ace at reading. She showed a big preference for illustrated books at first, and then we found out she had good drawing skills. When she drew a picture, she would meticulously, painstakingly draw and color details, including hands, eyelashes, and expressions. She had to do things her way and constantly questioned others' rationales for doing things a certain way. At preschool one day, during an art lesson, she refused to color some grapes purple. Her teacher tried to convince her otherwise. Elise stubbornly argued she was absolutely not going to color the grapes purple. I don't remember what color she finally used—or perhaps she simply did not color them all.

Although a good writer, Elise would take a very long time to write in class. She would become distracted; often she would pull a book out of her desk and start reading it instead. Or she would write and erase words and sentences numerous times because the letters weren't perfect. In second grade, she started outlining the same letter over and over again, which would cause her to take several minutes to write something that should have taken thirty seconds. Sometimes she would crumple up her paper and throw it away out of frustration. The end product was very good—if she finally got there. Often her teacher would send her in-class work home with her to complete before the next day. This way we would often experience Elise's writing style firsthand.

Her biggest problem was not the inability to write, it was that her writing process itself were being slowed down by what seemed to be excessive perfectionism and distraction.

Like me, Elise often has trouble getting to sleep at night. She would often come up to our bedroom (at this point she shared a room downstairs with her sister) and proclaim, "I can't sleep!" On her doctor's recommendation, we started giving her melatonin at bedtime, which helped but did not eliminate the problem.

Elise has exceptional musical aptitude. We began to notice she could listen to a song two or three times and have the music and lyrics completely memorized. She would often start singing songs during quiet times, while studying, at dinner—music was constantly playing in her head.

In second grade she began to take voice lessons with Callie and quickly showed an unusual stage presence and eagerness. Our girls both have great voices, but it became clear that Elise was a born performer. Callie eventually went on to other things, excelling in school and athletics, but Elise chose to keep going. As I am a fairly decent piano player, I became Elise's accompanist—one of the greatest joys I have ever known.

By the end of Elise's third-grade year, she was starting to perform on stage, impressing her school at a talent show and occasionally singing in parts of productions and the occasional solo at the Tim Noah Thumbnail Theater. That's where she took voice lessons from Cyndi Soup, a gifted instructor who was able to work with the stubbornness, constant questions, and distractibility that accompanied Elise's talent.

Elise has nearly perfect pitch. Early on she learned to sing "Over the Rainbow"—a song she has kept in her repertoire and keeps improving over time. I asked her to sing it a capella once— she didn't miss a note or a phrase. The song is keyed in E-flat, and, when she was done, I decided to see what key she had sung it in. I had not given her a starting note. I played an E-flat chord for reference, and, to my surprise, it was the key she had sung it in. It turned out that Elise could sing any song she knew in the exact key she had learned it, holding the exact pitch throughout the entire song.

During the summer after fourth grade, Elise's singing seemed to go a touch out of key during our practice sessions at home. And it seemed difficult for her to bring it up to the right notes. For some reason she was okay when she went to her lessons. We had our piano tuned partway through the summer, and the tuner informed us the piano had gone sharp due to the warmer weather. In other word, the piano had been out of tune—not Elise.

Elise's acting skills were strong too. She took a theater production class on *The Wind in the Willows*. She not only memorized her lines, she memorized the entire play. Whenever another child forgot a line, Elise would cue him or her.

Elise really has phenomenal talent. But did it come at a price, like mine?

Let's go back to second grade, to her writing process, talented but tortuous. Her inability for her products to "feel right" was an alarm bell to me. The slowness, the frustration, and her practice of tracing and retracing her letters added up to a tremendous waste of time and unhappiness on her part. She also had trouble sleeping. Her mind was always going a mile a minute, with constant thoughts and curiosities flooding through. I thought back to my old habit in elementary school of spending minute after minute drawing figure eight's because it felt good to get them just right.

Elise was starting to act a lot like I had early on. I had been as precocious as she was, as well, but as a piano player. We were much alike. Judy has always told me Elise has my brain. Actually she had far too much of it.

As Elise presented these symptoms, I started to talk with her about being aware of them, about the feeling of having to do something, and about separating her mind from her feelings. At least she was better educated about compulsions than I was, and my home therapy helped her to some extent.

I have described much about the anxiety I felt as a child. Besides her obsessiveness, her trouble sleeping, and her nonstop mind, something much worse hit Elise in second grade: anxiety. Frustrated with her slowness with her schoolwork, feeling like she was disappointing her teacher and her parents, and often bored with her subject matter, she developed a strong sense of hopelessness. She became constantly anxious, the feeling looping about and reinforcing itself. Our daughter was becoming very unhappy. She did not like much of her schoolwork, and she often hummed songs in class or read books of her own when she was supposed to be working out of textbooks. Sometimes she would put her head down on her desk and try to sleep. Finally, after an especially frustrating day at school, she came home in tears and made a frightening statement: "I hate myself. I wish I was dead."

Whenever a child makes such a statement, it is imperative he or she see a physician as quickly as possible. As a teacher, I am required to report to an administrator any such statement made by a student, as are all others who work with children, such as counselors and coaches.

Ironically, parents are not required to report such things. My own father, due to lack of education (of which there wasn't any at the time) had essentially told me to "suck it up" regarding my own anxieties and fears, which led to twenty-four years of severe OCD.

I was not about to let my daughter suffer my fate nor was my wife, having both suffered depressive issues. We took Elise into her pediatrician the next day. She referred us to Dr. Lawrence, an esteemed child psychiatrist who worked for the Everett Clinic's behavioral health department.

Dr. Lawrence talked with Elise, tested Elise, talked with us, and diagnosed her with anxiety and some OCD. His recommendation was similar to what my own doctors had recommended to me: medication and cognitive therapy. He is a master at drawing with a whiteboard, and he quickly illustrated to us dosages, the effectiveness of either treatment alone, and the clear advantage of both combined. He recommended starting Elise on Flouoxitine (Prozac), the same medication her mother uses and similar to the Citolapram I take.

We were a bit reluctant to medicate our child, because we had both seen our share of students we believed were overmedicated. But Dr. Lawrence had a sterling reputation, so we consented to his advice. He started Elise on a fairly low initial dose as a precaution to any adverse reaction, and we were to check back in with him in two weeks. We got the prescription and informed Elise on what it was supposed to do for her. She seemed eager to be helped.

Initially, we did not tell Elise's teacher that she was on medication. We did not want to set up any positive or negative expectations. After two weeks, Judy contacted Elise's teacher, Mrs. Iverson, to see how the last two weeks had been. Mrs. Iverson replied that she had never seen Elise so upbeat and happy and productive in class. She was still Elise, but was much less fettered by anxieties and repetitiousness.

Elise finished her second-grade year taking a low dose of fluoxetine and functioning better. The next year, there were continued issues with social interactions. While Elise was highly intelligent, socially, she functioned at a much lower age level than her peers—in some ways, again like her father (she had trouble expressing herself using appropriate language). But the remainder of second and the third grade went reasonably well. Her musical talent continued its swift climb during this period.

About halfway through fourth grade, Mrs. Lang, Elise's fourth-grade teacher approached us with several concerns. Among them was Elise's habit of eating rocks she would find on the carpet in the classroom. These were rocks carried in by the shoes of the other children from recess.

Elise started "skipping" recess; she would not leave the playground, but she did not participate with the other children in games and playing. Instead, she wandered on the outskirts of the recess area, closely studying the ground, picking up things of interest to her, and stashing them in her coat pockets.

I was informed of Elise's collecting habit by her older sister. Apparently one of the highlights of Callie's day was to go through Elise's pockets after school. One day, she invited me to participate. I was amazed at the Tom Sawyer-esque collection as Callie dumped—yes, dumped—out the pockets. Interesting rocks. Old buttons. Nails, screws, bolts left over from construction. Elise was a pocket hoarder. And especially a rock collector.

Elise was also seeking out the attention of her peers. Unfortunately, if she couldn't get attention in a good way, she was equally satisfied with negative attention. These concerns, among others, prompted us to start the process of getting Elise on a school 504 plan, which would provide her extra help in school. At some point in the evaluation process, we opted to have Elise fully evaluated for an individualized education program (IEP). By the time her IEP was complete, it was June of her fourth-grade year.

An IEP allows for such things as extra time and help to complete work and tests, counseling with the school's special education department (for which Snohomish is renowned), and extra education on appropriate behaviors. Like her father, Elise had trouble distinguishing correct interpersonal skills from those she perceived as correct—in other words, she needed to be taught how to act around others, not simply be able pick them up through her own observations.

The school's special education team began to put together an evaluation for Elise based on medical, parental, and teacher information. It also put her through a battery of tests designed to clarify her mental attitude, academic skills, and how the two worked together to affect her moods and efficiency.

As these early-elementary years went by, her issue of greatest concern continued to be feeling depressed. Dr. Lawrence presented us with convincing evidence that as a child grew, original doses became insufficient, and the child would fall back into old anxieties. And he was correct. We would up the dose, and she would feel better and be more amenable to therapy and school accommodations. Over several months we finally found a stable dose. It seemed high to us, but Dr. Lawrence pointed out that children's doses of medication sometimes must be equal to or higher than an adult's, as a child's metabolism is higher.

As Elise continued into fifth grade, her depression and OCD were being controlled, which allowed other issues to surface. Her impatience and trouble concentrating continued at times with the more challenging fifth-grade curriculum. She especially had trouble staying awake, or at least feeling awake. By now Dr. Lawrence had spent much time with Elise and was convinced that some attention deficit had been revealed. Although Judy and I had told ourselves we would never put a child of ours on Ritalin, there was a more modern, time-release form that avoided the sudden ups and downs of the previous form. Again we took Dr. Lawrence's advice. Again Elise responded positively.

We continue to evaluate Elise closely with Dr. Lawrence, and he suggests adjustments as necessary. Elise still sees a child psychologist, conveniently located down the hall from Dr. Lawrence. She continues to receive accommodations from her school and from brilliant teachers year to year as she moves through the grades.

I feel fortunate to be able to share my cognitive therapy with Elise. I am able to successfully talk my daughter down from anxiety attacks based on bad feelings or thoughts—something my parents or a physician could not have done for me. In fact, Elise's psychologist told me Elise was lucky in that her dad could actually help her overcome OCD.

Elise occasionally goes to bed worried she won't get to sleep. Then she can't—a self-fulfilling prophecy. She becomes very anxious from not being able to sleep. And then she's in the anxiety cycle, with her brain going Mach 5 and millions of random thoughts whirling around her head. Often this happens while my wife is tucking her in. It's my job to take over and calm Elise down.

A typical "talk down" begins with me encouraging her to verbalize her feelings and thoughts. Talking is a very good start with and OCD/anxiety attack, as it gets the person focused on the present and concentrating on the conversation itself, which is a significant distraction from being alone with one's thoughts.

Once we've talked about the anxiety and the thoughts, I explain to her the difference between her brain and herself. Her brain is a machine that produces thoughts and images, often without volition, and then proceeds to overreact to them due to an imbalance in brain chemistry. But her mind is the part of her that has the final control.

Her brain might tell her she'd feel better if she thrashed around restlessly in her bed, but it's lying to her. If she can step aside and let her mind, not her brain/feelings control her body, she can make herself lie still, and she will start to feel less anxious. But it might take several minutes for this to occur. I would stay with her and talk to her, telling her to be patient.

Elise has become very good at realizing the difference between her mind and her brain. Over the last couple of years, she has become much less vulnerable to and much more in control of her anxiety issues. This has allowed her to move forward further— to accept that she cannot control what comes into her head but she can control how she reacts to it. The episodes have greatly decreased.

Elise has become a successful young lady who has to work hard, supported by others who love children and work equally hard. But she will always be Elise—a gifted child who has been given the opportunity to express her gifts much more fully than her father was. And if my own school of hard knocks was to Elise's benefit—and hopefully to others' benefit—it was at least partially worthwhile.

* * * * *

I had been forced to confront my OCD for good in January of 1999. It took a full year of therapy using medication and cognitive therapy to finally, using a favorite word of Mark Twain, *lick* my OCD. I hope I didn't make it sound too easy, and I realize that for many, OCD is a lifelong battle. Why was my particular case so curable, so responsive to treatment? I don't believe I had a mild case. My conjecture is that I made choices along the way to develop myself mentally and physically, engaging in activities that improved my mental toughness and allowing me to fight it every step of the way. I'd been fighting it my entire life, and when an effective arsenal appeared, I was ready and willing to use it to my full ability. In the end, however, I will leave it up to the reader to decide.

My greatest relief and hope is that children no longer need suffer through OCD untreated—indeed, no one of any age does. I was in my late twenties before I received even preliminary treatment—when the disease was largely unknown. I was in my forties when I benefited from more extensive treatment. But there is no *complete* cure for OCD. It always stalks the back of your mind, waiting to pounce. It is by ignoring (yet being cognizant of) OCD that you render it ineffectual, giving it nothing to pounce on.

CPSIA information can be obtained at www.ICGtesting.com
Printed in the USA
LVOW12s1443150614

390125LV00022B/1070/P